STRATEGIC PLANNING
FOR FINANCIAL INSTITUTIONS

STRATEGIC PLANNING FOR FINANCIAL INSTITUTIONS

Edited by Bernard Taylor
and Guy de Moubray

THE BODLEY HEAD LTD &
HFL (PUBLISHERS) LTD
LONDON

This edition © B. Taylor & G. de Moubray 1974
ISBN 0 370 10457 9
Printed and bound in Great Britain for
The Bodley Head Ltd & HFL (Publishers) Ltd
9 Bow Street, London WC2E 7AL
by The Stellar Press Ltd, Hatfield, Herts
Set in 'Monotype' Times New Roman
First published 1974

ACKNOWLEDGMENTS

This book is based upon a series of presentations which were made to a National Conference on Strategic Planning for Financial Institutions organised by the Bank of England and the University of Bradford in July 1972. The Editors would like to thank the University of Bradford and the Bank of England for allowing the proceedings to be published.

The original papers by the speakers at the Conference have been augmented by the inclusion of a number of other articles and presentations. These other contributions are listed below, and the Editors would like to acknowledge the kindness of the copyright-holders in allowing these papers to be printed in this book.

The contributions by B. Taylor and G. de Moubray, Lord O'Brien of Lothbury, Sir Eric Roll, Sir Alexander Ross, S. T. Graham, P. H. Swan, Andrew Breach, Basil Robarts, C. H. Villiers, D. V. Weyer, A. Whittam Smith, J. E. Bolton, M. G. Kendall, R. L. Hopps, K. G. Addison, D. H. Maitland, A. Rudd, R. E. B. Lloyd and "The Structure of British Financial Institutions in the 1980s", by James Robertson. © B. Taylor and G. de Moubray, 1974.

"Thirty-five Years of Change for the Financial System", by David Peretz, was first published in *Futures*, December 1971. © *Futures*, 1971.

"Paying by Computer", by James Robertson, was first published in *New Scientist*, 23rd July 1970. © *New Scientist*, 1970.

"Competition for Consumer Credit", by A. Victor Adey, was a paper first presented to the Finance Houses Association Conference on the *Practical Implications of the Crowther Report*, October 1971. © B. Taylor and G. de Moubray, 1974.

ACKNOWLEDGMENTS

"Building Societies and the Demand for Houses", by B. H. Phillips, "The Function of Risk Capital in Insurance", by A. R. N. Ratcliff, and "Developments in the London Money Market", by A. J. Buchanan, were papers first presented at a Seminar on *Financial Institutions: Current Trends and Problems*, organised in London in March 1972 by Professor J. R. S. Revell, of the Economics Research Unit, University College of North Wales, Bangor. © B. Taylor and G. de Moubray, 1974.

"Pension Funds as Investors", by Michael Pilch and "Recent Developments in Investment Research", by J. M. Brew, were presented in January 1972 to the Annual Investment Seminar organised by the *Investors' Chronicle*. © B. Taylor and G. de Moubray, 1974.

"Financial Planning in U.K. Industry", by P. G. Nield, was first published in the spring 1973 issue of the *Journal of Business Policy*. © *Journal of Business Policy*, 1973.

"Investment Strategies for Pension Funds", by J. D. Skelton, appeared in the December 1973 issue of *Long-Range Planning*. © J. D. Skelton, 1973.

"Case Study of a Bank Merger", by R. E. B. Lloyd, was a paper presented at a Business Seminar on Mergers organised at London Graduate School of Business Studies in November 1970 by Professor H. Rose and Professor A. T. M. Wilson. © B. Taylor and G. de Moubray, 1974.

CONTENTS

CONTENTS

THE CONTRIBUTORS

A. VICTOR ADEY

A native of Wolverhampton, he began his business career as an articled clerk. In 1937 he joined Mercantile Credit as Branch Manager at Wolverhampton, becoming in turn Managing Director of the Irish subsidiary, a Director of the parent company and finally, in 1964, Managing Director. He is current Chairman of Eurofinas, an association of European finance houses.

K. G. ADDISON

Mr. Addison is General Manager, Home Division of The Sun Alliance and London Insurance Group. He holds a Bachelor of Laws degree of the University of London, is a Fellow of the Chartered Insurance Institute, an Associate of the Chartered Institute of Secretaries, and Fellow of the Institute of Arbitrators. He was President of the Institute of Arbitrators in 1968/69. He joined Alliance Assurance Company Limited in 1939, was appointed Assistant Secretary, Law Fire Office, a subsidiary of the Alliance in 1960; he became Organisation and Methods Manager of the Sun Alliance Group in 1964, and was appointed Assistant General Manager of the Sun Alliance and London Group in 1968. He was appointed General Manager, Home Divisions of the Group in July 1971.

JOHN E. BOLTON

John Bolton is Chairman and Managing Director of Solartron Electronic Group. He is also Chairman and Managing Director of Growth Capital Limited, Chairman or Director of many companies, and Chairman of the Foundation for Management Education. He was Chairman of the Committee of Inquiry on Small Firms from 1969 to 1971, and Vice-Chairman of the Royal Commission on Local Government from 1966 to 1969. He has been Chairman of Council, British Institute of Management, and is currently Vice-President. He was awarded the B.I.M. Bowie Medal in 1969, and was, until recently, Chairman of Council, Surrey University, and presently is Vice-Chairman of Council. Mr. Bolton was educated at Trinity College, Cambridge, and at Harvard Business School, where he was a Baker Scholar.

ANDREW BREACH

Mr. Breach has been Chief Executive of the Bristol and West Building Society since 1948, and was appointed Chairman in 1969. He has served as Chairman of the Building Societies Association (1963/65), as President of the Building Societies Institute (1969/70), and is on the Council of the International Union of Building Societies and Savings Associations. He serves on the Boards of various companies, is on the Bristol and District Board of Barclays Bank Limited, and is Chairman of the Regional Board of the Sun Alliance and London Insurance Group. Mr. Breach is also a Trustee or member of the Committee of Management of a number of charitable bodies. He is a member of the Society of Merchant Venturers and a member of the Court of the Worshipful Company of Basketmakers.

JOHN M. BREW

Since 1971 Mr. Brew has been Chairman of the Society of Investment Analysts, having been a Council member since 1967. He joined Grieveson Grant and Company (Stockbrokers) in 1953 and has spent most of his time there on gilt-edged and fixed-interest investment. He became a Partner in 1961. He was educated at Doncaster Grammar School and Trinity College, Cambridge.

ALISTAIR J. BUCHANAN

Mr. Buchanan is Managing Director of Allen Harvey & Ross Limited. He is a Fellow of the Institute of Chartered Accountants and was educated at Eton and New College, Oxford.

S. T. GRAHAM

Mr. Graham is an Assistant Chief General Manager of the Midland Bank, which he joined in 1938. After war service in the R A F he returned to the bank and served in various branches before taking up an appointment at the Head Office. Subsequent managerial appointments took him to branches in London and the provinces, and he returned to Head Office in 1962 for special executive duties and was appointed a Joint General Manager of the bank in 1966. His present appointment dates from 1970, and one of his responsibilities is the direction of the bank's planning activities.

RALPH L. HOPPS

Mr. Hopps is General Manager, Personnel Division of the National Westminster Bank. He joined the National Provincial Bank as a junior clerk in Bradford in 1934 and after service in several Yorkshire branches, was moved to London in 1950. He was appointed Manager of the new Automation Department in 1964, became an Assistant General Manager in 1965, and a Joint General Manager in 1967. On the merger of the National Provincial and Westminster Banks in 1968, he was appointed General Manager.

MAURICE G. KENDALL

Dr. Kendall is Chairman of Scientific Control Systems (Holdings) (formerly C.E.I.R.). Before joining his present company in 1961, he was a Professor of Statistics at the London School of Economics, where he is still a Visiting Professor. He is a Fellow of the British Academy and the Royal Society of Arts, and has been President of the Royal Statistical Society and the Operational Research Society. His publications include fourteen books and over a hundred scientific papers. In 1968 he was awarded a Gold Medal by the Royal Statistical Society for his outstanding contributions to statistics.

RICHARD E. B. LLOYD

Richard Lloyd is Chief Executive of Williams & Glyn's Bank, a Director of the Australia and New Zealand Banking Group Limited, Legal and General Assurance Society Limited and Peninsular and Oriental Steam Navigation Company. He is a member of the London and South Eastern Regional Council of the C.B.I. and of The Institute for the Study of Drug Dependence Council. He was educated at Wellington College and Oxford. After Oxford he joined Glyn Mills & Co. in 1952, becoming a Director in 1964.

DAVID H. MAITLAND

Mr. Maitland is Managing Director of the Save and Prosper Group. He was educated at Eton College. After war service, he was articled to a City firm of Chartered Accountants and qualified in 1950. In 1952 he joined the U.K. subsidiary of Mobil in a variety of accounting assignments. He joined Save and Prosper as Comptroller in 1961, became Secretary in 1961, Deputy Managing Director in 1964, and Managing Director of Save and Prosper Group Limited in 1966.

P. G. NEILD

After studying economics at Manchester University, Dr. Neild was awarded a Commonwealth Scholarship and gained his doctorate in econometrics at the University of Wellington, New Zealand. On returning from abroad he took up his present position as Economist with Phillips & Drew, London. In addition to contributing to several academic journals, Dr. Neild served on the European Commission established in 1972 by the European Federation of Financial Analysts' Societies which investigated the use of mathematical models for financial management.

LORD O'BRIEN OF LOTHBURY

Lord O'Brien is former Governor of the Bank of England. He joined the Bank in 1927, became Chief Cashier in 1955, Executive Director in 1962, Deputy Governor in 1964, and Governor in 1966. In 1967 he was created a Knight Grand Cross of the British Empire, and in 1970 he was appointed a Privy Councillor. He was elevated to the peerage in March 1973.

DAVID PERETZ

David Peretz joined the Inter-Bank Research Organisation in 1969, where he is now head of the Economic Section. Before 1969 he served for a number of years as an Administrative Civil

Servant in the Ministry of Technology, being involved in policy formulation on questions ranging from atomic energy policy to the costs and benefits of Government research. At IBRO he helps to advise at industry level on strategic issues arising for British banking; in particular, he is currently in charge of a number of projects concerning the development of public policy as it affects financial institutions, and changing financial institutional structure.

BRIAN H. PHILLIPS

Mr. Phillips is General Manager (Finance) of Nationwide Building Society. He joined the Society in 1967 and previous to this held senior financial appointments in a number of local authorities. He has published numerous articles on local-government finance and developments in the mortgage market.

MICHAEL PILCH

Mr. Pilch is a Director of Noble Lowndes & Partners Limited and the co-author of four books on pension schemes, the latest of which, *Company Pension Schemes*, has recently been re-printed by the Gower Press in a second edition.

A. R. N. RATCLIFF

A. R. N. Ratcliff is Joint General Manager of Eagle Star Insurance Company. He has written numerous articles on the subject of insurance, particularly concerning Pension Schemes in the E.E.C. and in the United Kingdom.

BASIL ROBARTS

Basil Robarts is Director and Chief General Manager of the Norwich Union Insurance Group. He is a Fellow of the British Institute of Management, a recent Chairman of the British Insurance Association, and a former Treasurer of the Institute of Actuaries.

JAMES ROBERTSON

James Robertson was educated at Sedbergh School and Balliol College, Oxford. He joined the Colonial Office in 1953 as an administrative civil servant. He accompanied Mr. Macmillan on his "Wind of Change" tour of Africa in 1960, and spent the next three years in the Cabinet Office. After two years with the Ministry of Defence, Mr. Robertson left the Civil Service in 1965, and joined C.E.I.R. (now Scientific Control Systems Limited), the computer consultants. From October 1968 until March 1973 he was Director of the Inter-Bank Research Organisation. Mr. Robertson published a book on the *Reform of British Central Government* in 1971. He served as Specialist Adviser to the Procedure Committee of the House of Commons in the Committee's 1969 investigation into parliamentary control of public expenditure.

SIR ERIC ROLL

Sir Eric is a Director of the Bank of England, a Deputy Chairman of the merchant bankers, S. G. Warburg, and a Director of Times Newspapers, Chrysler (U.K.), Dominion-Lincoln Assurance Company and several other companies. He has led U.K. delegations to the E.E.C. and the International Monetary Fund, and has held senior positions in the Treasury, the Ministry of Agriculture, and the Department of Economic Affairs.

SIR ALEXANDER ROSS

Sir Alexander Ross is Chairman, United Dominions Trust Limited, Chairman, Australia and New Zealand Banking Group Limited, and Vice-Chairman, Eagle Star Insurance Co. Limited. He joined the Reserve Bank of New Zealand in 1934, and was Deputy Governor from 1948 to 1955. He represented New Zealand in rowing at the Empire Games in 1930, and managed the New Zealand team to the Empire Games in Vancouver in 1954. Sir Alexander has been Chairman of the British Commonwealth Games Federation since 1968.

ANTHONY RUDD

Mr. Rudd is senior partner of a stockbroking firm, Rowe, Rudd and Company. He worked at the Bank of England from 1949 to 1955 in various departments, including a secondment to Washington D.C. From 1956 to 1959 he was a financial journalist in the City office of the *Manchester Guardian*. In 1959 he became a Member of the Stock Exchange, London, and was a partner in Rowe, Reeve and Company from 1959 to 1969. He became senior partner in Rowe, Rudd and Company (successor firm to Rowe, Reeve and Company) in 1969.

J. DEREK SKELTON

Mr. Skelton is a Fellow of the Chartered Institute of Secretaries. He was previously Company Secretary of Bradford Dyers Limited and of Associated Dairies Limited, and he is at present working with the University of Bradford Management Centre Post-Experience Programme.

PETER H. SWAN

After the war, Mr. Swan graduated in Economics at the London School of Economics. He joined Phillips & Drew in 1948, and was made a Member of the London Stock Exchange in 1954. For many years he has been the partner in charge of the Equity Department which now includes the Research section of the firm. He was elected to the Stock Exchange Council in 1963 and in 1971 was made Chairman of the Members Firms and Clerks Committee, and was on the Quotations Committee. In 1971 he was elected to the Council of the Federation of Stock Exchanges in Great Britain and Ireland.

CHARLES VILLIERS

Charles Villiers is best known for his work as Managing Director of the Industrial Reorganisation Corporation. He is now Chairman of the merchant bankers Guinness Mahon, Chairman of the Northern Ireland Finance Corporation, and the Federal Trust Group on European Monetary Integration. He is also a Director of several industrial companies, insurance companies and banks.

D. V. WEYER

Mr. Weyer is Senior General Manager of Barclays Bank, with special responsibilities for Marketing and Planning. He joined the Bank in 1941 at Filey. After war-time service, his first executive appointment was Assistant Manager of the Barclays' Water Street, Liverpool, Office in 1956. Following a period at the Bank's Head Office, and attendance at the Administrative Staff College, Mr. Weyer became Manager of Chester and Saltney branches in 1961. He was appointed a Local Director of the Liverpool District covering Merseyside, North and West Cheshire, and North Wales in 1965. Mr. Weyer spent six months at the Oxford Centre for Management Studies, and visited San Francisco to study U.S. banking methods, before being made an Assistant General Manager in 1968, and Senior General Manager in 1973.

ANDREAS WHITTAM SMITH

Mr. Whittam Smith is Editor of *The Investors' Chronicle*. He has been City Editor of *The Guardian* and Deputy City Editor of *The Daily Telegraph* and previously worked with *The Times*, *The Financial Times*, and *The Stock Exchange Gazette*.

THE EDITORS

PROFESSOR BERNARD TAYLOR

Professor Bernard Taylor has been closely associated with the development of Corporate Planning in Britain. He is Editor of two international journals: *Long-Range Planning* and the *Journal of General Management*. He has written numerous articles and has produced seven books dealing with various aspects of business strategy and planning. He lectures widely in Britain and on the Continent and in 1971 completed an assignment for the United Nations with the National Council for Applied Economic Research in New Delhi. He has held responsible positions in marketing and education and training with Procter & Gamble and Rank Xerox. He founded the Post-Experience Programme at the University of Bradford Management Centre and he is now Director of Planning and Development at the Administrative Staff College, Henley-on-Thames.

GUY DE MOUBRAY

Mr. de Moubray was born in 1925. After war service he read P.P.E. at Trinity College, Oxford. In 1948 he joined H.M. Treasury and in 1950 the Bank of England. He served with the

International Monetary Fund in 1953/54 and was Private Secretary to the Deputy Governor in 1955/56. From 1956 to 1959 he was Personal Assistant to the Managing Director of the I.M.F. in Washington. He returned to the Bank as Assistant Chief of the Central Banking Information Department, and from 1965/70 was Deputy Chief of the Economic Intelligence Department. In 1970 he was appointed to the newly-created post of Management Development Manager.

FOREWORD

by Lord O'Brien of Lothbury
Former Governor of the Bank of England

THE FUTURE DEVELOPMENT
OF FINANCIAL INSTITUTIONS

The Bank of England was a joint sponsor with the University of Bradford of the Conference on which this book is based. The involvement of the Bank of England in a Conference of this sort represented a breaking of new ground and I hope that, so far as the Bank was concerned, it was seen as a sign, if not of grace, at least of our readiness to accept new rôles in the rapidly changing world in which we live. The aim of the Conference was to promote thought about the future and how best we might prepare ourselves to meet it. It seems right to me that the Bank should lend their support to such an enterprise, and be particularly concerned about its application to City institutions.

There have been many changes and developments in City institutions over the past twenty-five years, despite the recurrent difficulties and declining rôle of sterling, and despite the official restrictions which have from time to time been necessary. In the main the financial institutions have not been daunted by these unpropitious circumstances. Ingenuity and innovation have not been checked – indeed in some directions they may at times have gone too far.

Now it seems we are at a watershed. After the turmoil of recent years thought is at last being turned to the possibility of a radical reform of the international monetary system which, if successful, should provide a more stable background for the development of trade and financial services in the world at large. In the United Kingdom the banking community has already entered an era of greater freedom and keener competition and membership of the Common Market is already bringing new problems and opportunities for many of our financial institutions.

I am not going to try to impart here my own private daydream of what changes these various influences are likely to bring about in the City. I am quite sure that the financial institutions will not simply stand still. Many may change their shape radically. The desire for harmonisation within the enlarged European Community may well present problems. The influence of the City of London will undoubtedly be great but influence will not be all one way. In so far as the Bank can guide the changes that must come they will, as always, be concerned to help the institutions, and the banking organisations in particular, to strengthen their ability to serve the nation as well as contribute to the fruitful development of the Community.

Industry has displayed a mounting interest in predicting the possible range of changes which may take place in the environment in which businesses will be conducted and hence the measures which firms may need to take in order to survive and prosper. As the contributors to this book testify, financial institutions may well be wise to follow suit.

Whether modern techniques of corporate planning would have helped the City to manipulate more skilfully the changes of the last twenty-five years it is hard to estimate. One is tempted to question whether in 1950 anyone could have foreseen a vast Euro-dollar market as a consequence of contingencies comprised in a corporate plan. But, if I understand correctly, the essence of corporate plans is not to make precise predictions or prescribe fixed courses of action or policy. They proceed rather by formulating sets of assumptions which help management to frame their strategy for the future and to gauge its likely consequences. It would assuredly be rash if the City, faced with changes such as the authors have depicted here, were to reject any such aid to prudent and far-sighted decision. The changes which speakers have foreseen spring largely from the greater competitive pressures which now face all financial institutions. These competitive pressures flow partly from the freedom associated with the new system of credit control, partly from our entry into the Common Market and partly from the ever-increasing number of competing institutions. These pressures will be more intense than any experienced in the past twenty-five years. They will lead inevitably to greater pressure on profitability, already squeezed from below by rising costs.

I want to mention two ways in which institutions may be expected to respond to these pressures.

The first concerns the structure of the institutions themselves. It seems to me that two divergent tendencies are likely to make themselves evident. On the one hand, there will be a movement to bring many diverse activities together within a single organisation, while on the other, in some instances, the urge to specialise will become more acute. The former will tend to blur the traditional lines of demarcation between one type of business and another. It is not possible for all business to be equally profitable simultaneously and a movement in this direction will increase the extent to which the less profitable business is carried by the more profitable. This will enhance the general stability of the system and help to reduce overall costs.

The urge to specialise will, I guess, come mainly from the pioneers. The prosperity of the City has been nurtured by men seeking out new ways of mobilising savings and deploying them profitably. The City can never afford to relinquish this traditional entrepreneurial expertise. It is, of course, displayed by organisations of all shapes and sizes, but the smaller, lightly-built enterprise frequently has the advantage of greater speed and dexterity. These are admirable virtues but they have their dangers. Brilliant innovation can be very impressive but in the City the basic requirement is to inspire and retain confidence and trust. This frequently takes a long time and makes young men in a hurry impatient, but there is no alternative and very few acceptable short cuts. Those who are far-sighted and careful in their strategic planning are more likely to reach their goal, and do so more quickly.

I am also concerned about another aspect of planning, namely its importance in the battle to contain or reduce costs in response to the pressure of competition. Since the war the composition of the staff of financial institutions has greatly changed. Women now outnumber men, whereas before they were no more than a tolerated and restricted minority. At the same time mechanisation has yielded steady if unspectacular savings in staff.

Nevertheless the financial sector is still markedly labour-intensive. For example, in the Bank of England labour costs account for some 70% of the total, and, I understand, that in some other large financial concerns the figure would be even higher.

Under the pressure of increased competition and rising labour costs a move towards greater capital intensity in the financial sector seems inevitable over the next decade. Computers, allied to modern management techniques such as clerical work measurement and methods study, are capable of making radical changes in work processes leading to substantial staff savings. If staff savings are to be made on a significant scale – and it is not inconceivable that the total clerical labour force of the financial sector could be cut by as much as a quarter to a third – they will cause distress and conflict unless the way is carefully prepared and unless we foresee accurately the balance between staff increases attributable to expansion and staff savings attributable to the adoption of new machines and methods.

Relations between management and staff in the City have been relatively trouble-free. Threats of redundancy, however, could beget feelings of insecurity against which these good relations would not automatically be proof. Indeed, the post-war changes in the relative prosperity of skilled industrial workers and higher clerical staff have already strengthened the move away from an informal paternalism towards protective systems in which staff associations and trades unions play a prominent part. If substantially reduced staff requirements are not to lead to redundancy – and we must, for all these reasons, try and avoid it – manpower planning must be given a higher priority than is now generally the case. The turnover of junior clerical staff is high and appreciable staff reductions can be made relatively painlessly through natural wastage. But this requires careful planning of future needs and future recruitment targets; and planning on the scale for which we must be prepared probably needs to be focused on at least a ten-year horizon.

If we achieve substantial labour saving with full recognition of the human problems involved for our employees we shall have strengthened the City's foundations. But in doing so we shall, in company with other industries, have contributed to a potential national problem. If our labour saving, added to the savings of others in face of mounting costs, is not to intensify national unemployment on an unacceptable scale, we must be concerned to see that in our other activities we contribute as effectively as possible to fostering the more rapid growth of the economy as a whole.

What of the other manpower issues which may be important during the next ten years? The raising of the school-leaving age and the trend towards more and more higher education are already changing dramatically the composition of the labour force seeking to enter the financial sector, bringing in above the junior clerical level more young people who have had full-time education after leaving school. More and more young men and women when they enter the City tend to have higher expectations than many who went before them. They have stronger expectations of early responsibility, look for a more consultative style of management and have a keener desire for job satisfaction. If the financial sector is to recruit and retain the people of the quality needed to compete effectively, domestically, and internationally, more emphasis will need to be placed on management development. But management development is not an end in itself; it has to be accompanied by a careful review of the ways in which information is communicated, both up and down the line; of the extent to which responsibility can be devolved; of the spirit in which subordinates and superiors treat one another; of the system by which performance and potential are assessed. This may call for measures which disturb well-grounded habits of thought and practice. But is is on such factors that the successful harnessing of human resources to the profitable development of this great financial centre will depend.

In the Bank of England, we have been turning our minds to the solution of some of these problems. We find ourselves increasingly constrained to focus on long-term issues; for example, to formulate contingencies which membership of the Common Market may bring with it and to anticipate developments likely to flow from the new approach to credit control.

We are also giving more systematic attention to planning our own domestic long-term developments. We recently completed a co-ordinated manpower plan estimating the demand for, and the supply of, staff up to a decade ahead. A plan of this sort is not a specific forecast, not a fixed blueprint, but an examination of the implications of various sets of assumptions about the future. Many of our personnel policies have already been significantly affected by the plan. The age structure of the Bank's staff, resulting from past recruitment patterns, is very uneven; and we have now a low level of normal retirements to be followed in a few years by an abnormally high one. This creates problems for staff morale and for management succession. The manpower plan has helped us to a partial solution through a special early pension offer to staff within ten years of normal retirement. The longer-term look has also significantly affected our recruitment targets for this year; a shorter horizon could well have meant higher targets and a greater risk of redundancy in the future. The plan is also helping us to reshape our staff salary structure.

Besides this we have established a management development programme, which provides for greater staff participation in career planning, encourages more delegation, and an expanded training programme designed to meet the needs identified by job evaluation and the manpower plan.

However, we are also concerned with training in a wider setting. We are familiar with the technical skills which the financial businesses of today demand: and this book provides glimpses of the new and evolving skills which will be required in the businesses of tomorrow. Equally, we see before us the massive changes envisaged by the contributors to the book: and these changes in themselves must be nursed along with the aid of management skills whose systematic foundation has only recently been laid.

The contributors to this book set the problems of the future in a great variety of fields and describe the practical experience they have gained in preparing srategic plans. I hope this will show that planning is not so much picking some winner in the meetings of the future as a means of moving more nimbly and more confidently through times which will still contain many uncertainties. Pasteur understood the place of planning in human affairs when he said "fortune favours the prepared mind". For, however sagaciously we examine the middle distance, we may still need a little luck to reinforce our plans.

INTRODUCTION

Bernard Taylor and Guy de Moubray

The 1970s promise a period of accelerating change which could revolutionise business practice in banking, insurance, building societies, stockbroking, and consumer credit. The aim of this book is to examine the issues which are likely to have a crucial effect on the growth and profitability of financial institutions over the next decade. A number of the papers are taken from a Conference on Strategic Planning for Financial Institutions, sponsored by the Bank of England and the University of Bradford, which was held on 6th and 7th June, 1972. Other papers, most of them previously unpublished, have been added to ensure that the study is comprehensive.

Most of the contributions to this book were written in the first half of 1972 and some of the references in them to what were then current affairs are now obviously out of date. The economy is in a different phase of the cycle; the level of interest rates is now significantly higher; the pound sterling has been floating since 23rd June, 1972 and we now have a statutory incomes policy. We have not attempted to bring the contributions up to date in this or in any other respect. In a book on strategic planning, details and facts about the present can only be a point of departure; what is important about these contributions is the light they can throw on issues and trends which are likely to affect future developments.

Contributors to the book are shown in the chapter headings holding the positions they held in June 1972. Where this is now different the new positions are shown elsewhere in the biographical notes on page ix.

The book is divided into two parts. Part One: *The Future of the Financial System* is concerned with trends in the business environment – national and international, social and economic, political and technological. The contributors attempt to assess the effects which these changes are likely to have on the future structure of financial institutions. Part Two: *Strategic Planning* examines the practical problems of organising, executing, and controlling long-term plans. Particular attention is paid to the use of computers, to the marketing of financial services, and to long-range planning for personnel.

MANAGEMENT IN FINANCIAL INSTITUTIONS

We hope that the book will help to foster teaching and research in the management of financial institutions. The starting point for the Conference was a remark made by Professor Harold Rose. In his report to the National Economic Development Office on Management Education in the Seventies, he has a chapter on the demand for courses by financial institutions in which he writes: "There is a strongly held view that external courses are aimed mainly at managers in manufacturing industry and are not designed to help managers deal with the special problems thought to be characteristic of the financial world. The implication is that there would be substantial support for courses regarded as being designed specifically for financial institutions."

Of the financial organisations participating in that survey, one third felt that suitable external management courses were just not available. Nevertheless, he predicted that among financial institutions the demand for external management courses would double between 1968 and 1975.

Managers of financial institutions have traditionally attained their position by virtue of their technical expertise, skilled, for example, at assessing credit risks, insurance risks, valuing property. Management's most important decisions tended to be day-to-day decisions committing the firm. But with the progressive erosion of the traditional barriers between different types of financial institutions and the development of institutions which are in effect financial conglomerates, there is a growing need to develop managers of resources; not just with technical skills in a relatively narrow area but capable of thinking in terms of a whole range of financial services.

Such considerations have led to the rapid expansion of demand for external management courses by financial institutions. Much of this demand has been satisfied by general management courses, for there is a dearth of courses and research specifically about the management of financial institutions. At present there are probably around 750,000 employees and 150,000 managers in financial organisations.[1] However, despite the number of managers involved and the obvious importance of the field, there are few useful publications on, for example, the Marketing of Financial Services, Personnel and Manpower Planning in Financial Institutions, or on the Use of Computers and Management Science Techniques in Financial Organisations. It is important, therefore, that the Business Schools and the City should co-operate to provide external management courses and research programmes specifically designed to meet the needs of the financial community.

STRATEGIC PLANNING

Institutions with short horizons and concerned with day-to-day decisions tend to have their future determined by a series of reactions to current external pressures; a future which, if unpalatable, is often discerned too late to remedy. We have no reason to think that financial institutions are any more prone to this tendency than many other types of institution; but the theme of this book is that the concept of strategic planning is a particularly important one for financial institutions facing, as Lord O'Brien has noted in his Foreword, more intense competitive pressures than any experienced in the past twenty-five years. The concept of strategic planning suggests that in a dynamic and competitive environment it may be necessary to re-appraise the fundamental nature of the business, to set more demanding objectives, to consider alternative strategies, and to produce action plans which will ensure its long-term development. Strategic planning usually involves making arrangements within an organisation which will ensure that the strategic issues are not neglected through the pressures of the day-to-day operation. This will certainly require the production of written plans with specific goals, time-tables and budgets for the long term. It may also require the formation of an Executive Committee of the Board, or even a full-time planning department to co-ordinate and monitor the formulation and implementation of these plans on a company-wide basis. Strategic planning is already sufficiently well established in large progressive companies for us to predict with some certainty that by 1980 it will be as much a part of management as budgetary control is today.

We hope that the book will encourage the development of

constructive thinking about the future development of financial institutions – in individual companies, in banking, insurance, building societies, etc., generally, and on a national or international basis.

FINANCIAL INSTITUTIONS IN PERSPECTIVE

In considering the future development of financial institutions it may be helpful to examine their present size and their rate of growth. The growth of the assets of financial institutions was relatively slow between the two World Wars, but has been very rapid since – more than keeping pace with inflation. More important than total growth, in the context of this book, has been the change in the relative share of these assets held by different types of institutions. Fully comprehensive and reliable statistics over long periods are not available. The two schedules of percentage shares (Table 1) and the underlying figures (Tables 2 and 3) which follow are based on estimates drawn from two different sources – covering different spans of years. Inevitably estimates for the year 1951 (common to both) differ somewhat, but mainly because their coverage is not identical: the first series (D. K. Sheppard) excludes important segments of the banking sector and includes national savings – the reverse being true of the second series (Bank of England).

However, both series tell much the same story; a steady decline in the share of the banking sector – in spite of the inclusion of the sterling equivalent of foreign currency deposits which have grown very substantially between 1950 and 1970. Whereas the assets of the Clearing Banks and the Discount Market represented 65% and 10%, respectively, of total Banking Sector assets in 1951, their shares of the total in 1970 had declined to 24% and 5%. In the same period, the assets of the Accepting Houses and overseas and other banks (largely the overseas banks) rose from 12% to 66% (Table 3).

Amongst the other financial institutions which have shown the fastest rates of growth are the Unit and Property Unit Trusts, Trustee Savings Banks and the finance houses. However, although the rate of growth of most of the institutions has been substantial, especially in the last decade, many were less well-established than the traditional deposit banks in the 1950s and

Table 1

Assets of Financial Institutions

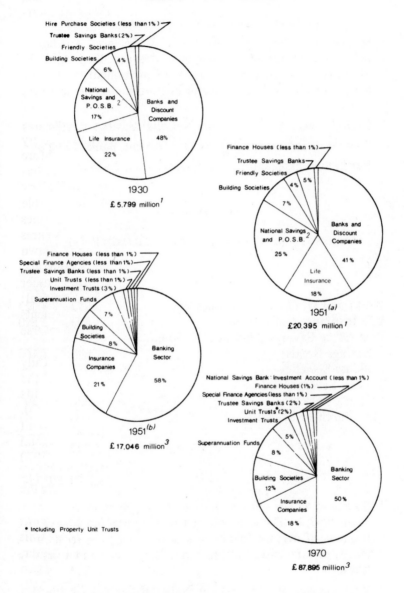

Hire Purchase Societies (less than 1%)
Trustee Savings Banks (2%)
Friendly Societies
Building Societies
4%
6%
National Savings and P.O.S.B. [2]
17%
Banks and Discount Companies
48%
Life Insurance
22%

1930
£ 5.799 million [1]

Finance Houses (less than 1%)
Trustee Savings Banks
Friendly Societies
Building Societies
5%
4%
7%
National Savings and P.O.S.B. [2]
25%
Banks and Discount Companies
41%
Life Insurance
18%

1951 [a]
£20.395 million [1]

Finance Houses (less than 1%)
Special Finance Agencies (less than 1%)
Trustee Savings Banks (less than 1%)
Unit Trusts (less than 1%)
Investment Trusts (3%)
Superannuation Funds
7%
Building Societies
8%
Insurance Companies
21%
Banking Sector
58%

1951 [b]
£ 17.046 million [3]

National Savings Bank : Investment Account (less than 1%)
Finance Houses (1%)
Special Finance Agencies (less than 1%)
Trustee Savings Banks (2%)
Unit Trusts* (2%)
Investment Trusts
5%
Superannuation Funds
8%
Building Societies
12%
Insurance Companies
18%
Banking Sector
50%

1970
£ 87.895 million [3]

* Including Property Unit Trusts

the assets of the other financial institutions are still only about the same size as the assets of the banking sector.

EXPLANATORY NOTES (TO TABLE 1)

[1] Source: *The Growth and Rôle of U.K. Financial Institutions 1880–1962*, by David K. Sheppard. Methuen. Excludes U.K. business of overseas banks, assets of investment trusts, unit trusts, private trusts and superannuation funds and accepting houses.

[2] Excludes accrued interest on National Savings Certificates.

[3] Source: Economic Intelligence Department, Bank of England.

For further explanatory notes – see Tables 2 and 3.

TABLE 2

ASSETS OF FINANCIAL INSTITUTIONS[1] (I)

	£ million	
	1930	*1951*
Banks and Discount Companies	2,772	8,423
Life Insurance Companies	1,293	3,590
Post Office Savings Bank and National Savings Bonds[2]	980	5,160
Building Societies	371	1,366
Trustee Savings Banks	139	959
Friendly Societies	226	795
Hire Purchase Societies	6	41
Total	5,799	20,395
	[5,787]	[20,334]

[1] Source: *The Growth and Rôle of U.K. Financial Institutions 1880–1962*, by David K. Sheppard. Methuen. Excludes U.K. business of overseas banks, assets of investment trusts, unit trusts, private trusts and superannuation funds and accepting houses.

[2] Excludes accrued interest on National Savings Certificates.

TABLE 3

ASSETS OF FINANCIAL INSTITUTIONS (II)

£ million

	End-Year 1951	End-Year 1970
Banking Sector		
London Clearing Banks[a]	6,396	10,618
Scottish Clearing Banks[b]	857	1,343
Northern Ireland Banks	138	352
Other deposit banks[c]	212	380
National Giro	Began 1968	58
Accepting Houses and overseas and other banks	1,229	29,267
Discount Market	1,031	2,352
Total	9,863	44,370
Other Financial Institutions		
Insurance companies[d]	3,590	15,452
Building societies[e]	1,357	10,940
Superannuation funds — Public[f]	.. ⎫	1,846 ⎫
Superannuation funds — Local Authority	250 ⎬ 1,250	1,273 ⎬ 7,792
Superannuation funds — Private	.. ⎭	4,673 ⎭
Investment Trusts[g]	620	4,469
Unit Trusts[h]	80	1,316
Trustee Savings Banks: s.i.d.s[i]	124	1,408
National Savings Bank: investment account	Began 1966	290
Property Unit Trusts	Began 1966	157
Special finance agencies[j]	103	479
Finance houses[k]	59	1,222
Total	7,183	43,525
Grand Total	17,046	87,895

Bank of England,
Economic Intelligence Department,
September 1972.

EXPLANATORY NOTES (TO TABLE 3)

The figures in the table refer mainly to the market value of total assets. However, in some cases, especially in the earlier period, only book values and totals of selected assets are available. Unless otherwise stated, the figures have been taken from the *Bank of England Quarterly Bulletin* (or the Statistical Abstract, Number 1) and Financial Statistics.

(a) 1951 figure taken from the Radcliffe Report, Principal Memoranda of Evidence 1, p. 131.
1970 figure as at 9.12.70.

(b) 1970 figure as at 9.12.70.

(c) 1951 figure refers to end-January 1952 statistics for the C.W.S. and S.C.W.S. banks, *ibid.* p. 131.
1970 figure estimated, and refers to C.W.S., S.C.W.S. banks and four other banks for which no published information available prior to 20.10.71.

(d) 1951 figure, *ibid.* p. 135.

(e) Figures at book value.

(f) 1951 figures at book value, *ibid.* p. 135.
1970 figures all at market value. The book value for public sector funds at end-1970 was £1,725 million. The figure for local authority funds is at end-March 1971; net cash transactions in the first quarter of 1971 amounted to £32 million.

(g) 1951 estimate is 1949 market value figure from Radcliffe Report, para. 262, p. 91. The restrictions on capital issues prior to 1953 were such as to allow little new money to be raised until that date. Market value at end-1953 has been estimated as £741 million (see Radcliffe Memoranda 1, p. 136).

(h) 1951 estimate is for 1938. Unit Trusts suffered from the capital issue restrictions outlined in footnote (g) above. Assets estimated at £120 million at June 1959 (Radcliffe Report, para. 284, p. 97).

(i) 1951 figure as at 20.11.51. Radcliffe Memoranda 1, p. 133.

(j) 1951 figure comprises A.M.C., F.C.I. and I.C.F.C.
1970 figure comprises A.M.C., F.C.I., I.C.F.C. and C.D.F.C. (formed 1953).
Based on accounts dated 31.3.52 and 31.3.71.

(k) 1951 figure estimated on figures for F.H.A. members only. The then F.H.A. members accounted for virtually all finance house business, *ibid.* p. 137.

It is clear from these figures that finance is a major growth area in the British economy. Over the period, the financial sector has enjoyed an average annual rate of growth of 9% (or, say, 6% in real terms), while the rapid-growth sectors such as Building Societies, Accepting Houses and overseas and other banks, Unit Trusts, Trustee Savings Banks and Finance Houses have grown at annual rates of between 12% and 18%. These average growth rates have hidden considerable fluctuations within the period. For example, the growth of the Finance Houses' business has been held back and stimulated by periodic changes in terms control.

We hope that this book will help to focus attention on the need for careful forward planning at all levels for this key area of business.

This book could not have been developed without the help of our colleagues at the University of Bradford, the Bank of England, and in the leading financial institutions. We would like to express our appreciation of the assistance and guidance which we have received.

BERNARD TAYLOR AND GUY DE MOUBRAY

August 1973

NOTE TO INTRODUCTION

[1] This estimate of total employees is derived from Department of Employment statistics. We have assumed that administrative and senior supervisory staff account for 20% of this total.

PART I

The Future of
the Financial System

Chapter 1

INTERNATIONAL MONETARY
DEVELOPMENTS AND
THE EUROPEAN COMMON MARKET

Sir Eric Roll
Deputy Chairman, S.G. Warburg & Co. Ltd.

It is only future historians possessing an adequate perspective who will be able to discern and evaluate which are the critical ones among the fissures that have appeared in the course of the evolution of the present international financial system. To the contemporary observer – and many of us are old enough to have been that over the whole post-war period – that evolution appears as a seamless garment where different patterns succeed one another in apparent inevitability. It is not possible to assess the current situation, let alone speculate about the future, without some reference to the past, at any rate the recent past. I hope, therefore, that you will bear with me while I first try to outline what seem to me to be the most significant aspects of the background against which the post-war system was set up, what were the principles on which it was founded, what hopes and expectations were placed in it, and how it has performed in the twenty-five years since it came into being.

The first thing to remember – particularly so at a time when everyone talks of the break-down of the present system and of the need to devise a new one to take its place for the longer term – is that it was precisely because of the experience of break-down of the international financial and trading system in the years preceding the Second World War that the Bretton Woods system was constructed.

The memory of the total disorder of the late Twenties and Thirties was still most vivid in the minds of those who set about the task – be it remembered to their lasting credit, in the darkest days of the war – to lay the foundation for a new and better system. The legacy of the world depression had been the disruption of world trade by restrictive and protectionist practices, the spread of bilateral trade and barter arrangements, the luxuriant growth of exchange restrictions of all kinds both for current and capital transactions. These were designed to sustain a structure of parities among currencies which had become largely artificial and which included both multiple and floating rates. Thanks to the fact that the financial strength of Britain, though greatly diminished compared with what it had been in the early years of the century, was still an important factor and that American experience and willingness to shoulder international responsibilities, though still rudimentary and quite out of proportion to the country's real strength, were beginning to emerge, co-operation between the new and the old financial centres, New York and London, developed rapidly. This alone prevented the complete collapse of the system even before the war totally changed the scene. But the need for co-operation between the major financial powers had been sufficiently established to form one of the basic elements in the construction of the post-war system.

Another was the much better appreciation of the connection, in modern economic conditions, between domestic economic policy – its desiderata and its results – and the international commercial and financial nexus. The builders of the post-war system were no longer inspired by the simple principles of the nineteenth-century gold-standard – the classic "mechanism" linking inflows and outflows of reserves *via* monetary policy with expansion and contraction of domestic economic activity. They had to take into account the duty of the state, newly acknowledged in all the major countries of the world, to ensure the maintenance of high and stable levels of economic activity. They also knew that the relation between monetary and other instruments of economic policy, or between international money flows and trade patterns was much more complex than was recognised in the economic theory prevalent in the Twenties and early Thirties. The "New Economics", largely associated with the name of Keynes, accepted that the "gearing", if I may so call it, of domestic and international policy had to be much more complex, given the powerful economic and political pressures for a higher degree of autonomy for domestic policy than could have been achieved by a return to the gold-exchange standard of the inter-war years.

Thus the system constructed at Bretton Woods must be viewed not simply as a financial one, which found its sole expression in the articles of the International Monetary Fund, but as a composite one in which there were two other equally essential elements. The first was a code of conduct in trade matters, and an institution to administer it; the second, one to deal with the twin problems of post-war reconstruction and development of the less developed parts of the world so as to make them better able to become members of the international financial and trading community and faithfully to observe its rules.

This is not the place to rehearse in detail the directly monetary objectives of the system. Essentially they were the maintenance of a degree of international discipline in domestic policy and at the same time to attenuate its severity by the provision of credit facilities. It was also hoped that this would ensure an adequate supply of liquidity for the system as a whole. But it is worth recalling that the ambitious total post-war construction did not immediately come alive. The International Trade Organisation was still-born and its work in trade liberalisation carried on at first in practice mainly by the O.E.E.C., later by the G.A.T.T. (though not as fully as was originally envisaged). Owing to the temendous disparity in economic strength between the U.S.A. and Western Europe, an "auxiliary engine", the Marshall Plan, had to be applied before any significant degree of economic co-operation through the Bretton Woods machinery itself could become possible. All this, however, should not blind us to the essential connection between these different parts whose joint operation was really a basic assumption for the full functioning of the monetary system itself.

That monetary system was constitutionally meant to be a dollar gold-exchange standard. In effect, as that distinguished central banker, Dr. Stopper, has recently pointed out, it was a dollar-exchange standard with gold playing a fluctuating but generally only residual role. Its functioning, undisputedly for fifteen years, was conditioned by the economic preponderance of the United States, by the concentration after the war of the vast bulk of the world's monetary gold reserves in the United States, by the willingness of the United States to accept the consequences of her position, namely to indulge in large-scale aid and to tolerate for a long time trade discrimination against herself, and by the close involvement of sterling as a subsidiary reserve currency most intimately linked in terms of balance of payments and, therefore, largely domestic economic policy, with the dollar.

After the first fifteen years of its existence, that is, since the early Sixties, the system came increasingly under pressure. As more countries improved their international trading position and strengthened their reserves, including the building up of the gold component, thereby diminishing the American gold reserves, both these countries and the United States herself became conscious of the difficulty of continuing to sustain American balance of payments deficits of the magnitude then experienced. Various measures were tried to remedy the situation. Attempts to enlarge the area of trade liberalisation by rounds of negotiated tariff cuts, like the Kennedy Round, American restrictions on capital movements, central bank operations, including a number of devices to diminish the convertibility of growing dollar balances in central reserves, were tried. These, however, proved unavailing, particularly in the face of continuing substantial outflows from the United States on account of defence expenditures and the persistent strengths of the balance of payments of some countries, notably Japan and Germany. The crisis finally came in 1971 when dollar convertibility was formally suspended and certain emergency trade measures instituted by the United States.

It was widely held that on 15th August 1971 the post-war monetary system had definitely broken down. It would be an idle semantic exercise to debate whether this is the correct description of what happened, though more and more people are now inclined to the view that what happened was not a sudden breakdown. It was more that some of the underlying facts and some of the accepted practices which alone had made the system workable had been eroded to the point where the mechanism required a complete overhaul notwithstanding that some of its working parts were still serviceable. Its basic purposes, however, continued to be still valid. At any rate a temporary realignment of parities, including a semi-theoretical depreciation of the dollar in terms of gold, together with the institution of wider bands of permitted exchange fluctuations was achieved in December; and the international monetary system has since functioned on the basis of this "Smithsonian" agreement.

It is recognised on all sides that this can only be a temporary arrangement and that pending a more thoroughgoing reform of the system which would promise to be at least as long-lasting as the previous régime, a number of important problems remain which such a reform must resolve. I would list these problems as follows, taking first those that fall within the strict framework of monetary arrangements. The first of these is the adequacy of the existing parities (allowing for the wider bands of fluctuations) and the future régime by which changes in parities are to be brought about. The second is what the future rôle of gold, the dollar and of special drawing rights should be in relation to each other, or in other words, what should constitute ultimate reserve assets. Within this problem are impounded both a short-term problem, namely the functioning of the I.M.F. mechanism under a régime of dollar inconvertibility, as well as the longer term problem of dollar convertibility *per se*. Third, there is the question of the régime, if any, to be applied to dollar balances already held by central banks as well as the methods by which future balances are to be dealt with, since these may well continue to arise at least for some little time ahead until there is a major reversal of current U.S. balance of payments trends. The fourth question is how the long-run needs for increased liquidity in the world as a whole are to be met on the assumption that a continuous replenishment through American deficits and dollar accumulations is in the long term not acceptable on either side of the Atlantic or Pacific. Finally, there is the problem whether the maintenance of the present régime, until a more lasting system is put in place, requires special measures in regard to money flows, both short and long term; and indeed whether the long-term solution needs to make provision for such controls to be applied in certain circumstances.

No doubt, this list could be enlarged, but these seem to me to be the main categories into which these and related problems can be grouped. Over and beyond, there are problems which the crisis of the last few years has brought to the fore, and which many people, including some of those responsible for fashioning their countries' policies, are tending to link with the purely monetary ones. There is, for example, the problem of how trade liberalisation can not only be maintained at the level so far achieved, but can be rapidly and significantly extended. Then there are the problems connected with international investment. These have not only a monetary aspect, that is, through the direct effects of long-term capital movements on balances of payments and international equilibrium; they raise the even more complex long-term economic problem – with its social and political overtones – of the effects of direct international investment, particularly as practised by the large multi-national corporations, on the location of production and employment as well as on the long-run currents on trade.

Even if all these, shall we say more transcendental, problems are left out of account (though they are unlikely to be wholly absent from the minds of the negotiators), it is clear that to bring a negotiation for a long-term reform of the financial system to a successful conclusion, be it in a group of twenty or in a group of ten, will take a considerable time. Meanwhile, we have to make the present régime work without undue disturbance. Meanwhile, also, the world does not stand still; in particular, despite the recent turbulence (which at present, happily, is not too intense) the Europe of the Economic Community has been trying, is trying, and will assuredly go on trying to evolve for itself a suitable monetary system to serve the needs of a customs union which is anxious to move rapidly towards a closer economic union of greater scope not only between its six original members, but within the wider framework of an enlarged membership of ten.

Let me first say a word about "the story so far". I do not mean by this that I want to give you a stage-by-stage account of the detailed negotiations that have taken place in the last few years, of the twists and turns of debate which are inevitable in an enterprise of this magnitude. I want rather to highlight what seem to me to be the significant trends and to set the effort towards a monetary union in the general context of the evolving Community.

The first thing to remember is that the objectives of the founding fathers of the Community have always been political.

That is not to say that the aim was always and has consistently been to work towards a European Federation, let alone one that would come into being in the foreseeable future, but the greater political cohesion of Europe was always the openly avowed goal, whatever the form this might in due course take. It followed that economic unification was a means to an end and moreover that each step in the direction of closer economic union was conceived of as a means of achieving the next and bigger step. Thus the Coal and Steel Community was an example of the "sector" approach, the essential precondition for moving towards the attempt to set up an Economic Community. Within the Economic Community itself, each step was designed to help establish a Community identity and to consolidate it by attempting successively more difficult tasks of economic unification. The first was to create the common external tariff, the second to move towards a full customs union with a common commercial policy, the third to produce a common agricultural policy, the fourth, *via* the agricultural fund, and the communalisation of customs receipts, to make major progress in the creation of a really significant Community budget. These steps, I should add, were being taken not necessarily in chronological order but were generally pursued simultaneously. Simultaneously, too, progress has been attempted and in a measure achieved in creating generally similar conditions affecting competition, harmonising taxation, social provisions and regulations of various kinds – all of which fall under the general heading of "economic union".

It was always recognised that monetary unification would have to play a major part in this process. But it was also accepted that this was a particularly difficult area in which to make rapid progress. In the first place, monetary policy, domestic and international, goes directly to the heart of the question of the abandonment of national sovereignty, though I should add at once that this is often a more apparent than real problem owing to the inescapable necessity for any advanced country of accepting the constraints of membership of some international system. In the second place, the international system includes as vitally important members many more countries not only than the six original members of the Community, but many more than were ever likely to become members.

Despite these difficulties, co-operation was begun some years ago by the setting up of the Monetary Committee, thus bringing together leading officials of the member countries and by regular meetings of Ministers of Finance and of Central Bank Governors. These meetings were designed to provide opportunities for exchanges of view on common problems, more particularly to attempt to harmonise the views of the members in advance of important wider international meetings, such as those of the Group of Ten, of Working Party Three of the O.E.C.D. or of the International Monetary Fund. It is no disparagement of all these efforts of the Six to say that for a number of years they had only achieved a very limited success. They were brought up short by successive alternations of crises in the major member countries, France, Germany, Italy, partly generated by domestic developments, partly as reflections of international disturbances, which required emergency measures of a unilateral character, including the imposition of controls and/or changes of currency parities. Not surprisingly also, when one surveys the monetary history of the last few years, the attempt to forge a common attitude in wider international negotiations rarely got very far. Given the disturbed conditions of the last decade, it was perhaps to be expected that the most ambitious plan for a step-by-step attempt at creating a complete European Monetary Union, the Werner Plan, evolved under the leadership of the Luxembourg Prime Minister, remained for some time only a blue print. For its emergence coincided, on the one hand, with a sharp intensification of the dollar crisis, and, on the other, with the sudden resolution, in a positive sense, of the long drawn-out debate on the enlargement of the Community. This was particularly important in the monetary sphere, since it would lead to the inclusion of Britain, the country with the strongest European financial centre, and with a currency which still had important trading and, to some extent, reserve functions to fulfil.

Perhaps paradoxically, though not altogether unprecedented in history, the crisis of August 1971 produced a greater coalescence, rather than an intensified divergence of views among the members of the Community and between them and the principal candidates for membership. Despite the fact that the first indications of crisis earlier in 1971 had evoked quite different reactions from the principal European countries affected, the resolutions adopted by the Six at the beginning of that year recording their determination to introduce within ten years an economic and monetary union was made into something of a living reality by the recent adoption, and implementation, of the first steps towards that end. From the 15th April, and, in the case of the British from only about two weeks later, the countries of the Community and the most important candidates have agreed to ensure that their exchange rates do not fluctuate beyond a range which is only half as wide as that adopted as part of the currency realignment of last year, namely $2\frac{1}{4}\%$ as against $4\frac{1}{2}\%$. This agreement is being operated for a period of about three months, but this must not be thought of as a trial period, but rather as a running-in phase: the intention is to continue this practice, indeed, as conditions make possible, to go further in narrowing the band as far as Community currencies are concerned.

Happily for all concerned, this major step in European uni-fication was taken at a time when there has been relative calm on the currency front: though the positions of European currencies in relation to the Smithsonian parities differ, none has been outside the narrower European band. That is to say that none seems to have required any intervention to "nudge" it into the new European range. The girth of the so-called European snake in the dollar tunnel was fortunately not outside the new permitted limits. One would, however, have to be very bold indeed to be quite confident that the maintenance of this dual-range system can be counted upon to continue for any considerable time without some definite action on the part of the monetary authorities. Not only is there the possibility that the fluctuating fortunes of the dollar may affect European currencies in different ways, but a glance at the disparities in economic and, indeed, social and political circumstances within the enlarged Community should suffice to show that pressures may arise which would tend to push this or that currency outside the new limits.

Nevertheless, the fact is that this is the system now in force, and that the authorities are committed to making it work. While no one would deny that to operate this dual system is a novel task and therefore that those operating the technique must necessarily be somewhat inexperienced, there can be no doubt that it will be pursued energetically. Failure to make it succeed, let alone failure to make every effort to this end, would gravely impair the credibility of this important attempt to make a great leap forward in European unification. This judgement must, I am sure, apply to Britain, not only as a new member whose practical commitment to the new Union will be carefully watched, but also as the member most experienced in international monetary management and, therefore, having both a special power and a special responsibility as far as success in this operation is concerned.

We thus find ourselves in a situation in which three important tendencies are at work at the same time. First of all there is the undoubted and universally acknowledged need to keep the world's monetary system as it has been patched up by the Smithsonian agreement in reasonable working shape and to avoid disturbances of the magnitude that shook the international order to its foundations last year or, even in some earlier phases, in recent years. In the second place, it is necessary to move with "all deliberate speed" towards a reformed international system whose long-term viability can be demonstrated not only intellectually but which will command a high degree of credibility in the world's markets. In the third place it is extremely desirable that these two objectives should be pursued in a manner which will not impede, but, on the contrary, will encourage progress on the European monetary front, or, conversely, that European monetary unification should proceed in a manner which will not militate against the achievement of a wider long-term solution.

It must be said that at first sight there are no solid grounds for expecting these three desiderata to be necessarily compatible with one another. As with so many important economic policy objectives, in this area too those things that are desirable are rarely obtainable at the same time. In this field of finance there are special difficulties. The needs of the longer term may militate against the best short-term solution and vice-versa. Let me take an example: in the short term it may well be that the problems of the proper functioning of the repurchase provisions of the International Monetary Fund may be solved, as they seem to have been solved in the case of the repayment of the British debt, without raising in an excessively acute form the question of the ultimate convertibility of the dollar or of the rôle that gold should play in the system. In the longer term, of course, these problems cannot be avoided, and it is easy to see that if very strong positions are adopted by different countries on these issues in so far as they concern a permanent solution, they would colour the attitude of the parties concerned in the shorter term, and may, therefore, contribute to aggravating current difficulties and increasing the general uncertainty.

Similarly, views on longer-term solutions and views on the validity of existing currency parities – which are already subject to divergent tendencies in different countries – may tend to get mixed up, thereby making more difficult the maintenance of that relative calm and stability in the short term without which agreement in the longer term is not possible or at least much more difficult.

In this connection, I would draw attention to another factor which is of importance. The debate on currency problems, whether long- or short-term, is now carried on in an environment which is completely unlike that which existed even forty years ago, let alone at the beginning of this century. Then, monetary problems, while freely discussed in academic circles and specialist publications, were negotiated between Governments and central banks very much in an atmosphere of secret diplomacy. Today, they are debated virtually in an open forum. We are all familiar with the reasons that have led to this state of affairs. Whatever one may think of the fundamental value of "open government" or at least open discussions – and I am certainly in favour of it – the fact remains that in currency matters, at any rate, public, semi-academic discussions and Government negotiations combined with continuous public comments, inevitably have an effect on markets. And the effect which they have is not necessarily always that which is desirable in itself, that which the authorities wish, or, above all, that which is consistent with the smooth functioning of the system over the longer term. Thus, a situation in which three major issues of the kind I have described have simultaneously to be dealt with in an atmosphere of continual public comment and debate is fraught with considerable difficulties.

As regards the first two of these three problems, this is not the place to pursue them in any detail. The needs, however, are clear enough. We must aim at stabilising the present *modus vivendi*, or, if modifications in the existing arrangements prove necessary or desirable, we must ensure that these take place in an atmosphere of calm and without exacerbating the conflicts, economic, political, and perhaps even personal, that often tend to lurk not far behind the openly debated issues. Clearly, also, there is a pressing need to arrive at a long-term solution and to achieve as speedy and as wide as possible an agreement on what reforms the international monetary system requires. The broad outlines of what that is are sufficiently well known and have recently been stated with great clarity and precision by Dr. Arthur Burns. I have already said that the maintenance of the existing system in reasonable stability, and the simultaneous active search for long-term reform may generate some friction and conflict. I have no ready prescription of how this can be avoided. I note that there is already some evidence that con-flicting views – and apparently strongly conflicting views – are held on the speed with which progress towards long-term reform should be made. But it should not be impossible, given the necessary political will, to devote adequate energies to the search for agreement on the reform of Bretton Woods, while at the same time making the existing interim system work smoothly. I have put the emphasis on the political will: I can only hope that this will be present in adequate measure.

Whatever may be the right view on all this, there is still the question of what room there is for progress on European monetary unification, the third in my list of items on the current agenda.

The first thing I would say is that it is important to distinguish between principles and practical problems. There is no doubt whatsoever in my mind that once the principles of the need for European economic union is acknowledged, monetary unifica-tion has to be accepted as an integral part of it; and every effort towards its practical achievement has to be made.

I would further say that one should not conceal from oneself the fact that monetary union cannot be sustained, even if it could be achieved, without a very high degree of unification in all the main aspects of economic policy. A narrow band of exchange fluctuations, *a fortiori* fixed parities, and, in the limit, a single currency, means one of two things. It could mean automatic responses of monetary policy in the different countries belonging to the monetary union to balance-of-payments disequilibrium, i.e. something equivalent to the classical "mechanism" in which outflows of funds lead to deflationary measures and inflows to expansionary ones. If, on the other hand, this is not acceptable, as it clearly would not be in the light of present-day requirements of economic management, then it must imply that the balance-of-payments problem of individual countries with other countries of the Community must be virtually eliminated. This means, in fact, automatic balance-of-payments support or, if one wishes to put it in more extreme terms, the pooling of reserves. As this is difficult to visualise without a high degree of unification not only of monetary policy but also of fiscal and, indeed, economic policy generally (since it is unlikely that a country would be given a blank cheque by its fellow members unless it accepted close surveillance of its policies), it is easy to see why, in the limit, monetary unification is virtually equivalent to total economic union.

I deliberately put the emphasis in the way I have, although in recent discussions the emphasis has been placed rather on the methods to bring about monetary unification than on its implications. While I cannot go into the detail of that debate here, I think it is fair to say that the point I have made about the relation of monetary unification to economic unification generally has a great relevance to it. In fact, the different methods that have been advocated essentially rest on different views as to what should precede what: pooling of reserves or a high degree of co-ordination of all monetary policies (involving that strong infusion of central authority which is a characteristic element in Community thinking) or an agreement to narrow exchange fluctuations. As long as one is clear about the intimate relationship between these various aspects of the financial nexus between the member countries, it is probably unnecessary to waste a great deal of time and heat on debating the precise sequence in which one should progress, for it is at least theoretically possible to make limited progress in each of these areas in turn: as I said earlier, each step leading to the next and making that next step easier to take. The fact that the emphasis has now been placed on the narrowing of exchange fluctuations is not surprising since it follows somewhat the pattern, adopted in connection with the successive stages of the agricultural policy, and thus corresponds to the philosophy that seems to underlie much of Community thinking, namely that once a mechanism has been put in place, the acceptance of certain policies which alone can make that mechanism work effectively will be virtually forced upon the participants.

I repeat, however, that one should be under no illusion that narrow exchange fluctuations or fixed parities can be anything more than a mechanism. The Central Banks will, I am sure, do all they can to make it function in a technically perfect manner, but they will be powerless to ensure its continued viability unless there is an assurance that there will be the necessary political will to implement the degree of economic policy unification that will be required. It is a platitude to say that this will not be easy, but it is, nevertheless, worth saying. It will not be easy, not only because co-ordination of national economic policies will have to overcome obstacles of national policy interests – whether rightly or wrongly conceived – but the requirements of economic policy in the various countries of the Community will be affected, and sometimes vitally affected, by their relations with non-member countries, and, particularly, with the United States.

This brings me finally to the equally important and, in the short term, more pressing problem, namely the relationship between progressive monetary unification within Europe and the international monetary order.

Narrow exchange-rate fluctuations in European currencies and even full monetary unification in Europe can, in theory, co-exist with more orthodox payment relationships with the outside world. If one visualises Europe as a single economic unit with a single currency, the problem becomes simple, namely that of the relation of one country with the rest of the world, and of the method of adjusting its payments terms within whatever the international monetary system is. But for some considerable time at least it must be supposed that this will not be the relationship and that we shall have to deal with a régime in which, while Europe is progressing towards monetary union, there is still considerable scope for individual payments relationships between each of their members and the outside world, or, to put it in another way, for the "collective" relationship between

"Europe" and the rest of the world to be only a partial one.

If these individual balance-of-payments relationships are allowed full scope in terms of their possible effect on exchange rates, yet another form of disturbance of the narrow range of exchange fluctuations within the Community that is aimed at will be present, additional to that which may directly arise from divergences in "autonomous" national economic policies. In the end, such a situation cannot be allowed to exist, since it would be disruptive of the whole idea of moving towards monetary union along the road of progressive narrowing of exchange fluctuations between the members. As Professor Cooper has recently shown, there are a number of ways in which this problem can be met. The first would be to have virtually all exchange markets concentrated in official dealings at announced buying and selling rates. This would, of course, destroy the competitive foreign exchange market; and if, in order to avoid this, official intervention were to be limited to keeping exchange fluctuations within the margins permitted in the international system, this would not only fail to achieve the narrowing of the Community range, but would involve continued use of the dollar as the intervention currency. The solution might be to use one of the Community currencies as the general intervention currency within the system, and that currency as the sole and "final" intervention currency vis-à-vis the dollar. Alternatively, an attempt can be made by all member Central Banks to intervene in a closely co-ordinated fashion both in respect to each other's currencies and in respect to the dollar with the object of ultimately reaching the stage when there are fixed parities in Europe which move together against all outside currencies, and particularly against the dollar.

Merely to state this proposition is enough to highlight the very great technical difficulty of achieving this objective in practice, particularly during the interim period before European parities are entirely fixed. A distinguished French expert, M. Guindey, has recently drawn attention to this point by calling for an early separation between intervention in European currencies for the purpose of maintaining the width of the "snake" and those in dollars designed to keep the whole European system within the required margins of fluctuations in relation to the dollar.

One may entertain the hope that despite the enormous practical difficulties that these problems pose, European monetary authorities would be able in a reasonable time to perfect their technical methods, including, what I believe would be essential, the forms of technical co-operation with the American monetary authorities.

But while the problem appears in a technical guise, it will be clear from what I said earlier that I consider it basically as a political problem, namely of the degree of willingness to progress in the co-ordination of economic policies to whatever level the successful accomplishment of monetary unification may require. Thus one must come back to the question of whether this collective European willingness will be forthcoming and whether it can at the same time be made sufficiently conscious of the needs of monetary co-operation in the wider setting of the future international monetary order. It is no use shutting one's eyes to the fact that there is a potential conflict here, moreover, one at two levels: between the pressure for autonomy in domestic economic policy and European unification; and between the need to make a reality of that unification without losing the benefits of an international system, a requirement which is probably more vital in monetary matters than in perhaps any other area of economic activity.

The danger that I see in this situation is that the will to accept the need for closer economic co-ordination may falter when put to a serious test and that in order not to abandon what successes monetary unification may by then appear to have achieved, recourse may be had to measures of exchange control, particularly as regards capital flows, either directly by setting up a two-tier exchange system or through attempts at control of intermediaries such as those operating in the Eurocurrency markets. It is not surprising that those of us with the experience and trading of London behind us should be sceptical, to put it mildly, about such possibilities; and I for one fully share the doubts in this regard which have recently been again expressed by the Governor of the Bank of England.

My own conclusions would, therefore, be that whenever the needs of monetary unification, be it in the more rigorous sense of a European community or in the more general context of reforming and reconstructing Bretton Woods, come up against the obstacle of real or imagined national interest, no effort must be spared to overcome this by an even higher degree of co-operation and co-ordination of policy and by the strengthening of the appropriate institutions to this end. I hope that in this process the European Community will assume an enlightened leadership both in its own interest and in that of the world.

SUGGESTED READING LIST

RINALDO OSSOLA Reflections on New Currency Solutions (*Banca Nazionale del Lavoro - Quarterly Review*, March 1972).

ARTHUR BURNS Some Essentials of Monetary Reform (address to the 1972 International Banking Conference, Montreal, 12th May 1972).

SIR LESLIE O'BRIEN The Problem of Control of Capital Movement (address to the 1972 International Banking Conference, Montreal, 12th May 1972).

LAWRENCE B. KRAUSE Sequel to Bretton Woods (The Brookings Institution).

RICHARD N. COOPER Sterling, European Monetary Unification and the International Monetary System (British North American Committee).

G. GUINDEY Pour un Rétablissement Rapide de la Convertibilité du Dollar (*Le Monde*, 30th April - 2nd May 1972).

Chapter 2

THE STRUCTURE OF THE BRITISH FINANCIAL INSTITUTIONS IN THE 1980s

James Robertson
Director, Inter-Bank Research Organisation

The objective of this paper is severely practical. It is to suggest the kind of way in which we can think about future changes in the financial system and elucidate the various possible courses of future events, so that we may take effective action in the present.

The objective is not to predict what British financial institutions *will* look like in the 1980s, so that it will be possible to say in twenty years' time "Haha! he was wrong" – or even, conceivably, "He was right"! Nor is the objective to suggest what British financial institutions *ought* to look like in the 1980s. There is no particular reason to suppose that individual value judgements on these matters would be of great interest. The aim is rather to highlight some questions about how the future *may* develop, and to suggest what we should do now to prepare for the kind of issues that are likely to arise – a more modest aim, in one sense, but more ambitious in another, because it points to action.

The paper falls into the following sections:

First, it illustrates briefly the kind of changes that are taking place in the financial system. It shows how these changes are inter-related and mutually reinforcing. It indicates the need to understand this inter-active process of change, and to plan for it as a whole.

Second, the paper discusses various kinds of structural change in the financial sector that are either taking place already or are clearly foreseeable.

18

Third, the paper briefly recapitulates (mainly in the form of questions rather than statements) the kind of changes in the structure of British financial institutions that may have taken place by the 1980s.

Fourth, and finally, the paper discusses what steps British financial institutions should now be taking to prepare themselves to meet future changes of this kind, given the very high degree of uncertainty that is involved in any attempt at long-term planning.

THE CHANGING FINANCIAL SYSTEM

Let us now look at the nature of some of the long-term changes that are taking place in the financial system. If we look back about thirty-five years and forward about thirty-five years[1], we can characterise these changes as in Table 1.

TABLE 1 CHARACTERISTICS OF THE CHANGING FINANCIAL SYSTEM

Aspect	Dominant characteristics in the past (*1936*)	Dominant characteristics in the future (*2006*)
Customers	Financially unaware, low valuation of time/convenience	Financially sophisticated, high valuation of time/convenience
Institutions, markets	Well defined boundaries, differentiated markets and services	Few recognised boundaries, integrated markets and services
Customer interface	Direct, face-to-face even for routine transactions. Extensive branch network	Remote communication. Customer-machine interface for routine transactions
Technology	Manual, paper-based information handling and processing	Automatic, computer/data communication based information handling and processing

Management	Operational, day-to-day, empirical, autocratic	Analytical, planning-oriented, participative
Employees	Fear motivated/security rewarded. Willing to perform clerical, repetitive tasks and to submit to autocratic hierarchies	Motivated and rewarded by job interest. Demanding changing tasks, participation
Regulatory framework	Historically and institutionally based, muddled, mysterious, implicit, national	Analytically and functionally based, clear, open, explicit, international
Geographical spread	Compartmentalised business in different countries	Integrated domestic and international business. Truly multi-national institutions

The various aspects of the financial system cannot, of course, be considered in isolation from one another. It will be noted that the first set of characteristics (for 1936) hangs together as a coherent whole, as does the second (for 2006). Changes in one aspect of the system thus have implications for other aspects. The whole process of change is inter-active. It has to be understood, and handled, not as a fragmented collection of changes in supposedly separate aspects of the business, but as a single totality.

Thus we must consider future developments in the round, whether for a single financial institution, or for a financial industry such as banking or insurance, or for the financial sector as a whole. (See Figure 1.) We should think of the business as consisting of certain types of *people and other resources*, *organised and managed* in certain ways, using certain *systems and methods of work*, to provide certain *services* to certain *markets and customers*. As changes occur in any of these aspects of the business, they will spill over into each of the others. At the same time the environment is changing: the *market*, the *employment environment*, the *framework of government regula-*

FIGURE 1

THE FUTURE OF AN INDUSTRY

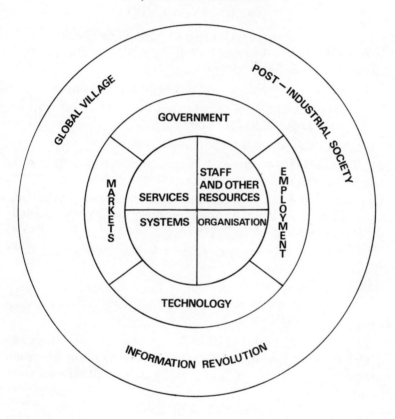

tion, and the state of the art in the relevant *technologies*; and the changing environment creates the opportunity or imposes the need for further change in various aspects of the business.

This is a continuing process of inter-active change, which will go on for ever. We have to learn to live with it, to understand it, to foresee what future course it may take, and to make effective and systematic arrangements to plan for it.

STRUCTURAL CHANGES

Turning now to structural changes and looking ahead towards the 1980s, we can distinguish three main types of change in the structure of the financial system:

(1) the trend towards all-purpose financial institutions;

(2) pressures to clarify the financial functions of government and the public sector; and

(3) the trend towards multi-nationalism.

The changing structure of financial institutions will also be influenced by:

(4) developments in computing and telecommunication systems, and the use made of these systems by financial institutions;

(5) developments in industrial relations and employment practices; and

(6) changes in the social rôle of large companies, including financial companies, and in the social rôle of the financial system itself.

The Trend Towards All-Purpose Institutions. The Radcliffe Committee, reporting in 1959 on the Working of the Monetary System, considered the following financial institutions in the private sector:

London Clearing Banks
Scottish Banks
Overseas and Foreign Banks
Finance Houses
Discount Houses
Accepting Houses

Issuing Houses
Insurance Companies
Pension Funds
Investment Trusts
Unit Trusts
Building Societies

The Committee said[2], "We have included all these groups of institutions in one chapter, despite the great differences in the activities which they undertake and the type of credit they offer, because we have been impressed in hearing evidence not by these differences but by the fact that the market for credit is a single market. Though each type of institution has its special type of business and may, by tradition or as a matter of commercial arrangement, state a preference for one form of lending rather than another, it does not seem that any hard and fast lines are drawn, for instance between the supply of short finance and the supply of long finance; and borrowers seem to be ready to switch to some extent from one to another if difficulties are put in the way of their obtaining finance from the source upon which they are accustomed to draw." Since 1959 we have moved further towards a single market, not just for credit but for other financial services too; as customers become more conscious of the need to manage their finances as a whole, the market becomes more like a single market for cash-flow management and advisory services; new types of financial activity (such as medium-term financing, international money management and the Euromarkets) have emerged to fill gaps in this market, thus integrating it even more closely; and the differences between the activities of the various institutions are not nearly so clear-cut as they were in 1959.

For example, clearing banks have diversified into many other types of financial activity. They are expanding their overseas activity and in some cases have emerged with overseas banks. They have linked with merchant banks or have formed their own. Looking towards the 1980s, it must be open to question whether the three-fold division of British banks into clearers, merchants and overseas banks will survive. Again, it is no secret that the clearing banks regard themselves as direct competitors of the Trustee Savings Banks, the National Savings Bank and the Building Societies in the market for savings, and that they are coming to regard themselves as direct competitors of the Building Societies in the market for house-purchase financing.

Again, in the last year or so the Crowther Committee on Consumer Credit[3] has stimulated institutional changes in that field. The former distinction between retail banking and other forms of consumer credit is softening, as a single integrated market evolves. Some of the more prominent finance houses have recently registered as banks under the Bank of England's new arrangements for "Competition and Credit Control", and are expanding their retail banking activities.

Insurance, too, is becoming more and more closely linked with other financial activities: with clearing banks, which have their own insurance broking subsidiaries or their own insurance-linked savings schemes; with house-purchase finance; with the finance houses, whose shares they hold; and with property finance. Earlier this month the following comment appeared in *The Times*[4]: "An institution like Commercial Union Assurance needs to go on increasing its United Kingdom assets and it needs to do so in fields where it has some expertise, which means the money business. Today that means a large trade investment in Mercantile Credit. In another five years it may mean a full-scale bid for that company. And in another ten years it could easily mean a merger with the same clearing banks which are currently divesting themselves of the hire-purchase interests which the insurance companies are buying." This kind of idea may seem fanciful to some people today, but it clearly cannot be ruled out for the 1980s.

It would be possible to continue thus with many other examples, showing that the traditional demarcation lines between one kind of financial activity and another are becoming blurred and that the trend towards all-purpose financial institutions is gathering momentum. It must even be doubtful whether the Stock Exchange will be able to insulate itself from these developments. As British financial institutions come to compete more closely with their European counterparts, and as a more closely integrated European capital and money market emerges, the continued existence of stockbroking as a self-contained financial activity may come under pressure.

It is appropriate to conclude this discussion of the trend

towards all-purpose financial institutions by referring to the recent report of President Nixon's Commission on Financial Structure and Regulation. The Commission not only recognised this trend in the United States but endorsed it too. They recommended that depository institutions should be authorised to engage in a wider range of financial services; viewed "the granting of new operating freedoms as a first step in an evolving process leading ultimately to the complete removal of socially harmful regulatory and statutory protection for particular types of institutions"; and concluded the introductory chapter of their report with the following paragraph:

"The Commission's objective, then, is to move as far as possible toward freedom of financial markets and equip all institutions with the powers necessary to compete in such markets. Once these powers and services have been authorized, and a suitable time allowed for implementation, each institution will be free to determine its own course. The public will be better served by such competition. Markets will work more efficiently in the allocation of funds and total savings will expand to meet private and public needs."[5]

Government and the Public Sector. Significant changes and much discussion have recently been taking place about various aspects of Government involvement with the financial sector. These include: the changes introduced last year by the Bank of England in their methods of monetary and credit control; the 1970 report on the Bank of England by the House of Commons Select Committee on Nationalised Industries; the Crowther Committee's report on Consumer Credit; the Page Committee's report on National Savings; and the prolonged deliberations over the survival of the National Giro. Also relevant are the reforms that have recently been taking place in the control of public expenditure, and the reforms of the tax system by the present Government.

In aggregate these developments represent a significant move towards the encouragement of a freely competitive financial system and towards more open and explicit forms of Government intervention in financial matters. But, so far, they only amount to a piecemeal aggregation of separate changes, most of which happen to be moving broadly in the same direction.

In the years ahead there could well be increasing pressure on the Government authorities to formulate a more coherent approach to the financial sector. Any such approach would have to examine the Government's various functions in the financial sphere.

Government's Domestic, House-keeping Functions. These include the raising of revenue by taxation; the disbursement of public expenditure; and the management of the Government's borrowing requirements. The institutions directly involved include:

(1) Inland Revenue Department
(2) Customs and Excise Department
(3) Paymaster General's Office
(4) Bank of England
(5) National Debt Office
(6) Post Office

Government's Social and Economic Functions. It is the Government's responsibility to arrange for resources to be channelled into activities that are socially and economically desirable, if these activities are not commercially sound enough to attract sufficient funds to themselves in the normal way. Broadly speaking, the Government can employ two different methods to channel funds towards such activities. The first is to subsidise them explicitly out of public expenditure (or by tax credits). The second is to intervene in the working of the financial system and, as some would say, distort its efficiency: either by persuading financial institutions to undertake commitments (such as export finance) that they might not be willing to undertake on straight commercial criteria; or by ensuring the existence and survival of certain types of institutions which are required to channel their funds in certain defined directions.

Public-sector Banking and Related Functions. A number of banking and related financial functions are now carried out in the public sector by institutions other than the Bank of England.

The institutions that serve personal customers include:

(7) National Giro

(8) National Savings Bank

(9) Trustee Savings Banks

(10) Building Societies

Building Societies may also be included in the private sector. There is room for argument about their status.

Other public-sector financial institutions serve corporate customers, such as:

(11) Export Credits Guarantee Department (E.C.G.D.)

(12) Crown Agents

There is also public-sector participation in bodies like I.C.F.C. and the Agricultural Mortgage Corporation. How far there may be scope for rationalising these public-sector banking and financial activities, and how far they need be carried out in the public sector at all, may well become live issues before the 1980s.

Government's Protective Functions.   It is the Government's responsibility to regulate the activities of financial institutions in such a way as may be necessary to protect the interests of shareholders and customers (including depositors, investors, borrowers and policy-holders). If such regulation is to be coherently framed so as to bite fairly on all financial institutions, one Government agency should presumably be responsible. Today (13) the Department of Trade and Industry is in the lead, but (14) the Registrar of Friendly Societies and (15) the proposed new Commissioner for Consumer Credit are also involved.

Government's Functions as National Monetary Authority.   It is the Government's responsibility to ensure the existence and development of an efficient national monetary system. This includes the existence of whatever physical "infrastructure" (such as coins, bank notes, clearing and settlement arrangements, etc.) is required. It also includes responsibility for the continuing efficiency and competitiveness of the financial system. The Government's functions as national monetary authority are at present carried out by the Bank of England and (16) the Royal Mint.

Government's Responsibility for Economic and Monetary Policy. The main instruments for carrying out the Government's economic and monetary policies have been mentioned in previous paragraphs: the levels and composition of taxation, public expenditure, and Government borrowing; and the central monetary authority's control of interest rates and the money supply. The policies, especially of economic demand management, which require the use of these instruments in one way rather than another, must be the responsibility of Ministers. The department concerned is (17) the Treasury.

There is no particular reason to regard as sacrosanct the present division of functions between all the various Government departments and agencies mentioned in the previous paragraphs. Some of these institutions (such as the National Debt Office, the Paymaster General's Office, and the Registrar of Friendly Societies) will not necessarily survive for ever. The Page Committee on National Savings may well find scope for some rationalisation of the routine banking and payments-handling functions carried out by the Bank of England, the National Giro, the Paymaster General's Office, the Trustee Savings Banks, the National Savings Bank, and the National Debt Office. It may be argued in the years ahead that, for reasons of operational efficiency, the production and distribution of coins and bank notes should come under one authority, not two separate ones. More generally, it seems likely that by the 1980s some attempt will have been made to examine comprehensively the functions of government outlined above and to re-shape the institutional structure for handling them. In short, we can confidently forecast that there will be no less significant structural changes in public financial institutions than in the private sector, although we cannot now predict precisely what form those changes will take.

The Trend Towards Multi-nationalism. There is no need to argue at length that a trend towards multi-nationalism is taking place. As international activity increases in all other walks of life, so it will inevitably continue to increase in the sphere of banking and finance. As international trade and travel grow, and as increasing numbers of international and multi-national companies come into existence, multi-national financial institutions are bound to evolve alongside them.

Among banks, we have seen the creation during the last few years of international consortium banks and of international groupings (such as that in which Banco di Roma, Commerzbank and Crédit Lyonnais are participating), which could well be the first steps towards the single, merged, multi-national banks of the future. Similar developments are taking place in the insurance world. The Chairman of the London Stock Exchange has said that he envisages the steady development of closer links between London and other European stock exchanges. The emergence of the Eurobond and Eurocurrency markets as important elements in the international capital and money markets have given a powerful impetus to the trend towards multi-national financial institutions.

As the world's financial and monetary system grows closer together, governments and central banks in different countries will inevitably find themselves working more and more closely together and becoming more multi-national in character. This seems likely to be particularly true in Europe, even if the route towards European monetary unification and commercial harmonisation proves longer and stonier than the enthusiasts would like. A European central bank and a world central bank (or something recognisably like them) will presumably emerge one day.

This trend towards multi-nationalism will itself stimulate change in the structure of the financial system in individual countries. As the British clearing banks, merchant banks and stock-broking firms come into keener competition (and also closer co-operation) with the German all-purpose banks, they may be compelled to consider whether the structural differences between them are still commercially advantageous. As the harmonisation of banking law, monetary instruments, taxation and company law proceeds in Europe (however fitfully), it can hardly avoid stimulating further discussion and debate about the structure of the financial system in all the various countries concerned.

Other Forces Relevant to Structural Change. As mentioned earlier in this chapter, developments in the *technology of computing and telecommunications* will have implications for the structure of financial institutions.

In the first place, co-operative computing and telecommunication systems require jointly sponsored enterprises to run them. Existing examples include Bankers Automated Clearing Services Limited (BACS), the computer bureau jointly sponsored by the British clearing banks; and the New York Clearing House Inter-bank Payments System (CHIPS), jointly sponsored by the New York banks. A considerable number of comparable systems are now being planned or are envisaged. They will give rise to new forms of co-operative enterprises in the financial sector, some of them multi-national in character. The research and study required for planning such enterprises is also giving rise to new organisations, like the Inter-Bank Research Organisation. Some of these, too, will have to take on a multi-national character.

More generally, the increasing use of automated systems for handling financial business, and the systems analysis that must precede their introduction, are likely to call in question the traditionally accepted demarcation lines between one sort of financial transaction and another. Again, the integrative potential of computers will enable financial institutions to widen the range of services they offer to their customers. Systems developments are thus likely to stimulate further thinking by financial institutions about the real nature of their business. In other words, systems developments are likely to act as a stimulus to further structural change among financial institutions.

Foreseeable developments in *employment and industrial relations* will affect the structure of financial institutions. Developments in trade unionism in the financial sector, including international and European trade unionism, and developments in industrial relations legislation and company law in this country and in Europe, may well stimulate or constrain future structural changes. The employees of financial institutions are likely to acquire increasing influence over the future development of the institutions in which they work, and become more strongly placed to encourage or inhibit structural changes such as mergers between one institution and another.

Finally, in this section of the paper, we must not forget the changes in the social rôle of large companies that appear to be occurring in the United States and may well spread to Europe. These changes can be summed up as a sharpening awareness of the social obligations of large companies. The multi-national, multi-purpose financial institution of the future is likely to have to pay close attention to such matters as individual privacy, and is likely to have to be demonstrably immune to conflicts of interest which could be prejudicial to its customers. Such considerations as these could come to exert unexpectedly powerful contraints on further structural innovation.

At the same time, the social function of the financial system as a whole is likely to come up for increasing discussion and debate. It would not be surprising if the notion were to take root that basically the financial system is an information system, whose functions are: to indicate the claims that people and organisations may make on the community's resources, in other words their entitlement to purchasing power; to enable them to trade present for future purchasing power, and certainty for risk; and to enable individuals, organisations, and the community as a whole to channel resources into the activities of their choice. It is by no means impossible that in due course such a concept of the functions of the financial system, and the idea that the financial system can be well or ill-designed to carry out these functions will itself exert a powerful influence on the future structure of financial institutions.

FINANCIAL STRUCTURE IN THE 1980s

How, then, will all these developments affect the structure of financial institutions in the 1980s? This question cannot be answered. It can only be clarified by making the question more specific.

How fast and how far will the trend towards *all-purpose financial institutions* go, in this country and others? (How much will this trend be inhibited by inflexibilities and rigidities in Government regulation? How soon will it be obstructed by anxieties about the power of large financial institutions and the conflicts of interest which they may involve?) How quickly will the pressures build up to rationalise the financial functions of

Government and the public sector? How quickly will the trend towards *multi-nationalism* gather momentum? How will these three main trends cut across one another? How will they be stimulated or constrained by other developments, for example in technology, employment and industrial relations, and by changes in the social obligations of financial institutions and in the social functions that we expect the financial system to perform?

How many of the present Big Four British clearing banks will still retain something resembling their present form by the late 1980s? And how many of the leading merchant banks, insurance companies, building societies, stock brokers and other financial institutions will be recognisably the same institutions as they are today? Will the Bank of England still combine the dual functions of Government banker and central monetary authority? Will the Bank of England have turned into the provincial outpost of a European central bank? And will such a European central bank have itself become the regional headquarters for a world central bank?

No one can give answers to these questions today. All we can do is to recognise that they are arising, and that the answers will be important. We have to regard them as the background of uncertainty against which planning must proceed.

ORGANISING FOR CHANGE

How should we organise for change? The question is applicable at the level of the individual institution. It is also applicable at industry level (for example, banking, insurance, or Stock Exchange), for so long as such industries continue to maintain their separate existence. It is applicable to the City of London as a whole, and also to the financial and monetary arms of government. It is becoming increasingly applicable to the international banking and financial community.

If an institution is to organise for change it must develop a capability for corporate planning, supported by corporate information, research and management services. Regular procedures, normally based on the annual budgetary cycle, must be introduced for creating and revising the corporate plan and for putting in hand the programme of research work required to support it. Other contributors to this book will, however, be discussing the arrangements needed for planning in the individual institution, and I shall say no more about them.

However, to organise for change at industry level requires the development at that level of precisely comparable capabilities and procedures to those in the individual institution. This is, in fact, what the clearing banks have been aiming to do in developing the Inter-Bank Research Organisation, and it may be of interest if I describe how the procedures work.

Putting matters very simply, IBRO is available to work for inter-bank committees and other inter-bank bodies with particular functional responsibilities, especially in the spheres of:

Automation Studies and Planning
Relations between Banks and Government
International Studies
Employment Questions

These committees and bodies correspond to (and indeed their membership consists of) the senior managers in the individual banks who are responsible for these areas of work. (See Figure 2.)

IBRO's work programme is made up mainly of projects carried out for these committees. The projects are decided in the following way. (See Figure 3.) First we set down as a working hypothesis the main events up to five or six years ahead that seem probable or desirable, and important. (An example in the field of inter-bank automation studies might be the introduction at a particular point in time of a computerised system for handling payments between financial institutions in the City of London.) Working back from those events, we then consider what prior inter-bank decisions and actions are required; and working back from those decisions we decide what studies are needed and how urgently. We repeat the process every six months, and a revised programme of work is submitted to the banks once a year for their approval. As each study project in the programme is completed, its results are submitted to the appropriate inter-bank committee.

It might be misleading to suggest that these systematic procedures for corporate planning and research at banking industry

FIGURE 2

IBRO COMMITTEE STRUCTURE

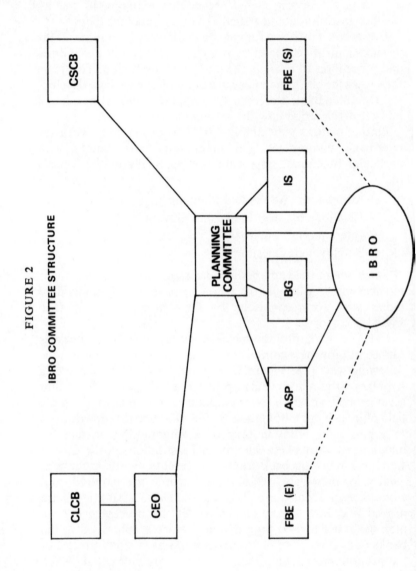

FIGURE 3

IBRO WORK PROGRAMME

CONCEPTUAL FRAMEWORK

DATE	STUDY PROJECTS	INTER—BANK DECISIONS	INTER—BANK ACTIONS	EVENTS
1972				
1973				
ETC.				

level are yet working quite as effectively as one would wish, or that their purpose is widely understood in every bank, or that they yet have a really effective counterpart in every bank. But, with patience and hard work, and close co-operation with a number of our sponsoring banks, we are making good progress towards a practical system of planning and research, geared into the decision-making processes of the banking industry. And with the full support and encouragement of the banks we are now becoming a fairly powerful research unit.

In my view, it will be necessary to evolve comparable arrangements for the City of London as a whole. It is impossible to lay down precisely what form they should take. They must emerge from a process of discussion and consultation between the various institutions and sectors of the City. The Bank of England may prove to have an important part to play.

CONCLUSION

The writer Ralph Waldo Emerson said that "The English mind turns every abstraction it can receive into a portable utensil, or working institution". In this chapter I have tried to suggest that we, who are concerned with the future vitality of British financial institutions and with this country's rôle in the future development of international financial institutions, should lose no time in turning our abstract ideas and speculative thinking about the future into working institutions for co-operative planning and research.

Such institutions are necessary if we are to cope with the processes of structural change that are now upon us. And they will themselves be an important element in the structure of financial institutions in the 1980s.

NOTES TO CHAPTER 2

[1] See *infra*, David Peretz, *Thirty-Five Years of Change for the Financial System*.
[2] Report of the Committee on the Working of the Monetary System, Cmnd. 827, August 1959; paragraph 125.
[3] Report of the Committee on Consumer Credit, Cmnd. 4596, March 1971.
[4] Christopher Marley, "City Conglomerates: Insurance Industry Broadens Money Base" (*The Times*, 5th April, 1972).
[5] Report of the President's Commission on Financial Structure and Regulation, December 1971.

Chapter 3

THIRTY-FIVE YEARS OF CHANGE
FOR THE FINANCIAL SYSTEM

David Peretz

Head of the Economic Section, Inter-Bank Research Organisation

The financial system is a large-scale information processing system. Like most such systems it is undergoing a major revolution with the introduction of the new information-processing technologies – computers and data communication. Because of the central rôle of the financial system in Western economies, such changes will have far-reaching implications, the significance of which has scarcely yet been appreciated.

It is surprising how little serious study has been devoted to the longer-term future of the financial system. The only major exception has been the discussion of the impact of developments in the payments mechanism, and the so-called "cashless and chequeless" society.[1] Whilst undoubtedly important, this is only one – and, I will argue, perhaps a relatively minor – aspect of the change that the "information revolution" will bring.

The point has been recognised by others, particularly in the U.S.A. In the words of Professor Harry Johnson: "The financial system will be the beneficiary of a technological revolution – computerisation – which is already proceeding apace but whose potentialities have scarcely been tapped. This is an important point the significance of which has scarcely been appreciated, either by governments and public or by many professional economists. . . . The financial sector might well do more to educate the public in the proposition that it is the high technology growth industry of the next decade."[2]

This chapter looks rather further ahead – somewhat arbitrarily thirty-five years ahead, up to the year 2006. Such forecasting is not an end in itself; its purpose is to show what future changes in the financial system may mean for actions and decisions to be taken now. Developments within – but to a lesser extent beyond – about a thirty-five-year time-horizon may have implications for today.

THE DEVELOPING SYSTEM

The elements of the future financial system are almost certainly already apparent, if only we can identify them.

One development in the *market* for financial services that seems to have been under way for some years is that towards increasing financial sophistication – corporate customers leading the way (for example in economising on the "idle" bank balances) and individuals following later. There is in fact some room for debate as to whether the present trends reflect a permanent change in attitude or simply result from changing cost and interest rate structures; and whether in the latter case the change is reversible. But there is apparent a real change in attitude, brought about by higher educational standards, and the increasingly wide dissemination of financial "knowledge" – this will be a continuing trend.[3]

Individual customers are also likely to place an increasing emphasis on convenience in financial services. This will be a force working towards "packaged" and integrated services.

The breaking down of traditional boundaries and lines of demarcation between financial *institutions* is, of course, already well under way, stimulated by the demands of consumers for the convenience of a single source of sophisticated financial service. The ability of computers and systems analysis to handle tasks of great complexity is likely to accelerate this trend, moving the balance of economic advantage away from specialised and compartmentalised operations towards diversified intercommunicating ones.

Advances in *technology* are never imperatives. Computer/communications technologies, and the associated systems analysis, will not of themselves revolutionise the financial system; but because of the nature of the business of financial institutions they will make a revolution possible. (Likewise, past revolutions are often not ascribed to the technical developments that have made them possible. For example, it is hard to see how the present proliferation of short- and medium-term domestic and international money markets could have developed without the telephone and telex; but these technologies are rarely cited as factors determining such developments.) Most of the activities of the financial sector can be described in some sense as information handling and processing (a theme to which I return below). Traditionally carried out by hand and on paper, more recently by telephone and telex, such activities are ideally suited to electronic computer and communications technologies.

So far as the payments system is concerned, this theme has been fully developed elsewhere. The so-called "cashless and chequeless society" is quite familiar[4] with its electronic money and terminals in shops linked directly to bank computer systems. But the same technologies may also revolutionise other aspects of the financial system.

Even today most decisions made by *management* in many financial institutions are almost literally day-to-day, and this seems to be true to a greater extent than in other areas of business or government. The need to plan and analyse, imposed by a changing environment, therefore comes particularly hard to such institutions. Nevertheless it seems safe to assume that by 2006 management in the financial sector will have undergone the same changes as are already under way in industry and government.

Computer systems cannot eliminate the need for human involvement or management judgement and decisions, but they are likely to contribute to a change in their nature. For example, decisions may be less directed at individual transactions, prices or interest rates, and more concerned with designing new systems for determining them automatically in response to varying circumstances.

Trends in *employment* and attitudes to work will also be important in this context. Demands for job interest and participation will lead to the elimination of dull, repetitive human tasks on the one hand, and on the other direct the course of automation to create satisfying rôles for employees and management alike.

The rôle of *government* is discussed at greater length below, but there are four points that should be made here. There is a clear move (in the U.K. at least) towards greater openness and explicitness in government. This has been apparent in recent years in, for example, the Government's attitude towards the objectives of nationalised industries, and in the increasingly sophisticated parliamentary discussion of public expenditure[5] and taxation. It is now beginning to manifest itself in changes in monetary policy, and in the regulatory framework for financial institutions.[6]

The present framework of monetary regulation has grown up historically. It seems unlikely that it can survive unchanged in an era of spectacular development in the financial system. Indeed it is improbable that any framework could survive that was not logically and analytically designed to be robust to a changing environment.

National regulations are not enough in a world of multinational companies and banks. Nor does any combination of unharmonised national regulatory frameworks necessarily provide a sensible framework for global operations. Recent international monetary crises demonstrate the problems of relying on co-operation between governments. Progress towards a truly international framework is difficult, involving as it does a loss of sovereignty by national governments. But events seem bound to compel considerable changes by 2006.

The "information revolution" may lead to demands for regulations for rather different purposes than the classical ones of monetary and economic policy – for example to protect personal privacy.

These developments – and others – are mutually consistent, and hence likely to be self-reinforcing. Placing them in a seventy year time-frame (thirty-five years back and thirty-five years on) we can construct a hypothesis for the year 2006, as shown in the table reproduced by James Robertson, page 19.

THE FINANCIAL SYSTEM AS AN INFORMATION SYSTEM

As Professor Johnson says, the significance of these changes has scarcely been appreciated.

Economists have always seen the financial system at least metaphorically as an information system.

Money (and more generally the "payments system") is seen as a means of transferring information about financial claims; in other words, entitlement to resources, between individuals, companies, etc. (economic units) – an efficient alternative to barter.

Financial intermediaries and markets are also concerned with distributing resources over time; they match information about the willingness of some units to forego immediate claims over resources with information about the demands of other units to bring forward their use of resources, thereby determining interest rates.

There is also the insurance function – trading certainty for risk – performed by insurance companies, unit trusts, banks and others, which contains a large element of pure information handling – matching risky investment opportunities with risk-averting investors.

Finally, there is the task of distributing resources to the "best" investment opportunities, thereby ultimately determining the pattern of real investment.

In the past such a view of the financial system has had little practical importance. Those who operate within the system have not seen their tasks in this light, nor have they needed to do so; each has been concerned only with a relatively small part of the whole. But modern information-processing technology and techniques could for the first time make it possible and economic to turn the metaphorical information system into an actual information system in a real operational sense. This raises a number of philosophical – but also practical – questions.

In collective economies essentially identical functions to these four are performed by hierarchies of state committees. Given that the social objectives in market and non-market economies are often similar (economic growth, etc.), it is interesting to speculate to what extent the logic of technology and systems analysis will eventually cause such organisational differences to dissolve.

THE NATURE OF MONEY

Historically, economists have discussed the nature of money

in terms of its functions in a primitive economy (means of payment, store of value and unit of account), and the properties of assets suitable for use as money (durability, recognisability, portability, divisibility, degree of confidence, etc.). For the future it seems more relevant to consider the functions required of "money" in a complex economy, and the technologies appropriate to these functions.

The prime function is that of an information system; payments transmit information about entitlement to resources, in accordance with implicit and explicit market and "social" decisions. In a sense all money flows result from some set of "social" decisions (usually implicit) about the distribution of real resources within the economy. It is already quite clear that the technologies most appropriate to this information-handling task will be computers and data communications; the costs of paper-handling associated with cash and cheques are becoming prohibitive. Relevant questions about this emerging payments system to some extent mirror those about the appropriate "properties" of money; confidence in the system's security, its accessibility from different locations, etc., will all be important (but solvable) problems.

There is one important characteristic in which the system will differ from the cash that it replaces. Cash is basically a decentralised information system; possession of cash is an indicator of entitlement to resources to the holder, and to those who sell to him; but cash itself provides no means of centralising (and then analysing) information about *all* holders and all transactions. An electronic payments/information system could offer such potential, perhaps at a relatively low additional cost.

This parallels the trend for social decisions about the distribution of resources to be made explicit through Government and parliament (prices and incomes policies, social security, etc.) rather than remain implicit in the workings of a "free" market economy. Potentially, then, the future payments system could provide much of the "management" information on which centralised social decisions about resource distribution could be based. This, in turn, of course, raises questions of personal privacy which are already well recognised. Like all new technologies, the system will offer opportunities for abuse and exploitation, as well as public benefit.

FINANCIAL INTERMEDIATION: LENDING AND BORROWING

The functions of financial intermediaries and markets can also be considered as primarily concerned with information processing. They take information about the willingness of some economic units to forego immediate consumption of resources to which they are entitled (saving), at a price (interest rate), and transfer it to others who are prepared to pay a price (interest rate) to bring forward their use of resources (borrowing). They also take information about the various risk (including liquidity) preferences of savers and match it with information about the riskiness of lending opportunities.

The functions of this system, seen as a totality, differ from those of the payments system in that, as well as being characterised by high volumes, they are also extremely complex. The traditional requirements of paper (and oral) based information-processing "technologies" have enforced decentralisation, and also a certain degree of simplification. Thus the financial sector has evolved as a series of largely compartmentalised markets and groups of institutions (commercial banks, merchant banks, building societies, insurance companies, the stock market, the money markets, brokers, etc.), different institutions offering and holding limited categories of carefully differentiated liabilities and assets (bank current accounts, deposit accounts, building society deposits, insurance policies, overdrafts, personal loans, mortgages, Government securities, equities, debentures, etc.), and abiding by simplified rules for matching the liquidity and riskiness of their assets and liabilities (liquidity ratios for commercial banks, equity/risk assets ratios for merchant banks, etc).

Even those financial groups that extend to several sectors of the market have tended to keep the various parts of their business differentiated, though some of the barriers are beginning to break down (for example, commercial banks are using their branches as selling points for their non-bank subsidiaries).

If these characteristics are the result of constraints imposed by today's technologies, then they can be expected to change under the impact of electronic technology, and its associated systems analysis and operational research. But what will replace them? Will institutions be able to offer complete ranges of "assets" and "liabilities" with characteristics carefully tailored to the needs of each customer, so that the categories of financial claims that we know today completely disappear? Will all the markets merge into one multi-faceted market, where each borrower and each lender can precisely specify all the various characteristics – risk, liquidity, interest, etc. – required or preferred, the market being "made" electronically? Will the remaining human functions (apart from organisational planning and control) consist largely of activities such as investment analysis, economic forecasting, operations research, systems analysis, etc? These questions certainly pose the extreme possibilities. But it should also be said here that the new technologies may well impose contraints of their own. In particular the lead-time for system modification, and hence innovation and change, could be increased considerably.

Which institutions will survive? The technology required for the borrowing and lending function appears to have much in common with that already being developed by the banking industry for the payments system. To take one example, it is quite likely that the floor of the Stock Exchange will in the medium-term future extend into a decentralised electronic information matching network; developments of this kind are already under way in the U.S.A.

A bank payments network might relatively easily be adapted to encompass such a function. Some commentators, therefore, argue that those who dominate the payments system will eventually come to dominate the whole financial system.

GOVERNMENT INTERVENTION AND "SOCIAL" POLICY

A distinguishing characteristic of non-market economies is that the functions of the financial system have been pre-empted by the State. In mixed economies, however, there are social decisions, made through Government, as well as market decisions about resource distribution; and in all such economies there is a degree of direct Government intervention in the financial system. One aspect of the current debate about monetary policy is resolving itself into the question of whether there should be such intervention (through directives to financial institutions, and Government operations in financial markets), or whether social decisions are better implemented through measures directed outside the financial system – for example, through subsidies or tax relief to savers, or for certain types of borrowing.

If the financial system is seen as a system for handling in-' formation about entitlement to resources, then this can be seen as a question about where in that system it is most appropriate for the Government to inject information about social resource distribution decisions. The answer can then be a pragmatic one, and may differ in different cases. Nevertheless, for the present at least, two points seem to weigh in favour of the second approach.

Government intervention should not be such as to disturb the mechanics and organisation of the financial system, at least not without very good reason.

It is probably best for such intervention to be explicit and aimed directly at the factor to be influenced. Thus direct incentives for productive investment are likely to be more effective than measures designed merely to direct funds from the personal to company sector.

MONOPOLIES, OLIGOPOLIES AND GOVERNMENT REGULATION

A question that remains to be tackled concerns the optimum form of organisation for the future financial system. In its bluntest form the question is: if technology makes it possible to operate the system as a single entity, should it be so operated (by the State, or in a regulated manner), or is there a continuing rôle for competition in the financial system? For the very long-term (2070?) this must be an open question, and even for the time-horizon of this article it will require careful examination.

Developments in the payments system are already pointing the way – and yet how can banks co-operate (necessarily) in developing a single system while competing on money transmission services? Similar questions seem likely to arise with the other developments discussed above.

Or take a rather different point. Financial markets are often so organised as to encourage "game playing" between a limited number of important participants. Such activities may have little true economic benefit, and new technologies can increase their costs. Thus if all participants in the market for Government securities buy computers to calculate differentials between bond yields faster and more accurately, none of them in the long run will be any better off. The market may be marginally more efficient, but possibly at a quite disproportionate cost in terms of computer investment.

The rôle of Government in setting correct ground rules for such activities has yet to be thought out. *Inter alia* there is a need for further investigation of the motivations of participants in financial markets. But it is clear that certain parts of the system may have to be brought under new forms of Government regulation, in order that competition in other parts can be to the public benefit.

IMPLICATIONS FOR TODAY

Finally let us return to the theme of the opening paragraphs. What are the immediate practical implications of such visions of the future, for decisions and actions to be taken now?

Frequently the management decisions with the longest time-span are those concerned with recruitment and manpower planning. Senior executives of financial institutions in 2006 are now in their early twenties. If the hypothesis about long-term developments is correct these executives will by then be running diversified, integrated, computer-based financial empires, where management is analytical and planning-oriented, rather than intuitive and operational. They need to be recruited and trained for this now. And similarly those who will occupy more junior rôles in 2006 need to be trained for them now.

Strategic business development is the other major area for action now by financial institutions. If new technology is to place a premium on diversified, multi-national institutions (with the capacity to integrate their various activities) then there may be room for only a few. Those already on this path may be those that survive. There will no doubt continue to be a rôle for small specialised institutions but it could turn out to be very limited.

There are, however, a number of important open questions, on which further research would be valuable. In particular we need to know more about the nature of the constraints that the new technologies will impose, and hence the institutional developments they will help to shape.

For Government there is a clear need to plan now to provide the proper framework within which such developments can take place. This framework should help to shape developments, not be shaped by them. Thus some of the apparently philosophical questions relating to the Government's rôle need to be considered now, as quite immediate and practical issues.

NOTES TO CHAPTER 3

[1] See Dennis W. Richardson, *Electric Money: Evolution of an Electronic Funds Transfer System* (Cambridge, Massachusetts, MIT Press, 1970), which also contains an extensive bibliography.

[2] Professor Harry G. Johnson, speech to the First National Conference of Canadian Bankers 1970, recorded in the *Institute of Canadian Bankers Bulletin*, Fall, 1970.

[3] For further discussion of one aspect of this debate see James Robertson and David Peretz, "The financial framework: pressures for reform", *The Banker*, November 1970, and also George Garvy and Martin R. Blyn, *The Velocity of Money* (Federal Reserve Bank of New York, 1969), Chapters 2 and 6.

[4] See Dennis W. Richardson, *op. cit.*

[5] See, for example, *The First Report from the Select Committee on Procedure: Session* 1968–69 (London, HMSO, 1969), and *Second Special Report from the Select Committee on Procedure Session* 1969–70 (London, HMSO, 1970).

[6] See the Bank of England's consultative document on *Competition and Credit Control* (May 1971), and their subsequent document on *Reserve Ratios and Special Deposits* (September 1971).

Chapter 4

PAYING BY COMPUTER

James Robertson
Director, Inter-Bank Research Organisation

The amount of cash in circulation and the number of cheques handled by the banks are both rising steadily year by year. During the next ten to twenty years, however, an electronic funds transfer system will be developed that will enable many of the payments today effected in cash or paper to be made automatically between the computers of different organisations. The banks are already well embarked on the early stages of developing such an inter-bank transfer system. This was one of the main reasons why the Inter-Bank Research Organisation came into existence in October 1968. The organisation is sponsored by the London clearing banks (Barclays, Lloyds, Midland, National Westminster, and Williams and Glyns) and also by the Scottish joint stock banks (Bank of Scotland, Clydesdale, and Royal Bank of Scotland).

As a basis for studies and planning, which is necessarily somewhat speculative at this stage, we are working on the hypothesis that computer-to-computer communication in the banking system will develop broadly through four phases (Figures 1 to 4).

An Inter-Bank Computer Bureau (I.B.C.B.) has been set up and a magnetic tape interface is being developed between this bureau and the computer centres of each bank. Bank customers with computers can put schedules of payments into the banking system on magnetic tapes generated by their computers and directly put into I.B.C.B.'s computer.

The I.B.C.B.'s role was originally conceived as a rather limited one. It was to handle schedules of standing-order payments generated each day by the computer centre of each bank.

48

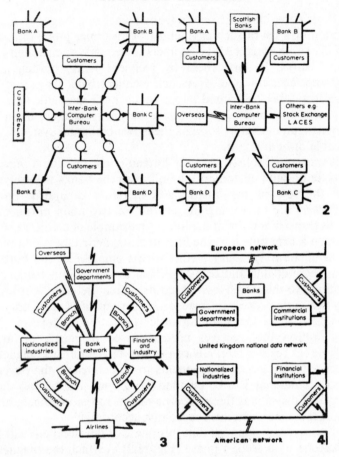

FIGURES 1 TO 4: PAYING BY COMPUTER

The British electronic banking network will probably develop along the lines shown in these four phases, although in practice each phase will gradually merge into the next. Figure 1 shows the first phase, in which customers' accounts are centralised at their bank's computer centres, and the Inter-Bank Computer Bureau exchanges magnetic tapes with the various bank computer centres and accepts tapes from some customers with their own computers. In the second phase (Figure 2), up to the middle 1970s, magnetic tape exchange will be replaced by data links. This will merge into the third (Figure 3), up to about 1980, in which Government departments, industries and others will have created data networks of their own, which will be increasingly linked to the bank network and each other. By the middle 1980s (Figure 4) the separate networks will probably have coalesced into one national data network, like the present telephone network.

Each day the bureau receives from each bank magnetic tapes containing a list of such payments (for insurance premiums and the like) authorised by its customers to be made to customers of other banks. It sorts them by recipient bank, branch and customer account, and gives each recipient bank its output in the form either of printed paper vouchers or magnetic tape as required. All banks should receive output from the bureau in magnetic tape form as soon as their own computer systems are capable of handling it.

It was soon realised that the bureau could provide a service directly to bank customers, as well as to the banks themselves, and the rôle of the bureau was therefore expanded. Bank customers are now using the bureau for two main purposes – credit transfer and direct debiting. An example of credit transfer is when a firm puts into the bureau a magnetic tape containing a list of monthly salary credits for its employees; the bureau sorts these credits and transfers them to the various banks for crediting to the employees' accounts. Direct debiting is essentially the same process in reverse – or perhaps it is more correct to regard it as the standing order operation in reverse. An organisation that receives pre-authorised payments in large volumes at regular intervals can supply to the bureau magnetic tapes containing lists of payments to be debited to the payers' bank accounts and to be credited to its own. The bureau then sorts and distributes these debit payments to the various banks, who debit their customers' accounts accordingly.

It is logical to suppose that this phase of development will be succeeded by a second phase (Figure 2) in which the magnetic tape interface between banks and I.B.C.B. will be replaced by data transmission links, thus changing the character of the I.B.C.B. installation from being a data-processing centre to something more like a switching centre routeing large volumes of payments data between the computer centres of the various banks. Also bank customers with computers or terminals will in future probably tend to deal directly with their own bank rather than with the bureau. Computer-to-computer communication, or computer-to-terminal communication, directly between a bank and its customers will increasingly provide a facility not just for handling the customer's payments but also for providing him with a wide range of automated accounting services of the kind now provided by many computer service bureaux.

However, the bureau is likely to remain the point of interface between the banking network and comparable computer systems being developed by organisations such as the Stock Exchange, whose members include customers of all the banks. The National Giro is another obvious example. We also expect to see a direct data-link in the middle 1970s between I.B.C.B. and the LACES system at London Airport which will be handling payments for goods imported and exported by air. Finally, by the middle 1970s data-links should be developed between the British banking system and banking systems abroad; I.B.C.B. seems the most likely point of interface at the British end.

This second phase will probably merge more or less imperceptibly into the third (Figure 3). By the middle 1970s other organisations and industries as well as the banks will have developed data networks of their own. Government departments – particularly the revenue departments, but also the major spending departments – will have linked their local and regional offices in country-wide data systems. So, no doubt, will the airlines and various nationalised industries such as the Coal Board, not forgetting the Post Office itself. During the later 1970s, if not before, these separately developed data networks will become increasingly linked to one another. This third phase of development will also see the introduction of computer terminals in almost all sizeable shops and offices, and greatly increased use of computer-to-computer communication between the British banking system and banks overseas. It will shade gradually into the fourth phase.

In this phase (Figure 4), which may be completed by the middle 1980s or later, the various separately developed data networks are likely to have become merged in a single national data-transmission system, linking all subscribers to one another in much the same way as the telephone system does today and providing a facility for direct communication between users of computers and terminals in any part of the country. Other countries will have developed similar data networks, and ours will be linked with theirs much as telephone and Telex systems are linked today.

As customers, developments on these lines will enable us, if we wish, to delegate authority to our banks to make and receive many more of our payments than we do today. Our regular payments for insurance, mortgages, and the like will be made more cheaply and at greater convenience by direct communication between our bank's computers and the computers of the insurance companies, building societies and so forth. Foolproof arrangements will, of course, have to be made to ensure that we have authorised the payments and to enable us to verify that they have been correctly made. Secondly, we are likely to make many of our retail payments through a new kind of cash register, which is in fact a terminal linked to the banking system.

You are at the supermarket, for example, and you reach the check-out point with your basketful of goods. There the girl totals the bill, recording the items purchased as required for the supermarket's stock control and re-ordering purposes, and communicating this information through the terminal to the supermarket's own computer centre. To pay, you insert your magnetised bank card into the terminal. At the same time you identify yourself – possibly by speaking, if voice-recognition techniques have developed sufficiently; possibly by imprinting your thumbmark on a sensitive plate on the terminal, if finger-print-recognition techniques have developed sufficiently; and possibly by simply keying in an authorising code. The terminal (or the bank computer holding your account, to which the terminal is linked) then verifies that the card does in fact belong to you. If the computer holding your bank account then verifies that you have the funds to match the bill, payment can be made. You press an activating key on the terminal, which instructs the computer holding your bank account to debit the necessary amount and transfer it to the supermarket's account held by its bank's computer.

Development of existing bank cards – including both cheque guarantee cards and credit cards as we know them today – will play a major rôle in the advance towards a "cashless and chequeless society". Apart from becoming one of the main instruments to identify us electronically to the banking system, they may also be used as a sort of portable bank account. In this case it will be the card itself, not the account held at the bank's computer centre, which is decremented as we make our payments. For example, a wage-earner might be paid not in cash but by being given a magnetically encoded card entitling him to make payments up to the value of his wages. Every time he makes a payment with his card or draws cash with it, the card is debited by the appropriate amount, the employer's bank account is debited by the same amount, and the payee's bank account is credited.

How will all this affect cheques? At present, cheques travel from the branch bank where they are paid in; to the clearing department of that bank (where they are read and sorted and the accounting information needed by that bank is captured); to the Banker's Clearing House (where they are handed over to the bank upon which they are drawn); to that bank's clearing department (where they are read and sorted again and the accounting information needed by that bank is captured); and finally to the branch holding the account of the customer who wrote the cheque.

Considering this as an operation carried out by the banking system as a whole, rather than as separate operations conducted by each bank, there is obviously a certain amount of redundancy in the procedures. The question for the future is how this present method of handling the flows of cheques and the information they contain should be developed, bearing in mind the possible future evolution of inter-bank data transmission as outlined earlier. One possibility, at least in theory, would be to obtain the information from the cheques at the point where they enter the system (i.e. on a reader terminal at the branch where they are paid in) and to convey this information as a total payment message through the inter-bank system to the various points that need it for accounting and settlement purposes.

The development of a banking and then a national data network in the general direction I have described will give rise to a whole host of problems. The most important of these will be about people: how to ensure that the new systems will be acceptable both to the people who use bank services and to the people who provide them. But in this article there is only space to touch on the technical and systems problems. These will include questions about the precise operational requirements of the data transmission network, the nature of the traffic which it will have to handle, the level of security and reliability it will have to provide, and the tariff structure to be adopted by the

Post Office. The network will have to cater for high-volume traffic with peak loads at certain times; it will be vital to ensure that no data are lost, that no spurious data are generated, and that no one can get unauthorised access to bank accounts. Highly reliable stand-by facilities will also be needed. There will be tremendous problems of standards and compatibility. And difficult problems of audit will arise for the accounting profession.

As the research arm of the banking industry, with a multi-disciplinary approach covering such areas as law and economics as well as systems analysis and electronic engineering, the Inter-Bank Research Organisation is well placed to help with most of these problems. The banks themselves have been co-operating since the early years of computing to achieve the necessary degree of compatibility between their computer systems. The electronic sub-committee of the Committee of London Clearing Bankers, formed in the mid-1950s, has evolved into the present inter-bank systems and development committee and its working parties. In 1968 the banks jointly established the Inter-Bank Computer Bureau, which – as I have suggested – may prove to be the nodal growth point for the electronic money-transmission system of the future. In 1970 they decided to set up a new, small, high-powered inter-bank steering committee on automation studies and planning to supervise a comprehensive programme of studies on all the various aspects of the longer-term possibilities I have described in this chapter. This steering committee is at general-manager level. To support it in master-minding its programme of "strategic" studies, the Inter-Bank Research Organisation has been strengthened by the creation of a new very senior post of Chief Consultant: Automation Studies and Planning. The magnitude of the task means that this post will provide a challenge to one of the ablest, most experienced computing men in the country.

Chapter 5

THE FUTURE FOR CONSUMER CREDIT

Sir Alexander Ross
Chairman, United Dominions Trust Ltd.

The Introduction tells us that the purpose of this book is "to examine the issues which are likely to have a crucial effect on the growth and profitability of financial institutions over the next decade". So we are to be concerned primarily with the factors affecting *growth and profitability*: and one of the four "topic areas" covers changes in markets and products in, amongst other things, *consumer credit*. Every examination candidate is urged to read the question before attempting the answer. He does not know how lucky he is – the questions are there and all he has to do is to provide the answers! In real life, the most difficult task is correctly to identify the questions. If one can do that, the answers are often relatively simple. I shall try to identify some of the questions – particularly those affecting growth and profitability – which will be faced by financial institutions engaged in the field of consumer credit over the next ten years. I will also hazard a guess at some of the answers.

Turning again to the Introduction, we read that "the 1970s promise a period of accelerating change which could revolutionise business practice in banking, insurance, building societies, stockbroking and *consumer credit*". This statement is certainly true of consumer credit: but change from what? In looking to the future, we are inevitably conditioned by what has happened in the more immediate past. There have been such wide-sweeping changes in almost every aspect of operations in the last two or three years that we might be tempted to believe that the pattern for the remainder of the decade must now have been set and that all we need to do to predict the future is to extrapolate existing trends. Unfortunately, it is not as simple as that. The available statistics are of little help to us. In the words of the Crowther Report, "Our consideration of the problems of consumer credit law and practice and of its economic and social implications has been hampered by an absence of statistical information in the form we required." The strategic planners of today are in no better plight. The trail has been muddied, mainly by changes in marketing methods: hire-purchase and credit-sale contracts are recorded where many similar transactions in the form of personal loans – particularly those written by the banks – are not. To quote historical statistics would be potentially misleading: to quote current statistics without a whole host of caveats and qualifications would be positively dangerous. I propose so far as possible to avoid them altogether.

Nevertheless, before we can begin to plot the possible areas and course of change, we do need to know something about the position as it is now and how it has come about. A basic question is, "What *is* consumer credit?" Many people tend to identify consumer credit simply with hire-purchase, but this is far too narrow a view. On the widest interpretation, "consumer credit" means the lending of money to individuals (either directly as a loan or by the deferment of payment of part or all of the price of goods or services) to cover personal, family or household expenditure. An economist might define it negatively as "borrowed funds used by individuals other than for the production of goods and services for sale". The Crowther Report defined it as covering: credit for house purchase; credit for periods of over three months, but not more than five years; and very short-term credit for three months or under. The market that *I* shall be examining will be Crowther's category "credit for periods of over three months but not more than five years".

By far the largest proportion of this credit is provided on instalment terms. I mention this because the word "instalment" is the one which will probably help immediately to visualise the kinds of lending and credit granting which I have in mind. I have deliberately excluded credit for house purchase because, although undoubtedly *consumer* expenditure, it can be regarded as "capital" rather than "consumable" expenditure. I have also excluded Crowther's category "very short-term credit for three months or under" because, in practice, this is largely provided by the retail trade under "open credit" terms and is therefore a topic which would be better left to a work which dealt with the finance of retail traders rather than of the consumer.

From now on, then, when I refer to consumer credit, I shall mean consumer instalment credit for periods of over three months but not more than five years. With this in mind, let me concentrate on the evolution of the market of today. In the past, the consumer credit market has been artificially distorted by monetary constraints and economic conditions which are unlikely to be reproduced in the next decade. The published statistics of outstanding consumer credit do not include any figures for credit extended by the banks: but they are a fair guide to what has happened over the past decade – at least until the restraints on the banks were lifted in September 1971. They show that, in the three years from March 1962 to March 1965, outstanding instalment credit expanded steadily from £888 million to £1,139 million. Then came the ceiling control imposed by the Governor's letter of May 1965, after which there was virtually no expansion for the next five years until March 1970, when the figure had grown only to £1,273 million. Since then, the expansion has been very rapid indeed. In March 1971, it was up to £1,356 million, and by March 1972, despite the exclusion of bank lending, it had leapt to £1,678 million. I believe that this trend will continue for the foreseeable future. The Bank of England's ceiling directive limited the supply of funds to finance consumer credit. This measure, far more than the Board of Trade's control orders, restricted expansion and inhibited competition between financial institutions. In 1971 both the ceiling control and the terms control orders were lifted – hopefully for ever.

In their place, we have the Bank of England's new scheme described in its green paper on "Competition and Credit Control". The introduction of this scheme has already meant more for the consumer finance market than it has for most other areas of banking and finance. We are, in consequence, currently enjoying boom conditions which are made to look all the greater coming, as they do, after so many years of repression. We are experiencing at the same time a rise in consumer spending, easier credit conditions, and some encouragement to spend on credit because interest on loans is capable of being claimed, in part, against income tax. Most of the financial lending institutions are presently flush with funds, and the authorities are busy increasing the money supply at a rate which the British consumer is finding difficult to absorb. Everything is working together to guarantee that there will be a rapid expansion of consumer credit. But economic conditions may one day dictate a return of tighter monetary control and it is this rather than any notional assessment of consumers' ability to borrow which will dictate the growth of consumer credit in the next decade.

In looking forward against this background, I feel that there will be two distinct phases of development. For a start, we shall see a continuation of the present boom. I expect that there will be a massive increase in the provision of consumer credit. This boom in credit will last, or perhaps I should say will be permitted to last, for as long as there are major reserves of under-utilised manpower and money in the economy. I am optimistic enough to expect a continuation of the present strong growth of consumer credit for the next year or two. But there will inevitably come a time when this boom will tail off. Perhaps it will slow down of its own accord; if not, then no doubt the authorities will be obliged to moderate its growth. The decade ahead therefore divides itself into two parts – the first, one of very strong growth, and the second of consolidation, with the rate of growth slowing down, or with some falling away in the level of consumer credit.

How far and how fast can the expansion of consumer credit go? Well, experience in the U.S.A. suggests that the United Kingdom has a long way to go before saturation point is reached, although, of course, national characteristics – and statistics – vary. The volume of consumer credit in this country is still far behind the per capita level of outstanding debt in many other countries. Moreover, the rapid rate of inflation not only escalates the price of goods being purchased on credit but also gives every encouragement to buy on credit rather than save up and pay later by cash.

The *cost* of money is also a consideration. We have been told that money costs and interest rates are likely to fluctuate considerably because of the new official policy in the monetary field. Most of the institutions engaged in consumer credit borrow money for a shorter term than that for which they subsequently lend. So we are exposed to the swings and roundabouts of interest-rate movements and must try to minimise the impact of fluctuating rates on our operations. This may eventually mean matching the borrowing period with that of the lending period to a greater extent than is at present the case. In the meantime, banks and finance houses have developed their own base rates as a means of relating the cost of money to the charge that they make for it. Fluctuating interest rates are more difficult to explain to the consumer than to business borrowers, particularly when they are fluctuating upwards.

Consumer credit institutions have a voracious appetite for money, and must plan the timing of their funding with special care. With the prospect of a tremendous surge forward in the demand for credit, and with money costs currently at a low point in the cycle, I would imagine that many such institutions must be contemplating a large-scale funding exercise at an early stage in their strategic plans. For there is a real prospect that the expansion in the demand for credit will provoke intense competition for the funds with which to meet it. The charge to the consumer for business which is low in value per transaction compared with commercial lending, and which involves considerable effort in monitoring repayments, is inevitably going to be high. Part of the cost of providing credit lies in the payment of commission to traders who introduce business. This has always led to criticism, because greater competition often means higher commissions. In an increasingly competitive world, the finance house will only be able to make such commission payments as can reasonably be related to the real saving in administrative costs which stems from the use of a trader as a means of access to the customer. If the alternative is to be massive and expensive advertising to attract business, or if it requires the maintenance of a national network of branches, then the cost is probably going to be much the same. This is one area where strategic planning based on factual evidence is going to be of vital importance.

I want to turn for a moment to another – and very significant – influence upon the present structure of the market – *the law*. I cannot hope to emulate the masterly exposition in the Crowther Report of the effects which the law has had upon the development of the consumer finance market. I wish only to mention three relevant areas of legislation, and then only because they give rise to problems which are of immediate concern at the present time. The solutions may well determine the structure and the operational methods of the market of the 1980s.

First, the *Moneylenders Acts*. These were responsible for the partition of the market into vendor and lender credit. At the turn of the century, only a very small proportion of the population had the credit-standing to borrow from banks. The rest – the vast majority of consumers – could turn only to licensed moneylenders unless they were in need of credit to cover the cost of new goods. Then, if they were fortunate, the retailer would offer them hire-purchase or credit-sale facilities. Looking back, it seems like a form of credit apartheid, with a closed banking establishment commanding the main part of the financial resources of the country but catering only for a small part of the market, and with the retail trade plus a very few small hire-purchase companies catering for the remainder. Even the rapid growth of the consumer durable market in the 1920s left traditional banking attitudes unaffected. The demand for consumer credit arising from the mass manufacture of cars, motor cycles, cookers, refrigerators, radios, and so on, was met by, for the most part, a new breed of financial institution, which we now call a finance house. This explains the classical pattern of finance-house operations whereby credit for the purchase of goods was provided through the trader at the point of sale: credit was secured by a hire-purchase agreement and the finance company's service was considered to be provided as much for the benefit of the trader as for that of the customer.

Second, the *Bills of Sale Acts*. These are still with us and, for all practical purposes, prevent the consumer from giving the security of goods in support of a loan. Had it not been for the Bills of Sale Acts, it is possible that the banks might long ago have lent money on the security of goods and established for themselves a commanding position in the market for the finance of consumer durables. But the banks saw little or no attraction in doing this: and the finance houses saw no attraction in lending as a legal means of providing consumer credit, because such lending would have had to be unsecured.

During the late Fifties and early Sixties, however, two events occurred to bridge the gap dividing lender from vendor credit. The first was the move by the clearing banks to buy equity participations in finance houses. This happened during a relatively short period between 1958 and 1959, and the catalyst was the boom in consumer instalment finance caused by the suspension of the control orders in 1958. One or two of the banks even crossed the divide for a short period by offering personal loan schemes on instalment terms, but these schemes were short-lived and were withdrawn when the economic and monetary climate began to deteriorate in the early Sixties.

The second event flowed directly from this brief foray. Some of the finance houses had noted the banks' competitive advantage in being able to offer personal loans with income-tax relief on the interest. By 1964 all the larger finance houses had introduced schemes under which their customers enjoyed tax relief on hire-purchase transactions. Some of these schemes involved the participation of a co-operating bank, and this provided the first real incentive for finance houses to seek exemption from the Moneylenders Acts: but, generally speaking, these new schemes were regarded simply as an extension of vendor credit facilities. What was really significant about this development was that, for the first time, it brought finance houses into direct contact with their customers.

The third consideration is the *Hire Purchase Acts*. These Acts significantly affected the development of the consumer finance market. The first Hire Purchase Act of 1938, and the second of 1954, were designed to do little more than prevent the "snatch-back" of low priced goods (£100 in 1938, extended to £300 in 1954). The 1964 Hire Purchase Act (now consolidated and re-enacted in the current Hire Purchase Act of 1965) was a different proposition entirely. First, its limit of £2,000 meant that, for the first time, the overwhelming majority of transactions involving motor cars and caravans were caught by protective legislation. Second, for a whole host of technical reasons, it further reduced the often marginal value for the finance house of possessing a security interest in the goods which it was financing. When the Act came into force on 1st January 1965, a number of the leading finance houses switched to handling their business on credit sale terms (that is, unsecured credit). At the same time, a new and special form of credit sale scheme was developed under which customers could obtain immediate income-tax relief on their credit charges, tax at the standard rate being deducted from the interest element of the instalments. What was more important, this scheme did not require the co-operation of a bank.

During the five short months when the finance houses were able to promote these schemes, they were immensely successful. However, in May 1965 the ceiling control on advances was imposed on finance houses. As a result, there was no longer a need for them to sell their facilities: it became simply a matter of rationing the supply of credit amongst existing customers. This went on for another five years, and during that time the clearing banks and the other commercial banks had to turn away virtually all their private customers for their personal finance needs. When at last the ceiling controls were lifted in 1971, the gap between vendor credit and lender credit institutions had been practically closed.

What had happened in the meantime was that, as a result of doubts arising from the case of *U.D.T.* v. *Kirkwood* in 1965, the Government had introduced a special provision in the Companies Act 1967. Section 123 of that Act specifically empowered the then Board of Trade to issue certificates of exemption from the Moneylenders Acts to those financial institutions which could establish that they were carrying on a banking business. The importance of Section 123 for the finance companies is that only those who have obtained certificates that they are banks for the purposes of the Moneylenders Acts can properly engage in the business of making instalment credit available in the form of personal loans instead of in the form of hire-purchase or credit sale agreements.

Over a hundred certificates have now been issued, and among those qualified to lend money other than as licensed money-lenders are virtually all the larger finance houses. As these institutions, together with the banks, collectively account for a very high proportion of consumer loan business, it can be said that the recommendation in the Crowther Report that everybody should be free to lend has, in practice, been anticipated. With the removal of any doubts as to their legal status, it was a logical step for finance houses to switch from credit sale to loans. This allowed a further simplification of documents; it made the tax-relief scheme easier to work; and finally, it avoided the risk, always present in point-of-sale business in the 1960s, that they would be held liable for innocent, inadvertent breaches of the control orders. The tax-relief privileges were withdrawn under the 1969 Finance Act, but the finance houses had by then begun to appreciate the full extent of the market for direct lending as compared with point-of-sale finance. As the banks were still constrained by the ceiling directives on lending, the finance houses were able to gain valuable experience of this (for them) new way of carrying on business in an orderly, stable and, at that time, only moderately competitive market.

A consumer looking at the market today could not fail to see the increased emphasis on the direct canvassing of loan business by a widening variety of financial institutions. He would notice no slackening in the readiness of traders to offer him competitive finance at the point of sale. He is being encouraged to borrow, not only by the financial institutions but also by the Government itself. In this new environment, he will need some protection: and this brings me to the Crowther Report. Both the Report and the Bank of England's green paper "Competition and Credit Control" have one theme in common – the need to stimulate competition. The Crowther Report recommends that anyone who wishes to lend in the consumer market should be free to do so, and that if the substance of a transaction is that of a loan and a borrowing, the consequences for the lender and the borrower should be the same whatever the form of the transaction. For example, a hire-purchase transaction would be treated as a loan secured on the goods, which in law at the moment it is not.

The Report defines a consumer loan as one for an amount not exceeding £2,000. For the purposes of consumer protection, it draws a distinction between point-of-sale credit arranged through a dealer intermediary, which it calls "connected" lending, and transactions negotiated directly with the customer, which it calls "unconnected" lending. The level of consumer protection recommended for connected lending – roughly equivalent to transactions covered by the Hire Purchase Acts of today – is materially greater than that proposed for unconnected lending. Where there is more than one level of consumer protection operating in the same market, there is a natural tendency for business to make for the less protected areas. So I think that greater protection than is at present proposed may be needed for the "unconnected" borrower to redress the balance. This adjustment will be all the more necessary if the present restrictions on entry into the market for unconnected lending – which have so far operated to control the calibre of entrants – are to be totally abolished. For one of the main recommendations in the Report is that *any* lender should be free to operate in both sectors of the market – by lending directly to his customer, or indirectly via a trader, as he wishes – and that the Moneylenders Acts should be swept aside.

Today, the capacity to engage in "unconnected" consumer lending is, for practical purposes, restricted to the banks, the Section 123 finance companies and licensed moneylenders. In terms of consumer protection, this may be no bad thing. But it does mean that, in the line-up of competitors at the beginning of this decade, there is one group of financial institutions under a handicap – those who don't possess any exemption from the Moneylenders Acts; for they can compete only in the connected point-of-sale area, which is certain to decline as a proportion of total consumer credit. They are unable to enter the market for direct lending, which will account for an increasing part of the total market of the future. This inequity will continue until such time as the Crowther Report's recommendations on this point have been implemented.

In the meantime, the finance companies which are able to make unconnected loans will need to make the most of that capacity, to meet the growing competition from the clearing banks. The rising tide which normally lifts all boats will, in this instance, lift some higher than others. The institutions which enjoy this advantage at present tend to be the larger ones, and the increasing importance of the computer is a further factor in favour of the big battalions in the business. How great any additional competition will be when the Moneylenders Acts are repealed it is difficult to estimate. The longer the delay, the less significance the repeal of the Moneylenders Acts is likely to have. Those who are at present free to make unconnected loans are likely to try to obtain as strong a foothold as they can whilst the going is good.

I would not wish to imply that the point-of-sale market is in any danger of disappearing. Although there are over ten million bank accounts held by individuals in the U.K., a significant section of the population does not maintain bank facilities, so that, even allowing for greater activity by the banks, there still exists a substantial market for credit at the point of sale. In absolute terms, it will probably increase in size, although as a proportion of the total consumer credit market, it may be expected to decline. Speaking very roughly, if the percentages of the consumer credit market accounted for by point-of-sale credit and direct credit were of the order of 70% and 30% today, it would not surprise me if these percentages were to be 50/50 – or even 40/60 – in ten years' time. Part of this decline will be accounted for by credit established on a revolving basis between a bank or finance house and its customer in conjunction with, for example, the use of credit cards.

Following the removal of the control factors, the market as a whole must surely grow considerably during the next ten years. And why not? The Crowther Report found no evidence to suggest that the level of consumer credit has untoward effects on inflationary pressures, on the volume of savings, or on the stability of the economy in general. As the Report points out, consumer credit accounts for only 9% of total consumer expenditure, which is itself only some 50% of the total spending in the United Kingdom economy. "On balance" – to quote the Report – "the use of credit to finance consumer expenditure does not pose any greater threat to the attempts of the monetary authorities to control the level of activity in the economy than its use for other forms of expenditure. We therefore do not view its potential future growth with alarm, and do not believe that there is a case on economic grounds for curbing the development of the consumer-credit industry."

The growth in population, the increasing demand for consumer durables, and the effects of inflation on the volume of money needed to finance them, are only some of the factors which will ensure that, barring unpredictable monetary restraints, the size of the consumer-credit cake will continue to grow. I am, of course, assuming that the standard of living in the U.K. will continue to rise. Personal disposable incomes will rise in real terms, and the section of the community which is at present too poor to obtain much credit may expect a growing benefit as the wealth of the nation becomes more widely spread. In future, too, the probable growth of disposable income in the hands of younger people will doubtless lead to a growing demand for credit – the young are more willing to go into debt than their parents. Increasing demand for labour-saving equipment in the home, increasing demand for cars, caravans, boats, television and hi-fi equipment, increasing demand for holidays, are all bull points in assessing the likely trend of the market.

As for the types of facility offered by the financial institutions, I'm sure that the underlying trend will be towards simplicity. Whether the Crowther legislation affecting consumer protection will upset this trend remains to be seen, but there is no doubt that the vast majority of consumers find the personal-loan type of contract most attractive, whether they obtain the facility by negotiation at the point of sale or directly with the lending company. Consumers are certainly becoming more financially aware and are prepared to shop around for their credit instead of considering it as part of the purchase of the goods. This trend will be accentuated if the Crowther Report's recommendations on "Truth in Lending" are accepted and implemented. Such facilities as medium-term loans secured against second mortgages, secured and unsecured revolving credit, and simple unsecured personal loans are already with us and are becoming widely acceptable, whether offered by banks or finance companies. And this is as it should be, because the Crowther Report, as its "first principle of social policy" urged that users of credit should be treated as adults capable of managing their own financial affairs. It has not always been so in the past. Economic restrictions on consumer credit have for many years operated to prevent many consumers from having access to credit that might otherwise have been available to them. With the present liberalisation of consumer credit there is a risk that the pendulum may be allowed to swing too far the other way. The forces of competition likely to be unleashed if the main recommendations of the Crowther Report were to be implemented could well prove to have been under-estimated. Certainly there will increasingly be a burden on the lender to see to it that the consumer does not fetter himself with debts that he should not be allowed to incur. Research will be intensified into better, quicker and more sophisticated methods of evaluating credit, as much for the borrower's benefit as for the lender's. With direct lending becoming an increasingly important part of the consumer-credit scene, I would expect to see the development of "financial counselling" for borrowers as an essential feature of the service to be provided by consumer-lending institutions in the days ahead. All such institutions will be aiming to establish and maintain a continuing link with good borrowers. The use and availability of revolving credit will increase as borrowers who have shown themselves to be sensible in the use and extent of the credit given them are encouraged to look to the institution with which they have established their credit for "top-up" facilities to meet their further requirements.

But there are always new types of goods and services appearing on the market and these may require a novel method of finance or some revision of an existing system. For instance, most people in this country obtain their television on rental. This practice seems to be peculiar to the United Kingdom but, with colour television emerging as a major growth-area of consumer spending in the Seventies, the trend towards rental in this sector will intensify. Personal credit is available not only for goods but also – and increasingly – for services. Shares and investment units can be bought on credit and the use of these facilities may be expected to grow. With the increasing importance of leisure activities, another major growth area lies in the provision of credit for holidays and the proposed change in the treatment of interest for tax purposes will plainly encourage all these developments.

When more experience has been gained of unsecured lending in a totally competitive market, there may well be a movement back towards the obtaining of security to support the personal covenant: and I think it possible that increasing competition may cause those who seek business from the weaker end of the market to reappraise the value of security as a stop-loss. Financial institutions are likely to seek ways of reducing the labour costs of their operations, but I believe that the branch network operation will prove to be an increasingly valuable way in which lenders can establish direct contact with their market. On the other hand, point-of-sale specialists may find less need for branch networks with the increasing use of computers and electronics as means of communication. In any event, closer attention must clearly be paid to the development of *marketing* techniques by *all* suppliers of credit.

What effect can all these things be expected to have on profitability? In the new environment, margins will tend to shrink and, to extract an acceptable level of profitability, we must not only do more business but also handle it more efficiently and economically. Fortunately, for the time being at least, the total market is growing so rapidly that there is enough room for everybody without having to tread too heavily on anybody's toes.

In the longer term, the auspices seem to me to favour the bigger companies and, in spite of the increasing competition, I see no reason why they should not maintain, if not increase, their return on net capital employed. I think that the disparity between the retail rates of differing types of financial institution will reduce as the market becomes increasingly rate conscious Similarly, a reduction can be expected in the disparity in the money costs of differing financial institutions. Freer competition will blur the distinctions between them. Finance houses have become banks and the banks are now heavily committed in what has been traditionally finance house territory. I hesitate to predict the future pattern of their relationship as further advances are made in the automation of the money transmission system, but *differences in organisation* remain. The banks, for instance, all run their finance-house subsidiaries as separate companies, and I would expect this to continue. So long as methods of marketing and administration remain different, we cannot expect to see a homogeneous banking unit. Indeed, one of the interesting features of the consumer credit scene is that there are so many widely different ways of providing credit, and all seem to be participating in the current boom – direct personal loans, point-of-sale credit, credit cards, check trading, rentals, licensed moneylenders, and so on. A key factor is the relative cost of administering each different method of providing credit. Rapidly spiralling wage costs will force institutions to consider the viability of those operations with a heavy labour content. The banks are reviewing their branch networks, and it would seem that, for them, the era of branch expansion is at an end for the time being.

But other institutions may be differently placed. Whilst banks are closing branches, building societies are expanding their branch network: and companies such as my own are developing new outlets known as "Moneycentres" as a means of engaging in retail banking directly with the consumer. Nor must we forget the possible entry into the market of new classes of institution which may already be very big in their own particular field. The Trustee Savings Banks and the National Giro might be permitted to offer credit. The dividing line between building society lending (consumer/capital finance) and consumer credit proper is already a thin one and could become thinner. And overseas companies – particularly the American banks – may seek to obtain a foothold in the British market. As Mr. Whittam Smith will refer to this subject in his chapter, I will say no more about it except, perhaps, to add that I would be surprised if either the building societies or the insurance companies were to make any significant direct contribution in the consumer credit market as I have defined it.

In looking ahead, we must, of course, take account of our entry into the European Common Market. It is difficult to be precise about the implications, but financial institutions will no doubt become more international in their outlook. This perhaps is of greater concern for some classes of consumer credit institution than for the clearing banks, which have always been international in concept. But whether Europe will become truly one market from the point of view of consumer finance seems doubtful. Financial institutions will, however, have to face up to greater mobility of labour and will have to adjust themselves to providing finance to someone who could quite well move to another country before the debt is repaid. Institutions will also have to seek out funds from the cheapest and most readily available part of the Market. One would expect to see organisations, systems and the general method of conducting business becoming uniform, or more nearly uniform, throughout the Common Market. This is, however, something which would be spread over a number of years and which would, I hope, be an area where British institutions could play a part in formulating the pattern of events. If it does prove possible to organise consumer credit on a Continental basis, then British institutions can expect to see a major increase in their market possibilities and, of course, a major increase in competition. The wide differences among consumer-credit operations in the various countries at present make it difficult to predict what may happen if competition and a uniform market lead to the disappearance of nationally different consumer-credit institutions.

To sum up in a few words, I would say first that, barring unpredictable official monetary restraints, the consumer-credit market must expand enormously over the next ten years. Second, that the present balance between point-of-sale finance and direct lending may be expected gradually to shift in favour of direct lending. And third, that competition will be fiercer than it has ever been and that the market shares of the different institutions presently serving the market or about to enter it will alter significantly under the influence of changes in the legal and economic environment.

But who can look into the seeds of time and say which will grow and which will not? Certainly not I! I have tried to identify the principal questions that will arise over the next ten years and I have given you *my* answers to at least some of them. At the end of the day, I have the uneasy suspicion that, whilst history may vindicate my choice of *questions*, the *answers* will prove to be somewhat different!

Chapter 6

COMPETITION IN THE

INSTALMENT-CREDIT INDUSTRY[1]

A. Victor Adey
Managing Director, Mercantile Credit

"Too many uncertainties exist to enable specific conclusions as to the future of finance houses to be drawn. Their strength lies in the expertise they have acquired in providing instalment credit and other financial facilities over many years in constantly changing market circumstances, surrounded by archaic law, at the mercy of the dictates of the institutions of Government and against strong flexible competition from many and constantly varying directions. The fact that finance houses have had to be flexible and resilient fits them as well as any other type of financial institution for the uncertainties which lie ahead."

The Crowther Committee intended to stimulate competition on the grounds that this was in the public interest. The Report does not attempt to explain how the methods it envisages for stimulating competition would give this result. It attempted no survey of the comparative strengths and weaknesses of finance houses within the financial community as a whole – all it did was to make an express statement that it hoped the clearing banks would enter the market (unsupported by any analysis of the possible consequences or even by an acknowledgment that such an analysis was necessary).

This chapter will survey the position of finance houses following Crowther in this broader context. Issues which Crowther did not consider are relevant to the validity of the conclusions reached in the Report. (The Bank of England proposals for the monetary regulations of finance houses and others referred to in their paper on Competition and Credit Control are crucial to the whole paper.)

FINANCE HOUSE

What is a finance house? Here we have a problem of definition. Is there any feature common to all finance houses but not to anyone else? – the answer is probably no. Who then do we refer to when we think of the future of finance houses – the thirty-two members of the Finance Houses Association (F.H.A.) whose membership includes some but by no means all of three types of finance company recognised in the U.S.A. – banks, sales finance companies and small loan companies. Should we include retailer-owned private-sales finance companies – of which there are hundreds, many of which are members of the Hire Purchase Trade Association? And where do the industrial leasing companies fit in – or the vehicle contract-hire companies? Perhaps the only common feature these possess is that they all finance the acquisition or use of goods.

The solution I propose for the purposes of this chapter is to talk about my subject from the viewpoint of a large independent publicly-owned group (i.e. one operating in both consumer and commercial markets and providing most, if not all, the types of financial facilities capable of being used to finance goods or services) for which:

(a) it holds a certificate under S. 123 of the Companies Act 1967, i.e. it can be treated for the purpose of the Money-lenders Acts as carrying on the business of banking and therefore exempt from the provisions of those Acts;

(b) it is not exempt from the provisions of the Protection of Depositors Act (relating to advertisements and accounts) under S. 127 of the Companies Act 1967;

(c) it is not a banking or discount company for the purpose of Part III of Schedule 2 of the Companies Act 1967 and thus not exempt from the provisions of that Act as to balance sheet and profit and loss account;

(d) under the Bank of England's new monetary policy (unless it seeks and obtains full recognition as a bank) it is subject to the 10% reserve asset ratio and can be called upon to make special deposits with the Bank of England.

I make my choice for the following reasons:

(i) Such companies are usually the ones the public, the financial press, the Bank of England, and the Government refer to when they talk about finance houses.

(ii) Such companies form the backbone of membership of the Finance Houses Association (though four of the largest F.H.A. companies are wholly owned by clearing banks).

(iii) It enables me to tackle my subject comprehensively and thus ensures that I include reference to the problems of the many other types of company which finance goods and services.

(iv) It enables me to speak with the greatest degree of authority since I am Managing Director of one such finance house.

THE FINANCIAL COMMUNITY

My first task is to sketch in the way in which Government regulations help to identify the constituent parts of the financial community because only by doing this can I illustrate the types of institution which either do compete or could, if they wished, compete with the finance houses and the advantages and constraints which the regulations give to each category. (I use the word "regulations" to cover that strange amalgam of Statute, Ministerial regulation – often exercisable on a discretionary basis in accordance with policy objectives unknown to and unascertainable by those affected – and "voluntary" directive which is so typically English.) In what follows I make no excuse for utilising some of the information and figures contained in the Report howbeit in a much condensed form.

The Clearing Banks. These are the members of that private total monopoly, the clearing (but the Giro is a competitor here). They can create credit and are now required by the Bank of England to keep 12½% of their assets in liquid form. They no longer operate a deposit-rate cartel; from 1st October 1971 each bank can quote independently for deposits. They are common-law banks and as such are exempt from the Moneylenders Acts. They and their principal deposit-gathering subsidiaries are exempt from the Protection of Depositors Act. Nevertheless they can be directed by the Bank of England under the general authority given to the Bank under S. 4 of the Bank of England Act 1946 and, from time to time, are required to make special deposits at the Bank of England to the detriment of their earning capacity. They also, somewhat reluctantly, subsidise export finance by low-rate loans. Potentially they are formidable competitors. The size of their resources and branch networks, their monopoly of the clearing which ensures face-to-face contact with customers using the money transmission system, their capacity both directly and through their subsidiaries to raise money at low cost and on long terms, their capacity to use persuasive powers for the introduction of retail business by retailers for whom they act as general bankers and the goodwill which their probity and power brings to them leave little doubt on the point.

Commercial, Foreign and Merchant Banks. Here we are considering the types of institution which provide a full service to industry and commerce ranging from financial advice and medium-term loans to foreign exchange and export finance. Usually they are "fully authorised" banks for the purposes of the Prevention of Fraud (Investments) Act, 1939 and the Exchange Control Regulations as well as holding certificates under S. 123 and 127 and exemption under Part III of Schedule 2 of the Companies Act, 1967. They are bound by the $12\frac{1}{2}\%$ liquid-assets requirement of the clearers and may be called upon to make special deposits at the Bank of England. They are not members of the clearing, but are on the Bank of England list and would be subject to directives issued under S. 4 of the Bank of England Act, 1946. These institutions are, in terms of resources, expertise and customers, a significant competitive force in the industrial and commercial market – many finance plant and equipment on hire-purchase or leasing terms already. Their cost of money is certainly no greater than that of the major finance houses and is often less – but they lack the extensive branch networks which the larger finance houses and the clearing banks possess. However, in the last year or two there have been signs that clearing banks and others are edging their way into the merchant-banking field with a result that the absence of a large number of branch outlets could soon change at least for some merchant banks.

We now consider those institutions which provide in general long-term secured credit.

Building Societies. Building societies provide a specialised service, mainly to private individuals to enable them to finance the purchase of houses or flats for their own occupation. The finance is secured by mortgage on the land and usually also on the dwelling. Societies are governed by the Law of Property Act, 1925, subject to supervisory legislation embodied in the Building Societies Act, 1962 and administered by the Registrar of Friendly Societies. They are exempt from the Moneylenders Acts, the Protection of Depositors Act and the Prevention of Fraud (Investments) Act, 1939. The total flow of funds in deposits and shares into building societies (almost entirely from individuals) and their mortgage lending activities make their operations a substantial industry. While Local Authorities and life assurance offices, among others, operate in the same field, building societies dominate it.

Subsequent lending by some building societies to their existing borrowers for home improvements and personal consumption bring them into a common field with finance companies. Further advances are usually covered by the first mortgage deed. In general, a building society does not lend on a second mortgage unless the first mortgage is in favour of the society.

Building societies will continue to be substantial competitors for individuals' savings, which in itself is likely to cause many societies, in particular the large ones, to continue to extend their branch networks. About 50% of houses are now owner-occupied compared with 30% some ten years ago. The number of new houses built in the years ahead is likely to increase, as is the proportion for owner-occupation. This coupled with inflation will necessitate a very large increase in building societies' funds.

In the unlikely event, at least in the early years ahead, of building societies finding themselves with surplus funds, they could offer plans for home improvements, particularly to past and existing borrowers and in the case of the latter it could of course be with security under the existing mortgage deed and probably subject to tax relief on the interest. Their contact with many millions of investors and borrowers places them in an excellent position should they ever wish to canvas such business.

Life Assurance Offices. This is the group of institutions which is largely comprised of companies incorporated in Great Britain and, to a lesser extent, foreign companies, industrial and provident societies, collecting friendly societies and, in a relatively small way, ordinary friendly societies, all of whom issue life policies in some form.

Assurance companies are governed by the Insurance Companies Acts, 1958–1967 and are exempt from the Moneylenders Acts. Friendly societies are governed by the Friendly Societies Acts, 1896–1968 and are exempt from the Moneylenders Acts and the Protection of Depositors Act. Industrial and provident societies are governed by the Industrial and Provident Societies Acts, 1965–1968 and are exempt from the Protection of Depositors Act but their position *vis-à-vis* the Moneylenders Acts is not entirely clear.

As a by-product of their business many life assurance offices give credit, the greater part of which is lending to individual customers for house purchase against a first mortgage in parallel with an endowment life policy. They also provide loans on a life policy within its surrender value. Such loans are usually available without specification of purpose for which the money is required. There is little risk to the lender, the rate is usually not much more than Bank rate and repayment may be irregular. The amount of policy loans made is small in relation to the assets of assurance offices and their total business. Potentially there could be considerable scope for secured lending probably at attractive rates to policyholders of a few years' standing with value in their policies.

Other Lenders on First Mortgage. These include a small number of commercial companies which do not come under the building societies' legislation but carry on the business of making long-term loans for the purchase of houses (usually of the type in which building societies are not interested) and secured by mortgage on the house. The companies are usually exempted from the Moneylenders Acts under Section 6 (e) of the 1900 Act and can advertise for deposits under the Protection of Depositors Act. The exemption from the Moneylenders Acts precludes them from charging in excess of $12\frac{1}{2}\%$ simple interest.

General insurers (i.e. non-life insurance companies) also come under this heading, as do commercial and industrial companies who make mortgage loans to their staff for house purchase. There is also a considerable amount of first mortgage finance, a large part for business purpose but some for house purchase, put up by trusts and trust companies and private persons. It is estimated in the Report that the total lent in 1969 by all these groups was £40m. with some £430m. outstanding at the end of the year. There is no reason why the commercial companies should not lend money secured by mortgage for purposes other than house purchase. General insurers do lend a little for purposes other than house purchase and no doubt could lend more if they wished. Commercial and industrial companies do make personal loans to their staff.

Second Mortgage Brokers and Lenders. This is a group of upwards of some eighty firms (brokers and lenders) engaged in the industry of lending money secured by second mortgage on the equity in the borrower's house. The business has increased considerably in recent years at a time when terms controls have made it difficult to acquire goods on hire-purchase and credit sale and when, largely because of inflation, equity in an individual's house already secured by mortgage has built up fairly quickly. Some second mortgage lenders hold a certificate under Section 123 of the Companies Act, 1967, others as corporate bodies are exempted by the Board of Trade from the Moneylenders Act, 1900 under Section 6 (e). Money borrowed, usually over five to ten years, is frequently spent on home improvements, but in most cases there is no tie to the purpose for which the loan is used. At the end of 1968 it was estimated that there was at least £14m. outstanding on second mortgages. The Association of Finance Agents believes the figure is nearer £25m. Without terms controls potential might reduce, particularly as the cost of borrowing by second mortgage must of necessity be higher, at least initially, than unsecured lending. On the other hand, with continuing inflation an increasing number of people are likely to have an increasing equity in their house and may be inclined to utilise it as security in return for a loan possibly over a somewhat longer period than that over which an unsecured loan could be obtained.

Other Long-Term Lenders. These are some forty small companies normally lending on the security of share certificates and other documents of title; a few specialise in loans on reversions. Many of the loans are for business purposes. Most of the companies are exempted from the Moneylenders Acts under Section 6 (e) of the 1900 Act. In 1969 they lent possibly £1m. (excluding mortgage loans in which some companies are engaged) and had £8m. outstanding at the end of that year. Potentially such specialised companies are unlikely to be significant competitors in the general credit instalment field.

We now consider those institutions and bodies whose main purpose is to provide credit (either lender or vendor credit and generally unsecured) for consumer transactions.

Check and Voucher Traders. This is a group of around four hundred or so firms specialising in a form of trading where a document called a check is issued by a check trader and purchased by a customer which entitles the customer to buy consumer goods at specified shops. The customer pays for the check by instalments over twenty weeks (usually £1·05 for each £1 face value of the check). The check trader reimburses the retailer after taking a discount.

Agents are usually employed to sell new checks and collect customers' payments. More expensive goods are sometimes covered by a hire-purchase agreement or by checks with a larger repayment period or by vouchers which are also for a longer period and sometimes for a specified article at a specified shop.

The legal position of check and voucher trading is not definite. The trade tends to claim it is not moneylending or credit sale, although one County Court has held it is moneylending. Check traders are not exempt from the Protection of Depositors Act or from the 1967 Companies Act accounts regulations. Growth in check trading and particularly its extension to the more expensive goods has to some extent been stimulated in recent years by the fact that neither check trading nor voucher trading was subject to terms control.

Future business without terms control is likely to be confined to that section of the community requiring low to medium priced consumer durables who like to have someone calling on them each week to collect payments. However, if there is a demand among their customers and check traders have the funds or can obtain them and are prepared to extend into the higher-price goods trades and accept payments over a longer period, there might be some growth in check trading or even personal loans. In this latter field, however, there would be no trader discount and rates would have to be higher than general if the cost of doorstep collections had still to be covered. In 1969 checks issued amounted to at least £130m.

Credit-Card Issuers.   By comparison with other credit granting institutions those issuing credit cards are a recent development. We are concerned only with businesses specialising in credit cards who issue "three-party" cards for use at a list of shops, hotels, airlines, etc., and where the credit-card issuer reimburses the suppliers of the goods and services after deduction of a discount. Under one type of card an annual charge is made to the holder and, in general, no more credit is provided than the short period between purchase and billing. Under the other type, though no charge is made for the card, credit is offered to the holder each time his account is presented for payment and if he chooses to pay by instalments interest is charged to his account.

There are no specific legal provisions affecting credit-card transactions. The legal aspects of such transactions have not come before the courts in England and the relationship betwene the card issuer and the card holder is uncertain but possibly one of lender and borrower, i.e. credit by means of credit card is moneylending. In general, card issuers are free to advertise their cards and solicit or canvas for new card users. Companies, other than banks, have to conform to the provisions of the Companies Act, 1967 as to the balance sheet and profit and loss account.

In the United States the use of credit cards in general has grown rapidly and therefore the credit given by hotels, shops, etc. In Great Britain the number of institutions issuing credit cards is also likely to grow. Three of the four big banks have indicated their intention to issue a joint credit card.[2] It is reasonable to suppose that finance houses could well become involved in this field possibly in association with trade groups for their customers and particularly with the type of credit card under which instalment credit may be utilised.

Pawnbrokers. This is a community of businesses, licensed by the local authorities on the authorisation of magistrates, who make small loans (not exceeding £50 but on average very much less) against a pledge (often of clothing) for a short period (not exceeding six months). If the pledge is not redeemed within the prescribed time it is forfeited to the pawnbroker if the loan is £2 or less, but must be put up for auction if the loan exceeds £2.

Pawnbrokers are governed by the Pawnbrokers Acts, 1872–1960 and specifically exempted from the Moneylenders Acts in respect of business carried on in accordance with the provisions of those Acts in relation to moneylenders. The legal position of loans secured on a pledge for amounts exceeding £50 is not clear but may come under the Moneylenders Acts. Pawnbrokers rely on their own capital resources to finance the advances they make and do not rely much on borrowing from banks or other sources.

A large proportion of pawnbrokers are engaged in some other form of business, most often the sale of jewellery. In 1966 the turnover of licensed pawnbrokers was £8m. but pawnbroking was thought to be only about a quarter of this. Pawnbroking appears to be declining; only around 400 pawnbrokers were licensed in Great Britain in 1968 compared with 1,400 in 1950. Pawnbrokers as such are obviously not competitors in the unsecured personal loan field; their business is specialised and utilised by a particular section of people to whom normal credit facilities would not in general be available. It is, of course, possible that pawnbrokers could enter the personal loan field but in general it is doubtful if they have the resources or the expertise for granting such unsecured facilities.

Moneylenders. These fall into two classes. There are the licensed moneylenders whose number has increased steadily in recent years and is now about 2,500. Many of these are small proprietorships but there are a few sizeable incorporated licencees. Just under half are engaged in other business, notably check trading. Their lending is mainly unsecured, is risky (loans are frequently made to cover exceptional outlay by the borrower or to meet an urgent demand to pay off a debt) and at a high rate of interest. In recent years a few companies stimulated by severe terms controls on hire-purchase have lent solely to purchase cars over two or three years with a bill of sale on the car as security. Licensed moneylenders are required by the Moneylenders Acts to conform to various requirements, including prohibition on agents and canvassing and restriction on advertisements. They appear to rely mainly on their own capital resources and do not raise funds by bank advances or by seeking deposits. In the Report it is estimated that loans amounting to about £38m. were made in 1969 and possibly about £28m. was outstanding at the end of the year.

The other class of moneylender is the company exempted from the Moneylenders Acts under Section 6 (e) of the 1900 Act, who as a condition of exemption must not charge more than $12\frac{1}{2}\%$ simple interest on loans. There are about 190 exemptions granted to various companies, many of them small and not in a position to claim exemption as a bank under Section 123 of the Companies Act, 1967 or otherwise. Their business is varied and they include finance companies, companies lending on first and/or second mortgage or other security and companies providing loans to businesses and business and professional men.

As long as there are people who over-commit themselves or require money at short notice for exceptional expenditure which they can probably not obtain elsewhere there will be a place in society for the licensed moneylender but not as a competitor of other money-granting institutions – it is unlikely that moneylenders in general would enter the normal competitive personal-loan market.

The Post Office National Giro. In 1970 the National Giro started to make personal loans available to its account holders through an arrangement with Mercantile Credit Company. The loan is credited by Mercantile Credit to the customer's giro account and repayments are made to Mercantile Credit by standing order on the customer's giro account. The transaction is a form of revolving credit because as the loan is repaid it can be "topped-up" to the original credit limit. Interest is calculated on the outstanding loan each month and if the loan account goes into credit by £10 or more for a month or more interest is credited. Potentially any lender could make arrangements with the National Giro to provide facilities to its customers or others through the medium of the customer's giro accounts.

Small Loan Societies and Companies. This is a varied group and generally declining number of loan societies, small loan companies (including credit unions) and friendly societies who had their origin in mutual aid movements. Small loan companies take deposits from their members, friendly societies are engaged in mutual insurance functions and all make small loans[3] to their members.

Loan societies certified by the Registrar of Friendly Societies under the Loan Societies Act, 1840 and friendly societies governed by the Friendly Societies Acts, 1896–1968, are specifically exempted from the Moneylenders Acts. Some small loan companies are incorporated under the Companies Acts, others under the Industrial and Provident Societies Acts, 1965–1968; in each class some companies hold an exemption order under the Moneylenders Acts and others have no exemption. Friendly societies and industrial and provident societies are exempted from the Protection of Depositors Act. In total the volume of loan business is relatively very small; it is estimated in the Report that in 1969 their collective lending amounted to little more than £1m. and outstandings at the end of the year were only £657,000. By virtue of the closed and mutual manner in which this group operates it is unlikely that the companies and societies would extend credit to other than their members and therefore become competitors in the general field of consumer credit.

Finally, we consider those institutions whose main purpose is selling (or renting) and to whom the extension of credit is incidental:

Retailers. Under this heading we consider that very large group, including shops, of suppliers of goods and services to the consumer. Credit may be extended in one of many ways. We are concerned, however, only with forms of instalment credit. Included among these are budget accounts, a form of revolving credit which has grown considerably in recent years in the retail trade. An alternative to the budget account is the option account where the customer, on receiving his account, has the option to pay in full or by instalments of not less than a specified amount, in which event a charge is made. The agreement with a budget account customer is not hire-purchase and probably not credit sale and therefore not covered by legislation. In England a retailer giving budget account facilities is by some thought to be lending money; if so, this would be outside the Moneylenders Acts since the lenders would fall within Section 6 (d) of the 1900 Act – "persons *bona fide* carrying on any business not having for its primary object the lending of money".

The retailer may also extend formal credit in the form of hire-purchase or credit sale either himself, in which case he may assign his interest in the contract to a finance company, or as an intermediary for a lending institution. The Hire-Purchase Act, 1965 will apply to such consumer transactions except credit sale agreements where the total purchase price is not more than £30. Retailers may also make credit available to their customers by agreeing to accept the checks or vouchers of a check trader or the cards of a credit card company. In recent years some larger retailers have set up their own credit card or check trading subsidiaries and some have their own small finance company to finance their instalment credit transactions.

Retailers are subject to the general law on sales, notably the Sale of Goods Act, 1893. They have two sources to meet their financial needs, bank advances and trade credit, but these may not always be available to finance consumer credit since there will be other needs such as stocking.

Potentially it is doubtful whether the general body of retailers will enter the consumer-credit instalment market on a larger scale than now. In addition to raising the funds necessary to finance the consumer credit required there would be the problem of expertise in underwriting credit and collection of repayments. Unless a trader was prepared to subsidise the cost of his consumer credit by his retail operations, his costs, including that of money, would mean his customers in many cases would be paying more for their credit than if they borrowed from one of the large lending institutions.

Mail-Order Houses. "Mail-order house" covers a wide range from the large firms whoe names are household words to small one-man businesses. There are the "catalogue houses" who rely on catalogues to introduce their wares to the public, some through agents, others direct. There are also the direct-mail houses who rely on advertising, chiefly in the press, of specific items; much of their business is on a cash basis. We are concerned with credit and therefore mainly with the catalogue companies and particularly those who work through agents. These companies trade almost entirely for credit – repayments are generally over twenty or sometimes thirty-eight weeks. Agents, who play a large part in the business and are paid commission, are largely housewives who solicit business from their friends.

There are no special legal provisions affecting mail-order trading. The Hire-Purchase Act, 1965 applies to mail order in so far as it regulates credit-sale agreements. Standards of quality are maintained by strong competition between mail-order houses and the principle that a dissatisfied customer can have his money back. The advertising industry, backed by the Newspaper Publishers' Association, is vigilant to ensure standards of honesty are maintained. Mail order has grown particularly since 1945 (in recent years growth has probably been helped by terms control on hire-purchase and credit sale) until today it is used probably by more people than any other form of credit. The attraction of shopping by looking through a catalogue in one's own home is unlikely to diminish and could well increase as mail-order houses extend their range of goods. Agents also have the added incentive of commission.

Doorstep Sellers.   Under this heading we have nearly 3,500 itinerant credit traders or tallymen who operate by regular calls on their customers with samples or catalogues from a central warehouse. Credit rarely exceeds £30 or £40 per customer with repayment over twenty weeks. Usually there is no written agreement. Goods are mostly clothing and household textiles. Most itinerant credit traders are independents and not multiples, although there are a few large businesses with branches.There is also the doorstep seller where the sale is a once-only affair usually for cash – we are not concerned with these – but some selling such as vacuum cleaners and encyclopaedias is on credit. If the contract is credit sale with a total purchase price exceeding £30 or hire-purchase, the Hire-Purchase Act, 1965 applies and in particular a customer signing the contract in his home has the right for a short period to cancel it. As long as people like to buy on their doorstep and are prepared to pay the higher credit charges to cover the cost of an agent calling and giving personal service, there will be a place for the itinerant credit trader, but he is unlikely to be a competitor in the general credit instalment field of personal loans.

Rental Companies. Here we are considering those who offer medium- and long-term rental of consumer durables. (We can forget the short-term hiring of cars, television, radio, etc., to consumers for holiday and other purposes and for my particular purpose here we can set aside the large-scale hiring of plant and long-term leasing of industrial machinery and equipment.) While there is some sign that long-term car rental to private individuals is developing, the main area of activity by rental companies is, and has been since 1950, in the television field. Rental contracts under which the hirer is not given the option to purchase the goods but is obliged to surrender them when a contract comes to an end are not subject to any form of legislative control. There are no restrictions on the owner's right to repossess the goods pursuant to the terms of agreement or upon termination and a purchaser, even a private one, buying in good faith from a hirer does not acquire good title.

A survey referred to in the Report indicated that 37% of respondents said they had at some time rented a television receiver and estimates indicated there are probably at least 6·5 million and may be as many as 8·5 million receivers on rent. This widespread rental of television is a phenomenon unique to this country and was probably stimulated by the absence of terms control on renting in the early days of terms control, and the system of investment allowances for rental companies. However, the business would probably not have grown or survived its later inclusion in the Control of Hiring Orders without the advantage of maintenance being the responsibility of the renting company and that until technical developments were more advanced it was probably safer to rent than to buy a receiver. These facts must have some bearing on the extent to which colour television receivers, at a much greater cost than black-and-white, are now rented and are likely to continue to be rented for some time to come. Multiple rental companies with 3,000 branches and 750 other rental companies and over 360 relay companies who also rent their receivers make a formidable total in addition to the considerable number of general radio and electrical dealers, some of whom also do a fair volume of rental business. Total rental income in 1969 was estimated at possibly £200m. and with the growth of colour television this must increase considerably in the years ahead, particularly as there is now no statutory control on the payment of advance rentals.

The table on page 88 summarises the magnitude of the institutions referred to in this part of my chapter and their operations.

CROWTHER AND THE FUTURE

This survey raises two specific questions:

First, to what extent are these graduations of privilege and obligation justifiable on logical grounds – i.e. what social economic or monetary policies do they serve to implement and how? Are the Crowther recommendations relating to free entry into the lending market consistent or even sustainable in the context of the conclusions reached? Particularly, what inducements does the ready availability of chattel mortgages in the consumer market provide for an invasion in force by such institutions of the consumer markets and what would be the consequences in terms of social, economic and monetary policies of such an invasion? Second, what have finance houses to offer which justifies their continuance as separately identifiable institutions in such circumstances?

The first of these two questions raises issues which, though of great importance to finance houses, are of a wider and more fundamental nature than fall to be considered at this Conference. Nevertheless, they are totally ignored by the Crowther Committee and thus make suspect, or at least call into question, the Crowther thesis that public policy demands unrestricted competition. If the Crowther recommendations were to be adopted the result would be a banking and financial community in general less regulated in its deposit-gathering and lending operations than any other in Europe or North America. Although, as we have seen in the United States, banks can be regulated at times – witness regulation "Q" under which they were compelled to limit the rate of interest they paid on deposits and current accounts – this lack of regulation may be a good thing. But have the fuller implications been considered? I doubt it and so must urge caution.

The answer to the second question would appear to rest solely upon expertise and resources – particularly in relation to point-of-sale finance. Is Crowther justified in his view that point-of-sale finance should be discouraged (ignoring for the moment some of the inconsistencies in terms of consequences which the detail of the Crowther recommendations give rise to)?

Having said this I am quite confident of the strength and resilience of the finance houses to continue in business whatever the legal environment imposed upon them. What I cannot do is to attempt any assessment of market developments – the technical difficulties and uncertainties of the Report leave so much scope for choice as to the final picture which will be adopted and these hold the key to the future of finance houses just as they do for any other industry. However, what I can do is to review some aspects of the Report affecting consumer credit and attempt to gauge the result they will have in a competitive sense, on finance houses and certain other financial institutions.

Funds. Although in this chapter we are concerned with the practical implications of the Crowther Report, equally important, particularly to finance houses, are the changes in monetary policy and its control over credit announced by the Bank of England on 10th September, 1971 and giving effect to the basic principles of the arrangements outlined in the Bank's paper *Competition and Credit Control.* Impediments to competition between banks and finance houses which have existed in recent years as a result of ceiling and other controls are now removed. The Report welcomes competition and so, I am sure, do finance houses in a free environment.

Finance houses (except those with liabilities of less than £5m.) are now in a similar position to that of banks in general. They are subject to liquid-asset reserves but will only retain 10% of their assets in liquid form compared with $12\frac{1}{2}\%$ by the banks and when required, for the purpose of credit control, they can

COMPARISON OF CONSUMER INSTALMENT CREDIT IN 1966 AND 1969†

ADVANCED BY		Extended During Year £m.		Outstanding at End of Year £m.	
		1966	1969	1966	1969
FINANCE HOUSES		466	492	508	499

OTHER LENDERS (generally secured)

		1966	1969	1966	1969
Banks	House Purchase	(65)	(76)	(323)	(378)
	Other	500	550	497	501
Building Societies	House Purchase	(1,217)	(1,515) ⎫	5,219*	7,705*
	Other	33	33 ⎭		
Insurers	House Purchase	(147)	(180)	(886)	(1,080)
	Other	34	51	128	184
Local Authorities	House Purchase	(134)	(70) ⎫		
	Other	4	5 ⎪	1,042*	1,176*
Other First Mortgage Lenders			⎬		
	House Purchase	(39)	(40) ⎪		
	Other	1	2 ⎭	384*	430*
Second Mortgage Lenders		3	18	10	25
Other Long-Term Lenders		1	1	7	8
	House Purchase	(1,602)	(1,881)	(7,854)*	(10,769)*
	Other	576	660	642	718

OTHER LENDERS (generally unsecured)

		1966	1969	1966	1969
Check and Voucher Traders		76	130	52	93
Credit Card Issuers		1	5	1	2
Pawnbrokers		6	6	3	3
Moneylenders		35	38	25	28
Small Loan Companies		1	1	1	1
Private Loans		5	5	10	10
		124	185	92	137

SELLERS

		1966	1969	1966	1969
Retailers and Traders		354 ⎱	488	345 ⎱	405
Doorstep Sellers		138 ⎰		86 ⎰	
Mail Order Houses		374	448	111	167
		866	936	542	572

OVERDUE DEBTS		68	80	46	54

		1966	1969	1966	1969
	House Purchase	(1,602)	(1,881)	(7,854)	(10,769)
	Others	2,100	2,353	1,830	1,980
	Total	3,702	4,234	9,684	12,749

† A combination of Tables 2.1 and 2.9 appearing on pages 52, 53, 58 and 59 of the Report.
* Includes Home Improvement Loans.

be called upon to make special deposits with the Bank of England. Deposits are a large proportion of the liabilities of many major finance houses and it is obvious that although they may be more free in future to compete in the money market for deposits, the overall cost of money to them is likely to shade upwards due to the necessity for maintaining such reserves. Similarly, the London and Scottish Clearing Banks having abandoned their collective agreements on interest rates, the rates they pay for at least some deposits from the public (previously 2% below Bank rate) will certainly rise. (At present the authorities propose no upper limit to "protect" the savings and building society movements.) The overall effect of this, as I see it, is that banks and finance houses (particularly the larger finance houses) will be able to compete in the same commercial markets for deposits and broadly obtain funds at similar rates, but the banks will always have the edge on the overall cost of their money because of the use they have of the extremely large volume of money in their transmission systems and customers' current accounts.

At the present time banks are under-lent and though as the country's economic condition improves industrial investment is likely to increase and with it the need for working capital, in the longer term industry may well turn to the capital issue market and banks can thus be expected to continue to press on with their marketing of consumer credit. In the personal-loan field, in their current-account customers banks have as much of the cream as they can be expected to canvas. Rates for bank loans may go up a little as they pay more for their money, but they are still likely to have just that edge on finance house rates which may in time ease down a fraction to compete with a resulting lowering of profit margins. For other than their own customers, banks are also likely to remain competitors of finance houses through their credit-card scheme where, though the rates are higher than for their personal loans, they are comparable with those for personal loans from finance companies and through the Post Office Giro – a truly national competitor of the clearing banks with 22,000 points of sale.

Public Demand and Supply.   With the removal of ceiling control on banks and finance houses both classes of institution will aim to lend more. The Report welcomes competition and the proposed legislation aims broadly to place all lenders on an equal footing. No longer will some lenders be at a disadvantage as they have been in the past during periods of terms control. Pressure by all categories of lender upon the public to borrow more will increase, not only because some lenders will want to lend more but because others will endeavour to maintain their volume of the market even if they do not want their share to increase. Banks will try to make personal loans to the cream of their current-account customers and Barclaycard will no doubt step up the appeal of its instalment-credit facility. Finance companies with ceiling restrictions limiting their growth in the past six years will want to see their capital more fully employed and will encourage their good customers against bank competition to "come again". Motor traders can offer 25% deposit and three years to pay or easier terms. Rental companies are able to supply colour television with few, if any, rental payments payable upon delivery. Retailers can offer electrical appliances and furniture with small or no deposit and at least three years to pay. Mail order houses, aided by their friendly agents, continue to grow with a wider range of goods reaching a greater proportion of the population. And so the list can go on. But, what about "the poor old consumer"? Does he want the goods? Can he afford them? Is there not a danger that he will be encouraged to over-commit himself? Will the pressure of mailing, doorstep canvassing, press and magazine, and television advertising be too great? In the last few years we have been through a period of economic unrest, contracting industry, redundancies, high unemployment, reduced overtime, low capital investment, during which the consumer durable market has somewhat stagnated. In spite of increasing inflation people have tended to save rather than buy – building societies have record funds and national savings have increased. Many people, I would suggest, have been afraid to buy; with less overtime and doubt about continuing employment they have thought twice about committing themselves to continuing payments. Is the position likely to change suddenly?

After so many years of restraints on credit it is obvious that many people will fall for the attraction of easy terms, but I venture to suggest that at the present time there is far more money available to be lent than there are creditworthy people to consume it. Competition between lenders is therefore likely to be all that more severe with a shaving of rates and easier terms with a resulting reduction in profit on funds employed. Easy terms not only encourage bad debts but could, in the long run, rebound on traders. Take the case of a motor car; when the customer comes to trade in his old car for a new one he finds that because of the low deposit terms and longish repayment period he has little equity in it towards the deposit on the new car. New car sales could suffer in two to three years hence. A change in the law to place all lenders on a competitive footing is to be applauded, but if that competition becomes so strong that lenders cut each others' throats, any Government control required to right the situation would be embracing upon all lenders under the new law and therefore more restrictive than ever before.

Licensed and Unlicensed Lenders. It will be an offence for anyone to engage in the business of making consumer loans without having taken out a licence from the Commissioner. There will be no exceptions or exclusions (as under the Money-lenders Acts) from the necessity to be licensed, of any special class or defined category of lender, though some institutions will exempt themselves by not entering the field of consumer credit. Retailers accepting checks or credit cards will not, by that reason alone, require to be licensed since (so the Report says) they are not responsible for introducing the customers to the check trader or card issuer. But surely retailers accept checks or credit cards because they hope these will bring increased business which will more than offset the discount which they have to give to the check trader or card issuer. Retailers are not slow to indicate to a hovering customer that they will accept a check or a credit card which could make the difference between a sale and no sale or a more expensive sale and a cheaper sale. Retailers display in their windows the check trader's or card issuer's symbol. It is a thin line to imply the retailer is not responsible for introducing customers to the check trader or card issuer. After all, the check traders and card issuers are connected lenders.

Those engaged in consumer rental business (for some purposes consumer rental agreements are within the Consumer

Sale and Loan Act) are excluded from the licensing requirements though the Report recommends that the new Act should provide for their inclusion at a later date if, e.g., there was a great increase in doorstep canvassing by rental companies. But will this be fair competition for the general body of traders in domestic goods, radio and television, who, however little instalment credit they offer, will have to have a licence?

A bank will not in general have to be licensed unless it operates a personal-loan scheme or credit-card scheme providing for repayment by instalments. Loans by way of overdraft or loan account to a customer and made by a Clearing Bank as an independent lender at a rate of charge not exceeding $2\frac{1}{2}\%$ over Bank rate will not in themselves require the bank to be licensed.

Generally, it will not be necessary for building societies to be licensed. Loans made to consumers for the purchase of real property or made as an independent lender at a rate not exceeding $2\frac{1}{2}\%$ above Bank rate will be outside the Consumer Sale and Loan Act. If a loan is made by a society as a connected lender, i.e. the sale is a financed consumer sale, the society will require to be licensed irrespective of the rate charged, although loans over £2,000 will be outside the Consumer Sale and Loan Act regardless of the rate and whether or not such loans are made by the society as a connected lender. There seems little wrong in the traditional rôle of lending by building societies being outside control, but if there was any substantial growth in unconnected lending to existing borrowers which could well be used for general purposes (and possibly not connected with home improvements) I am sure we would be concerned that it would appear to escape regulation if the new facility regardless of the rate was added to an existing loan of £2,000 or more. Is there not some ground here for any additional loan, or at least one not being used for house purchase or home improvements, to be treated as a separate loan in a manner similar to that proposed for revolving loans, although there might still be problems of regulation if the rate did not exceed $2\frac{1}{2}\%$ over Bank rate.

It is proposed that insurance contracts shall be excluded from the Consumer Sale and Loan Act and it is assumed that loans made to policy-holders will also be exempt from the Act. It is not unreasonable to exclude loans for house purchase, but if loans for other probably unspecified purposes should increase there could certainly be an element of competition to finance houses, particularly as the loan is provided with little risk to the lender and at a relatively fine rate.

Advertising, Canvassing and Mailing. At present, legislation specifically controlling the advertising of instalment credit facilities comprises the Advertisements (Hire-Purchase) Act, 1967 which regulates the advertising of hire-purchase and credit sale and the Moneylenders Acts which regulate advertising, canvassing and mailing by moneylenders. It is proposed that these Acts should be repealed. The Committee's proposals in relation to advertisements, which will cover all lending whether or not it is subject to the Consumer Sale and Loan Act, and also canvassing and mailing are fairly straightforward. Under the proposals finance houses appear to be in a fair position to compete with banks and lenders in general except possibly those engaged in doorstep canvassing – a field which is unlikely to be of general interest to them.

Terms.
   Statutory. In his July 1971 mini-Budget the Chancellor of the Exchequer revoked all terms control on hire-purchase, credit sale and hiring. This was in line with the recommendations of the Crowther Committee, but the Chancellor did not accept the Committee's further recommendation and go so far as to repeal the enabling legislation. Thus, at this point of time, terms control could be re-introduced. The inequity of the controls in recent years, their limited application to only a few fields of instalment credit, their ineffectiveness as an instrument of economic control and the extent to which they have been evaded are all well known. For these reasons alone we would not want to see a return of statutory terms control and from what we read in the Report there would be little justification for such an action. However, if for any remote reason control was reimposed it must apply to all classes of lending, otherwise, particularly with the growth of personal loans, evasions would be more extensive and competition between lenders more unfair than we have already seen.

   Trade Terms. Without statutory control lenders are free to decide their own terms for credit trading in a competitive market, a market which under the Crowther Committee's proposals will otherwise largely place all lenders on an equal footing. But of what value is terms competition if the end result is the lender's bankruptcy or liquidation. In the early 1960s we saw the effect on finance houses, including some of the largest, of that "free for all" period between the end of 1958 and early 1960 when no statutory control applied. It could so easily happen again and to any lender, particularly if in somewhat dull market conditions lenders tend to make terms too easy just to aid or make a sale. Almost any consumer can afford a single item of goods on no-deposit and minimal weekly or monthly payments over, say, five years, but think of the effect if he had three, four or five such transactions all running at the same time – you might say a lender would take steps to ensure his customer was not over-committing himself, but our credit-rating systems are not yet so developed as always to tell us the full commitments of a potential borrower.

I contend that it is not unreasonable to ask a borrower for a deposit at least to cover the initial depreciation in the goods; it gives him a stake in them, it makes him think twice if he can really afford them. And, by adjusting the period to not more than the reasonable life of the goods, if trouble should come, there is some chance that if the goods have to be "repossessed" and sold the proceeds will be somewhere near the balance payable by the borrower and both the borrower (other than losing the goods) and the lender will suffer little.

With some industry at low capacity there are some who feel easy terms can increase immediate sales and therefore production, but this could leave a flat period a year or so hence, with little or low stocks, while manufacturers were trying to catch up. If, as a result of increased sales repossessions also increased and had to be sold, these could be added competition to new sales, particularly in a field such as that of private cars. Without statutory control on terms, competition can be fierce and possibly unfair, but in the long run prudent underwriting should prevail.

Life Insurance. The offer of "life insurance" to many borrowers is increasing. In some cases the borrower is asked or even obliged to pay a premium, in other cases "free" life cover is provided. In all cases the cover generally provides that if the borrower should die before he has repaid his loan the balance, excluding arrears at the time of death, will be met by the insurers. Obviously life cover is in the interest of the borrower, particularly where his loan is to be repaid, e.g., in the case of central heating, over a long period, possibly up to ten years. The cover is also in the interest of the lender because in the event of the untimely death of his borrower he would be repaid the debt almost immediately compared with the delay which would likely arise with payment from the deceased's estate. The inclusion of life cover in a loan agreement may raise problems in that as a possible service its cost may be included in any calculation of the true rate of interest charged for the loan, although the Crowther Committee make no specific recommendation on this point. This could make it a little difficult for prospective borrowers to compare terms and services.

Cost of Credit.

Truth in Lending. The Committee has recommended that the cost of credit in all consumer credit transactions be expressed not only in terms of a sum of money but also as an effective rate of interest. For revolving credit, where the effective return depends upon the manner in which the customer chooses to operate his account and for mail order, where no cash price is quoted, modified provisions apply.

Exclusions. Although there may be practical difficulties, I do not think we disagree with the broad principle of truth in lending, provided it is simple to apply and it is applied across the board.

Under the Committee's proposals loans made by a bank or building society as an unconnected lender with a rate of interest not exceeding Bank rate plus $2\frac{1}{2}\%$ will be exempt from the true-rate disclosure requirements. It is possible that with competition the rate charged by finance houses for personal loans will differ little from that charged by, say, a bank and if the potential borrower is to be fully informed surely he should be aware of the true-rate equivalent to the lower bank charge. Also in such cases finance houses would no doubt like people to know that their costs are little more than those of a bank. It is proposed that the provisions regarding advertisements should apply to all lending irrespective of whether the loan is within or outside the Consumer Sale and Loan Act. Should not the same apply to true rate disclosures?

While there are arguments for excluding connected loans not exceeding £30 from the provisions and, in particular, that the charges must be higher than for loans of larger sums, surely a potential borrower should be in a position to compare the rate offered by one lender with that offered by another for a loan of £30 or under, just as much as, if not more so, than for a loan over £30. The variation between rates would be much larger for small loans than for large ones and the small-loan borrower may well be less affluent than the large borrower and entitled to that additional protection which the Committee proposes he need not have.

The Form of Loan Contract. At the present time there is a sharp distinction between purchase-money loans and sales on credit which, particularly in the past ten years or so, has given rise to unfair competition between lenders and hardship and injustices to the contracting parties and at times to third parties. All this has not been helped by the legal fiction of the hire-purchase contract. Under the proposed new legal framework the Committee view the extension of credit in a sale or hire-purchase transaction as a purchase-money loan and the registration of title under a hire-purchase or conditional sale agreement (or finance lease) as a chattel mortgage securing a loan. Further, they replace the present distinct set of rules for different security devices by a legal structure applicable to all forms of security interests.

Contracting parties will continue to be free to use the form of financing instrument of their choice but, whatever the form of the credit transaction, it will be governed by the Lending and Security Act, under which it will be viewed as a security transaction and regulated in the same way as a purchase-money chattel mortgage. In other words, the end product will be broadly the same for all transactions.

Broadly, it would appear that the proposals are fair to lenders and borrowers alike and finance houses in particular have little to worry about from the aspect of competition, although I am not too sure that in the case of commercial transactions they wouldn't prefer a little more freedom. The Committee recognises that where a transaction involves credit, bargaining power usually lies with the supplier. No doubt lenders will use one or two forms of contract of their own choosing which the potential borrower will have little choice but to accept or go elsewhere for his credit. However, when he does go elsewhere he may well find that, under the proposed new law, any other form of contract offered to him will not be so different, at least in its implications, as he might find today between, say, hire-purchase and personal loan.

Secured and Unsecured Lending. Under the proposed Lending and Security Act all lenders will be able, if they wish, to take security for a loan, but whether the environment of competition will be favourable in all cases for them to do this is doubtful. We have already seen a trend particularly by banks and finance houses towards personal loans without security, a trend which is likely to continue under the proposed legal framework, particularly as all lenders will truly be able to lend money.

Without security, the creditworthiness of the borrower becomes more important. It is unlikely that banks will seek security for personal loans to their customers where the amount is a few hundred pounds or even a thousand pounds; they have ample evidence of how the customer handles his financial affairs and can, with little difficulty, assess whether he is likely to be able to meet the repayments without being too concerned about security. In such a market it is therefore more than likely that finance houses will continue to expand their personal loan schemes without security at least where the amount involved is not large. However, they do not have the advantage that the banks have in being able to see the customer's bank account and thus they will have to take extra care in underwriting, particularly as there will probably be a tendency for the cream of customers with bank accounts to turn to their bank for a loan at a lower rate of interest than a finance house may be able to afford to offer. In those cases where the credit-worthiness of a potential borrower is felt to be not quite up to the commitments he would incur if the loan he requires is granted the lender may decide the risk is a reasonable one to take with security. In other cases where the loan is for a larger amount some security may be required as matter of policy by some lenders. Also some lenders may be prepared to reduce their rate of interest for security and in such a market it is obviously not easy to see how the volume of lending will be spread between the various participating institutions. Only time will tell.

Connected v. Unconnected Lending. Mr. Wilcox in his talk delivered at *The Financial Times Investors' Chronicle Conference* in July 1971 suggested that one result of the Committee's proposals with regard to connected lenders could be to cause a lender to see the merit in advertising the special advantages of borrowing from a connected lender and feel able to cover the loss he might make by a higher charge which the borrower seeking such facilities would doubtless be willing to pay. On the other hand, there will be many creditworthy people who will be prepared to accept lower rate personal loans from banks and finance houses as independent lenders and by buying from reputable and financially sound traders be prepared to forego the connected lender protection.

It has also been suggested that, in order to obtain goods or services quickly, a potential borrower might negotiate a loan from the seller or a connected lender of the seller, but having obtained it would shortly afterwards repay it with a personal loan from an independent lender obtained at a lower rate. But depending upon the rebate terms (statutory or otherwise) for his first loan it may not pay the borrower to carry out this switch.

In several quarters it has been suggested that competition between lenders will encourage a switch from connected to unconnected lending. I contend the trend was already in being several years ago and will continue irrespective of whether or not the Committee's proposals regarding connected lender responsibilities become law. Nevertheless, connected lending will always be with us because there will, of course, always be some people who do not have a bank or finance house contact and when buying goods will rely upon the seller to introduce a lender and in such cases the lender will usually be a connected lender.

The Motor Trade. I think we should give special consideration to the motor trade because their position in the consumer credit field is, in some respects, different from other traders. Also for many finance houses the motor trade has been one of their main sources of business if, in fact, not the main source for very many years. Many consumers may turn to personal loans from banks and finance houses to finance the acquisition of their cars. Both these institutions will encourage their existing customers to apply for personal loans for all their requirements and for reasons I have already mentioned, banks may well tend to take some of the cream of finance house business. It is also relatively easy for banks to increase their customers in other directions. However, in the past, finance houses have relied upon and must to a very large extent in the future continue to rely upon traders for their new customers. I do not think the time has yet come when many people not previously having dealt with a finance house would approach one direct for a loan unless possibly in response to an advertisement.

Finance houses in dealing with reputable traders have welcomed their introductions, the goods have been of known quality and the customer, often a local person known to the dealer, has been valued because of his creditworthiness. In return for the value of the traders' introductions finance houses have paid commission. The Committee considered commission payments, particularly to the motor trade, and came to the conclusions that such payments of commission should not be prohibited, that a ceiling should not be placed upon the amount of commission that can be paid and that there appeared to be little value in insisting that the fact that commission will be paid should be disclosed to the trader's customer.

With increased competition for business generally and in particular from motor traders, finance houses may tend to increase their commission payments, but any increase can only be matched by savings in their administrative costs and a lower customer default level, otherwise it will be the customer who will have to pay, something he is unlikely to do if he can avoid it when he sees the relatively lower cost of personal loans. Alternatively, perhaps the day is not far off when finance houses will offer to handle motor traders' business at a stated rate net of commission close to that for personal loans. The trader will then charge his customer a rate of his own choosing within a maximum laid down by the finance company, who will allow the trader to retain the difference as commission.

Consumer Protection.   I have already covered several aspects of consumer protection in this chapter. The general body of measures to protect the consumer which the Crowther Committee proposes be included in the Consumer Sale and Loan Act are already familiar to us as, broadly, they are those applicable to hire-purchase, conditional sale and credit sale as set down in the Hire Purchase Act, 1965.

On the whole, I think we must agree that the extension of the 1965 Act protective measures to all forms of consumer lending is right and proper; it is in the interests of the consumer and places all lenders on the same competitive footing. There are, of course, a few classes of credit transaction which are not regulated by the Consumer Sale and Loan Act and therefore will not be subject to the consumer protective measures. Included among these are unconnected loans with a rate of interest not exceeding Bank rate plus $2\frac{1}{2}$%. Possibly finance houses need have little to concern them as long as banks, building societies and insurance companies confine their lending to the traditional rôle of house purchase, but if these relatively low-rate bank loans and overdrafts and building society and insurance company loans to existing borrowers for purposes other than house purchase (and possibly home improvements) should increase, then I think finance houses would justifiably feel that such lending should come within the Consumer Sale and Loan Act. A solution to this may be to give the Commissioner power to bring such lending within the Act if the volume of such lending, according to some measure, exceeded a certain figure either in total or for each lender.

The "Poor" Borrower.   I want to say a few words about the "poor" borrower, I mean the man who probably has no bank account, is in possession of a reasonable but not large income, has dependants, probably lives in tenanted accommodation and who, because of industrial unrest in the last few years, may have been unemployed recently or made redundant. He is honest but not too well educated, lacks knowledge of credit matters and is possibly improvident, his credit record is good, but he is not in a position where he can easily obtain, say, an unsecured personal loan, but he is good for credit provided the repayments are not too large. Weekly payments as can be made under the arrangements offered by check traders and mail order houses may well suit this man and some finance houses are prepared to consider requests for small loans or to block discount such credit instalment agreements entered into by traders with their customers. But however this man obtains his finance he needs as much protection as anybody, if not more, and therefore, as I have mentioned elsewhere, it is wrong in his case that a number of measures of consumer protection will not apply to loans amounting to £30 or less. In a more competitive market it is in the social interests of the country that the poor borrower is not encouraged to over-commit himself. Here lenders have a duty to society to ensure their lending is properly controlled – they must not be reckless.

Service. At the beginning of this section I asked what finance houses have to offer which justifies their continuance as separately identifiable institutions under the proposed new legal framework of consumer credit. In time, when all lenders can truly lend money, the first thoughts of many may be, is there any need for finance houses, cannot banks take over all lending? Several of the largest finance houses are already wholly-owned subsidiaries of Clearing Banks and it may not be difficult to integrate their activities into those of the bank generally.

I say without hesitation that finance houses have a place in Crowther's new world of lending. They have an expertise which has been built up by men of experience of many years which would take a long time to replace by anyone coming fresh into the industry. Further, in the competitive field we are likely to see in the years ahead that experience counts – it goes a long way to successful underwriting, efficient collection of repayments, particularly from the slow payer and ultimately avoiding bad debts. In addition, there is the commercial field often with specialised equipment requiring tailor-made finance – hire-purchase, commercial loan, leasing, factoring, etc., where security has to be considered carefully and is more important than in the consumer field. Although banks will undoubtedly make an entry into the consumer market, I venture to suggest their main objective is an efficient money transmission service. It is only secondary that because of the large sums of money in their systems it is convenient for them to lend as a means of increasing their profits.

Service to the Trade I have already referred to the motor trade and generally there will be many other traders who, for as far ahead as I can see, will look to finance houses to provide some facility for those of their customers requiring credit who may have no bank account or finance house contact to enable them to get a personal loan direct. I think it is unlikely that banks are going to set themselves up in such a way that they will investigate a particular trader and say to the trader, we will finance any of your customers' credit requirements. Some traders finance their own credit paper and then block discount – a field in which finance houses have considerable skill.

Service to the Public. However much banks may succeed over a period of years in encouraging a larger proportion of the population to have a bank account it will be a long time before every working man and woman has such a facility. In any case, the Post Office Giro is a competitor of the banks and with the large number of Post Offices mostly open for longer hours than banks and in particular on Saturdays, the Giro offers a service which will suit a not insignificant proportion of the population better than the banks are likely to. Many people without bank accounts will look to the trader from whom they acquire goods or services for an introduction to a finance house, others will turn to a finance house with whom they have already had credit dealings and who, as a good payer, the finance house has already encouraged to go back to them.

In this chapter I have repeatedly referred to the banks as competitors of finance houses; I make no excuse for this because if anyone is going to make inroads into finance house lending it will be the banks, not only the Clearing Banks with their large branch structure, but also possibly the foreign banks who, though the number of their branches is very much smaller, will I am sure seriously consider a larger and wider entry into the consumer market once the legal framework is right for them. There will, of course, be other competitors; obviously mail order will continue to grow and possibly check trading, but these are not likely to make such inroads into finance house consumer lending.

CREDIT BUREAUX

With the growth of lending in a free environment as envisaged in the Report it is essential to all lenders and in the interests of all consumers who want to borrow that we have a national credit register or bureau or whatever you may like to call it, which can aid lenders to grant credit promptly to the creditworthy and put them on notice where information indicates they may be at risk because of a bad payment record and/or because the potential borrower may over-commit himself.

Until a few years ago much short and medium-term consumer credit was on hire-purchase under which the lender had security in the goods. With the growth of unsecured personal loans, the creditworthiness of the potential borrower becomes of significant importance compared with the purpose for which the loan is required and which, in any case, may not be known. For a long time finance houses and others have been able to obtain a reference from a customer's bank and they have been able to rely upon it as an important aid when assessing that customer's creditworthiness. However, in the more competitive field in which we now find ourselves and which the Crowther proposals set out to make still more competitive, intending lenders may hesitate to seek information from competitors. In this competitive field an independent national register of credit information available for use by all lenders is an essential if bad debts are to be avoided. The Crowther Committee recognise the need for an efficient system but make few recommendations other than "proceed with caution".

This whole matter of credit registers raises questions of privacy which are, of course, of particular concern to the individual. It is right and proper that any credit information recorded in any register about any person should be treated with some confidence. When new consumer credit legislation is prepared it is essential that the Government's intentions regarding credit bureaux are also known.

What do Lenders Want?   For a credit register to be fully effective and truly useful to all lenders it must contain as much information as can be reasonably recorded about an individual, i.e. a record of his credit commitments and a record of any default in payment and legal action against him. I will return to this a little later. Further, all lenders should participate in providing this information as a *quid pro quo* for the information which they can all obtain from the register.

In a country the size of the U.K., and having regard to the number of people who move home each year, it should be possible to have a central register so that filing by name will aid any search for a person who has moved. Obviously a computer with branch terminals for input and output would be the ideal instrument of filing, but the cost of its operation would have to be such as could be borne by its users. One would hope that the greater use made of the register the cheaper it would be to use.

While it might be useful if all lenders were required to file certain information, for the sake of consumer privacy and any thought that "big brother" is watching, it would be preferable for the credit register to be in private hands and possibly run as a non-profitmaking organisation. The National Credit Register operated by the United Association for the Protection of Trade obviously provides an excellent base from which such a development could spring, but it will require a tremendous effort and considerable investment in equipment and may thus require closer liaison with banks and finance companies to achieve a comprehensive register.

Credit Information.   From a lender's point of view, his main concern is not to lend money and then finish up with a bad debt. Just as a bad record of payment is a warning against lending again, so is a potential borrower's record of satisfied commitments a valuable guide in assessing whether he can afford the additional credit he seeks. A complete file record of all instalment credit agreements of each individual would be ideal. Some existing credit registers obtain information from the courts of County Court judgments and transfer the details to their own records. This would continue. In addition, all lenders would be asked (possibly obliged under statute) to register default information under various categories; once having registered a default it would be essential that any payment by the debtor to liquidate his debt should also be recorded. Again, those lenders with computer accounting should not find it too difficult to supply a computer-produced record of such information which could be fed into the credit-register computer and thus help keep staff required for the preparation of input information to the minimum. Retailers and small lenders could possibly provide monthly lists.

Privacy and Consumer Rights   Any information regarding an individual's financial affairs is, of course, private to him, but in the broadening field of consumer credit it is, as I have said elsewhere, as much in the consumer's interest as that of the lender's that details of recent past and current credit transactions are recorded correctly in any credit register. To facilitate this and particularly if consumer participation is to be encouraged in supplying information, the consumer should have the opportunity to check the information on record, particularly if he finds difficulty in obtaining credit. I would therefore suggest that however inconvenient it may be to the staff of a credit register, that provision should be made for every person, should he so wish, to have access to the contents of his record. This would not only enable him to satisfy himself that his record is in order but where there is an error he can be given the opportun-·ity to have it corrected. Where there is a bad record there may, in some instances, be justification for recording the debtor's side of the picture in order to place his file record in perspective.

NOTES TO CHAPTER 6

1   This paper was originally presented to a Conference on the Practical Implications of the Crowther Report held in October 1971 by the Finance Houses Association.

2   The Access credit card was launched by the Midland, Lloyds and National Westminster Banks in the autumn of 1972.

3   Loan societies are limited to lending not more than £15 to any one member; in the case of friendly societies the amount is £50; there is no limit in the case of societies incorporated under the Industrial and Provident Acts or the Companies Acts.

Chapter 7

THE FUTURE FOR BANKING

S. T. Graham

*Assistant Chief General Manager, Midland Bank
Limited*

In trying to assess how the banking system will develop over the next decade or so it is useful to identify, so far as one can, the most powerful influences that seem likely to be making themselves felt. I begin by noting some underlying trends which will determine the environment in which the banking system will be operating, trends which on the whole, and rather reassuringly, may be counted as growth factors.

THE CHANGING ENVIRONMENT

First, the population of the United Kingdom is forecast to increase by about 2½ m. between 1971 and 1980 to 58 m., with a continuation of migration away from Scotland, Wales, Northern Ireland and the North of England towards the Midlands and the South. This movement may be modified by official regional policies, but is unlikely to be stopped entirely. Meanwhile the proportion of the population in the age-group 15–19 is expected to increase significantly from 6·8% to 8·1% of the total.

Secondly, there is the expectation, or perhaps one could say "safe assumption", that the national income as a whole will continue to increase. If we assume that growth averages 4% per annum, then the national income would be half as large again in ten years. An annual growth of 7·18%, which does not seem an unrealistic assumption if we are thinking in terms of current prices, would represent a doubling over ten years. At the same time it seems likely that the long-term trend for wealth to be

106

redistributed more equally will persist. Although redistribution may be less certain than an increase, history is against any marked or sustained reversal of the redistribution process.

The growth of personal disposable incomes, and a continuing trend towards more even distribution of wealth, will in turn bring significant changes in expenditure patterns, and especially increases in home ownership and in demand for consumer durable goods. It has been estimated that within fifteen years or so virtually every house in the country will have central heating, against about one third today; about four fifths of households will have refrigerators against two thirds; at least three quarters will have their own cars against about one half, and the proportion of houses in owner-occupation, now around 50%, will increase significantly further.

In the business sector, another trend which can be assumed is that the broad existing movement towards larger units, which has become pronounced in recent years, will continue, both through growth of successful companies and more particularly perhaps by way of mergers and takeovers. The latest available statistics show that the total value of net assets of companies quoted on the Stock Exchange involved in manufacturing industry and the distributive and service trades almost doubled between 1957 and 1967 – partly because of inflation – but the number of companies involved fell by nearly 40%. In 1957 one half or more of the net assets in each of the twenty-two main industrial categories were held in total by 142 companies; ten years later this proportion was held by 100 companies.

The formation of bigger units may be prevented in particular cases by official action to prevent the emergence of monopolies, and also perhaps by availability of managerial capacity. But the general trend is likely to be maintained. An increasing concentration on multi-national representation may also be expected, whether by direct links, the establishment of joint enterprises – particularly with European companies – or by formalising and developing existing export marketing networks, possibly including the setting up of overseas subsidiaries.

In line with the trend to bigger units, the Clearing Banks themselves have been developing into larger groups, and some notable mergers were effected in the late Sixties. Each of the Clearing Banks operates a number of subsidiaries undertaking particular functions, and has associations with other banks and financial institutions both at home and abroad. In this chapter it is the activities of these banking groups with which I am concerned.

All these broad movements will affect the banking system, but the way in which it develops will be influenced by more particular factors, some of which are being discussed in other parts of the book; for example, changes in the needs of our customers, the evolution of the international monetary scene, and Britain's membership of the E.E.C. I would also note two influences of special relevance to the banks. One is the new methods of credit control that were introduced in September 1971 and with which we are still coming to terms. The second is advances in technology and the ways in which we can exploit them to the best advantage of ourselves and our customers.

FINANCIAL NEEDS OF CUSTOMERS

It is relatively easy to indicate, as I have done, what are likely to be the main forces for change over the next decade, on the assumption of continued stability of our political, social, economic and financial structure. I must now move on to their possible effects. What are the most important developments that can be foreseen today?

Some of the implications of my opening remarks are self-evident. For example, the estimates regarding changes in consumer expenditure patterns indicate the kind of scope that is opening up for development of the business of financial institutions in the personal sector. We are likely, too, to see further development of special schemes geared to particular customer groups or needs such as holidays and student loans. As part of this development the banks will be engaging in medium-term and even longer-term personal finance to a greater extent than hitherto.

As for the corporate sector, on the basis of an analysis by the Board of Trade of "Company assets, income and finance in 1963" – which unfortunately has not been up-dated – "it is evident that large and growing companies rely less on internal finance than other companies".[1] However, resort to the various external sources of finance can vary widely from year to year, and in the past the proportion of total needs met by the banks has been relatively small. But this picture could be changing.

A significant change in the banking scene over recent years has been the move away from specialisation in the direction of universal or all-purpose banks. Indeed, most financial needs of both companies and individuals could today be met from any of the "massive financial conglomerates" as the Clearing Bank groups have been described.[2] As a corollary, with continuing concentration of resources among the largest companies in British industry, the demand for bank services from the business sector can be expected increasingly to call for larger and more varied types of finance facilities, and for guidance on a wide variety of corporate financial problems.

Thus, one can confidently expect further development of the range of services offered by these groups in response to and tailored to the needs of their customers. Increasingly the banks will be able and indeed will seek to provide "packages" of services covering short-, medium- and long-term financial requirements, particularly for companies but also for the personal sector. Among other things, this will involve further encroachment by the Clearing Banks into what have traditionally been the preserves of the merchant banks and other financial institutions, either directly or by taking participations.

The widening of the range of the kinds of financial support provided by the Clearing Banks, to include especially lending at medium and even longer term, will bring some important practical consequences. Our position as bankers and the lending criteria to be applied will be different from those appropriate to the traditional in-and-out overdraft which, at least nominally, is repayable on demand. We shall become much more concerned with the borrower's cash-flow projections for some years ahead, and the possible shape of his budget at the end of the borrowing period. So our involvement with financial planning or "engineering" is likely to become much closer, and for an extending range of customers. It will be necessary in any event if we are to be able to provide the financial package most appropriate to the customer's needs. In all this, we shall be filling a rôle hitherto associated more especially with the merchant banks.

Expertise to undertake broader and longer-range assessments of financial needs is already being brought together and developed by some of the banks. Such financial services will, I think, have become an accepted and welcome feature of the banking scene by the 1980s, and include the offer of specific financial consultancy services, such as cash-flow analysis or budgeting and stock control, which are currently being developed. One area where there is a particular need for such services is among the smaller businesses, judging both by our own experience and the report of the Bolton Committee. For these, it may be that we shall need to go somewhat further than for the larger customers.

PROVISION OF EQUITY FINANCE

The development of these kinds of lending and financial services leads to a particularly interesting question that has been under discussion recently, and especially since the new régime of credit control was introduced in September 1971. This is to what extent the banks themselves should or will become involved in the provision of equity finance and in actual company management. Some of us have already begun to provide venture capital to companies in anticipation of their going public. But on the question as to whether we should go further there are sharp divisions of opinion among bankers.

In this connection reference is often made to the situation on the continent, though it should be noted that the arrangements vary considerably from country to country. In France, Belgium and Italy, for example, participation of deposit banks in the affairs of their customers, whether by equity holdings, directorships or involvement in management is minimal. In Holland, and even more so in Germany, by contrast, associations are much closer. The large German banks between them are said to own about 5% of the total share capital of the country's joint stock companies, and in some of them they hold a majority of the issued share capital. Representation on boards is common.

My own view is that any moves we might make in this direction will be fairly limited both in scope and extent, and will be related to our capital resources rather than deposits. We are bankers and not investors, and it seems to me inappropriate that we should use more than a limited part of our deposit resources to provide equity capital, even though prospective returns may be greater than on our investments in gilt-edged securities. We shall, too, be mindful of disadvantages such as that expressed by a German banker who has been quoted[3] as saying: "Shareholding in industry has become a trap for the banks. We have to take part in every capital increase to maintain our voting percentage, and that pulls more of our lending resources into particular companies than is justified by creditworthiness or profitability." Moreover, in the United Kingdom we have longer-established and more highly-developed markets from which companies can obtain equity and loan capital than in other European countries. More generally, it can be argued that the channelling of capital through the market makes for a more efficient use of resources.

What I would expect is that growing amounts of equity finance will be provided for the smaller companies which are not yet large enough to go to the market but have expectations of doing so, and in these circumstances the banks or their subsidiaries as appropriate will normally seek board representation. Again, I would expect growing provision of some equity finance as part of a general package for a major capital development. Beyond this the Clearing Banks could well include some selected equities in their investment portfolios, at present virtually confined to gilt-edged securities.

INVOLVEMENT IN COMPANY MANAGEMENT

If I am right in thinking we shall not, except in limited and special cases, be taking on the rôle of providers of risk capital, then it likewise seems unlikely that we shall wish as a general rule to become involved in company management to the extent of appointing directors to the board. However, whether we are providing equity finance or not, there is no doubt in my mind that we shall require more information and knowledge than in the past of the progress of businesses to which we are lending substantial sums. This will be especially so as term-financing for periods of up to ten years and perhaps beyond, and the provision of "packages" embracing a range of facilities, become accepted functions of the Clearing Banks. In other words, we shall need to exercise a closer surveillance of the progress of the borrower, and over a longer time-scale than when short-term finance is being provided.

Whether something more than "surveillance" will be required will depend on the circumstances of each case. Many businesses of their own volition have always kept their bankers fully informed of their progress and important changes in their situation. But some do not accept this moral obligation, and the banks could well require to be represented on the boards of such companies. A number of recent events have pointed the need for closer involvement and exercise of influence by lenders in the management of large borrowing undertakings. Such developments have also provided the impetus for the initiation of discussions between a number of representative bodies, under the chairmanship of the Bank of England, on the relationships between institutional investors and industry. These discussions represent a considerable step in the direction which individual banks, as I have indicated, will wish to go.

DEPOSITS AND SERVICES

So far I have been mainly concerned with aspects of the banks' lending activities, but in order to sustain these visualised developments we shall need a corresponding expansion of our deposit base. This implies the maintenance of our branch networks if we are to continue to attract the most liquid assets of the community other than cash itself. However, the size of these branch networks will continue to receive searching scrutiny, particularly having regard to the expected movements of population to the Midlands and the South. Moreover, with the growing range of sophistication of services offered, we may have to consider moves towards differentiation of branches.

It is particularly important that we remain in close proximity to our personal customers since their accounts provide a large and growing proportion of our total deposits, and are considerably in excess of our lending to the business sector. The importance of personal-sector deposits means that we shall be continuing to seek to improve and extend the ancillary services that we are well placed to provide, quite apart from special credit schemes and arrangements. Provision of investment and savings advice is one field which we may wish to develop on a wider and more formal basis than at present.

Companies will increasingly be seeking out the most remunerative outlets for their liquid funds, continuing the trends of the past ten to fifteen years, and the banks and their subsidiaries will continue to bid for these funds. Companies will, however, need to maintain "transactions" balances at the branches, primarily because we shall continue to provide the most efficient and widespread system for transfer of payments. Indeed, full automation of the payments mechanism will be speeded up and find widening applications. There will be greater linkages between the banking system and the business world, not only within the United Kingdom, but also with other financial centres and especially with banks on the continent.

Alongside all this we may expect to see a significant expansion in the provision by the banks of computer-based services for companies which are themselves unable to meet the high costs of installation and obsolescence of equipment which cannot be used to capacity. The obvious fields for further development are company share registers and pay-roll accounting, services which the banks are already providing on a growing scale. Expansion might be especially rapid among medium-sized companies for computer-based services such as factoring and stock record and control programmes.

INTERNATIONAL LINKS

The future of the banking system cannot be contemplated without reference to the international scene. British banks have always been as internationally-minded as comparable institutions aboard, and perhaps more so than most. For the most part development has traditionally been by the establishment of extensive networks of banking correspondents, and to a varying extent by the setting up of branches abroad. Over the past decade or so new patterns have developed for a number of reasons, but principally in response to the needs of the large multinational companies, in order to take advantage of the rapid expansion of the Euro-currency markets, and in anticipation of U.K. entry into the Common Market.

As a result we have seen a proliferation of consortium banks, operating as quite separate entities from the shareholding banks. These new institutions have quickly established themselves, operating in the various money markets and catering particularly to the needs of multinational companies for medium-term finance. There would seem to be considerable room for a widening of the range of activities undertaken; the number of such institutions could also grow further. Although the major British banks already have participations in consortia based on London or the continent, they are also likely to be involved in the establishment of groupings in other parts of the world. This is already happening to some extent, but I would expect considerable further activity of this kind.

Parallel with the formation of the consortium banks has been the establishment of less formal associations with overseas banks, not involving exchanges of share capital or any other direct financial link, though such associations have provided the basis for a number of joint ventures. Since the associations which have been initiated so far have a strong European bias, they are likely to be strengthened by U.K. membership of the E.E.C., and new participants may be sought to provide a wider geographical spread. But in this area the options are wide open; indeed not all the Clearing Banks have sought associations of this kind, but they seem to me to be a more logical line of development than establishing a branch network on the continent.

Further development of financial links between the partners in such groupings may well have to wait on progress in harmon-isation and integration in the E.E.C., more especially in the fiscal, company-law and monetary fields. When this stage is reached, then the way will be open for the formation of real multi-national European banks, exercising overall control through the setting up of holding companies and involving exchanges of share capital. This may not come about this century, unless the obstacles to monetary, fiscal and legal integration in the Community can be overcome much more quickly than seems likely at present. But a deepening of the content of the existing associations could well occur, as the partner banks harmonise their working arrangements and develop reciprocal facilities, for example by making credits readily transferable between themselves and by providing "service intermediation" facilities for each others' customers. Integration of intra-European payments arrangements, however, is more likely to be on a universal basis, moving towards a system similar to that now operating in Britain.

An important factor in the future development of the banking system, both generally and in relation to the kinds of links I have just been discussing, will be the way in which the City of London's position as an international financial centre is affected more particularly by membership of the Common Market. Any assessment here must be based on a number of assumptions of varying degrees of uncertainty. It is reassuring to note, from a special study by the Committee on Invisible Exports[4] that "as the largest financial centre in Europe (London) may increasingly be regarded as a focus – perhaps the main focus – of a closely-knit continental financial network" after entry.

The same report echoes other assessments that the City should be well placed to compete on the grounds of its well-recognised expertise in the provision of financial services. But it would be a mistake to be complacent here; other influences may be working in the opposite direction, and much will depend on the flexibility and liberalism of monetary developments in the enlarged Community. Moreover, it seems important that London should be able to offer more than intermediation services, which has been its outstanding rôle since the war; it should also be able to supply capital resources if it is to realise its full potential and establish itself as the undoubted capital market of Europe.

ASPECTS OF OFFICIAL POLICY

Having considered briefly both domestic and international aspects of banking, I can now draw the threads together and refer to official policy, which in an economy such as ours must play a significant rôle.

Following the Clearing Bank mergers of the late Sixties, the decisions relating to disclosure of profits and reserves, and then in 1971 the introduction by the authorities of new credit-control arrangements, the banking system has clearly entered a new era, and one which is likely to see radical changes in banking practices and structures. An immediate effect of the new régime of credit control has been the introduction of a more flexible rate structure, and this will result in continuing pressures on the margins between rates charged and allowed. They will reinforce the search for new forms of lending which can carry a higher rate of return than the traditional overdraft, both in the company sector as already indicated, but more especially perhaps in the personal sector, where we can raise our return and still undercut other sources of finance. Pressure on margins will also intensify the need for proper costing of all the ancillary services we provide, e.g. cash handling, and generally these will be required to pay their own passage.

Inter-bank competition is expected to increase significantly over the next few years as services are expanded and made more attractive to potential customers, and as foreign and other banks also broaden the range of their activities. This will further encourage the existing trends towards strengthening and widening links between commercial banks, merchant banks, finance houses and other financial institutions both at home and abroad. In other words the move towards "universal banks" and away from specialist institutions is likely to continue.

The extent and direction of the changes in the institutional framework that seem bound to occur in the Seventies will depend in part at least on the acquiescence of the authorities. So the answers to such questions as whether further mergers of banks will take place, how relationships between deposit and merchant banks, discount houses and non-financial institutions will develop, will not rest wholly with the banks themselves. But there seems little doubt that pressures will persist towards closer integration of the financial system, in order to exploit the benefits of size and technology, and so as to be able to provide, from under one umbrella, a comprehensive range of financial services.

Changes in operational procedures and organisation will no doubt take place within the Clearing-Bank groups. Since September 1971 some banks, and particularly my own, have moved towards more centralised control of the deposit-taking function, especially as it relates to the wholesale money markets, whereas others have preferred to leave such activities in the hands of specialist subsidiaries. It is too early to say whether a common pattern will develop, though in any event subsidiary companies will continue to be responsible for specialist activities akin to merchant banking, factoring, leasing, and instalment credit.

The new system of credit control has yet to be tested in conditions when the authorities are seeking to restrict credit. The arrangements could be effective if the authorities are prepared to accept the implications of the principles laid down, and in particular that interest rates – the new "rationing" mechanism – may have to rise to levels which in the past would have been regarded as unacceptable. It should be noted too that although the use of lending ceilings as a monetary instrument has been abandoned, hopefully for ever, we must still expect from time to time that our ability to extend credit will be restricted.

Another factor that assumes importance once the United Kingdom is a member of the E.E.C. is the rate of progress made towards monetary union, and with it the prospect of harmonisation of methods of controlling credit in the Community. Despite the ambitious proposals and plans in the monetary field, my own view is that little will be achieved over the next decade that will directly affect us in a major sense. Some aspects of the proposed progress towards monetary union, and greater freedom of capital movements, will of course have implications for our business. But for a long time to come the changes seem unlikely to affect to any great extent our own course of development except, as I indicated earlier, in the way of associations with continental banks.

Finally, to recapitulate the main future trends as I see them, they are continuing strong growth of the banking system, but in a highly competitive environment; a continuing trend towards "universal" banks; a closer involvement of banks in the affairs of their corporate customers who are borrowing on a large scale; and a strengthening of international banking links. For the most part, however, development will be gradual; I do not think we shall see any dramatic overnight changes. Nevertheless, the net result over a period of years is likely to be substantial, and ten years hence the banking scene could well be as different from that of today as today's is as compared with that of the early Sixties. What I have tried to do is to indicate what will probably be the main features of the banking landscape of 1980, but not its precise configuration.

NOTES TO CHAPTER 7

[1] *Board of Trade Journal*, 27th August 1965.
[2] *The Banker*, February 1972, page 199.
[3] In "German Banks Look Outwards", by Richard Fry; *The Banker*, January 1971.
[4] "How entry into the Common Market may affect Britain's Invisible Earnings", Committee on Invisibile Exports, July 1971.

Chapter 8

THE FUTURE FOR

THE LONDON STOCK EXCHANGE

Peter H. Swan

Stock Exchange Council

The London Stock Exchange is run as a privately controlled organisation, although it is recognised by legislation for certain purposes, and whilst no doubt in the past it was concerned primarily with the benefit of its Members, today that concept has completely changed and it sees itself as one of the leading national and possibly international financial institutions. It is controlled by a Council of thirty-six Members, who come up for election every three years. They sit as a Council each Monday and throughout the remainder of the week are divided into various standing committees reporting to the Council at its weekly meeting. The Chairman and his two deputies meet each morning and act very like the executive directors of any large company. There is a permanent staff numbering some six hundred people, many of whom have professional qualifications and act as secretaries and advisers to the various Committees, as well as operating the various central departments which aid the settlement of business.

Business is regulated by the *Rules & Regulations of the Stock Exchange*, which run into three hundred pages with some two hundred individual Rules. As existing Rules are altered and new ones made these are circulated to all the Members. These Rules are far from being restrictive but enable Members to carry out their business properly. They cover items such as the commission which Brokers charge, the various procedures for settlement and delivery of stock, the regulations for becoming a Member, regulations regarding a firm's financial affairs and many other aspects of conducting business. If any of these Rules are broken the culprit receives the displeasure of the Council or in certain areas the Firm would be fined, and in more serious matters the Members or the Firm could be formally censored or suspended for a period of time. The final penalty is complete expulsion from the Stock Exchange.

The Members are divided into two distinct Groups; first there is the Jobber, who acts as a price maker in securities – normally there is more than one Jobber in the securities which are quoted and consequently because of the resulting competition between them the prices quoted are extremely close. The Jobber has his capital at risk and is therefore trying to make a profit or minimise a loss. He may only deal with another Member, who of course is normally a Broker, and must not deal with the public. The second Group is the Broker, who deals on behalf of the public as an agent and is remunerated by a commission which is laid down by the Council. Occasionally a Broker may act as an agent between two of his clients and even this comes under one of the Rules, but the vast majority of the business of a Broker is done with the Jobbers. It is this distinct division between the Jobber and Broker which is unique in any securities market of the world. As there is more than one Jobber in the majority of securities a Broker can find a price which is the most suitable to his client. The Jobber on being asked the price by a Broker is not told which way the Broker's business is likely to be. The profit which the Jobber may make in his trading is a small price to pay to have such an efficient market covering the small private-client business up to the large institutional orders. In most other financial markets the person handling the client's business acts in a dual capacity. In other words, he becomes a principal for the purchase of a stock and the agent when he places it with his client. This is a practice which could be open to abuse. Because of our efficient secondary market it does mean that our primary market itself has reached a very high standard. Clients know, when subscribing for new issues, that they can always sell their allotment if they so wish or finance the transaction by the sale of existing securities. This means that industry can borrow more cheaply when both these markets are working so well in harmony.

The Issuing Houses Association have been investigating the

possibility of Merchant Banks subscribing to a computer system whereby large orders may be done outside the Stock Exchange. Without being carping, this suggestion means they would have to use the Jobbers' prices for any large transactions and prices are not made just by large orders. It is my belief that the criticism is not made at the Jobbing system or the usual business undertaken by the Brokers in their normal day but at the large amounts of commission which Merchant Banks have paid to Stockbrokers when big lines of shares have been bought in the market in the middle of a take-over battle. This, of course, is not general business of the Stock Exchange and it is brought to it by the Merchant Bank. It may be the answer lies in reducing Brokers' commission in these particular areas.

A few figures are necessary to understand what the size of the Stock Exchange is. In the first place there are 540 Members acting as Jobbers and 2,900 individual Members acting as Brokers and to this number there are some corporate bodies as Members which gives a total of a little over 3,500. Those that are either Partners or Directors have formed themselves into organisations and at the moment there are 168 Broking and 24 Jobbing firms. Apart from the Members there are others on the floor of the House. These are young men starting their career and are called Unauthorised Clerks. They take messages and are able to get prices for Partners transacting business with clients. There are also Authorised Clerks which, as the name implies, are people who are authorised to deal on behalf of their firm. At the same time in the offices there are many men and women processing the various pieces· of paper which are necessary with the legal transfer of securities and again there are many in the Brokers' trading, research and other departments. In total it has been estimated that the population of the Stock Exchange is around 20,000 to 25,000.

To make a comparison with this relatively small number of people, it is of interest to know that there are about 9,000 quoted securities. Of these there are 1,394 gilt-edged securities valued at £25,000 million and 3,300 equity securities with a market value of £116,000 million. The balance of the figure covers the debentures and preference shares and other categories of securities. The turnover per day in the London Stock Exchange is approximately £225 million. Naturally, the year's figure is quite staggering. Turnover last year (1971/2) in the gilt-edged market was £51,000 million and in the equity market £13,000 million.

The standard of entry to Stock Exchange membership has improved tremendously and young men with university degrees or professional qualifications are now normally the rule. At the same time the Stock Exchange itself has instituted examinations and these must be passed before a person can become a Broker. There are naturally exemptions for certain sections of the paper which are given when an applicant holds a professional qualification, but all must do examinations on Stock Exchange principles and practice. This has meant a higher standard of service to the Brokers' clients and this is a move which will continue. In view of the high turnover just mentioned the liquid resources of the Jobbers has been stretched and because of high taxation it has made the creation of capital nearly impossible. Recent liberalisation of the Rules has enabled firms to get outside capital in one way or another. Various regulations must be complied with, such as that the control must always be held by the individual personal Members and no interference in running the firm from outside shareholders is allowed. At the moment there are ten firms trading as limited liability companies and fifteen as unlimited companies. Whilst the object of these changes in Rules was mainly for the Jobbers, Brokers themselves have also taken advantage of this facility. Although a Broker's business is primarily agency and charging a commission, the cost of running a Broking firm has risen rapidly and these days where computers and other sophisticated machines are being used Brokers have found the need for extra capital themselves. This is a move which will extend in future years. There are sixteen firms which have opened branches or have subsidiary companies abroad and no doubt with the increased interest in the facilities of the London Stock Exchange further offices will be opened. These sixteen firms have offices as far apart as Luxemburg or Brussels, New York and San Francisco and Sydney and Bangkok. Once upon a time the London Stockbroker had the "square mile" as his parish but today it is the world.

Although Stockbroking is not really a profession its Members have fairly strong views on the merits of paid advertising. It was only recently that a recommendation of the Council put before the Members to allow paid advertising was rejected. However, firms that have offices abroad have been able to advertise their services in local newspapers and periodicals provided they are printed abroad. The Council also recently allowed firms based in London to advertise their services in overseas newspapers, as many firms do not wish to have overseas offices and yet still do a very considerable amount of investment on behalf of overseas clients. The general move is towards advertising and now we are part of the Common Market no doubt overseas institutions will advertise in London newspapers. It looks therefore as though it will not be long before the Rule will be changed and London Brokers will be able to advertise in our national press.

All Brokers charge a commission, the rate of which is laid down by the Council. Although it is a minimum commission in actual fact all Brokers do charge it. From time to time it is said that Brokers themselves should negotiate commission with their clients on the particular business. This is a feeling which is growing in America. It seems quite easy to take this view, but fixed commissions were actually brought in by clients early in this century as they wished to know what was the rate for the job. At the moment the maintenance of a sophisticated research department costs quite a lot of money and institutions rely on the information which they get from Brokers. If commissions are cut, therefore, specialist brokers in particular would have to reduce their research, which would necessitate the institutions having to take on this rather expensive job themselves. I am not saying in certain areas, as I mentioned earlier, that Brokers' commissions are not too high, but I think it is only reasonable that any reductions or concessions should be made unilaterally among all clients. There is a tremendous amount of competition between Brokers and expansion of a Broker's Firm can only come through maintaining a good service to his clients. The word "service" covers many things. It might, for instance, be a very efficient and price-getting service, it might mean becoming leaders in a specialised market and also it means expanding and maintaining a good research department and providing an efficient settlement of paperwork following Stock Exchange transactions.

Investment research as a subject started as long ago as the

late 1950s, but in recent years the trend has intensified and most large Firms of Stockbrokers employ highly-skilled teams of investment analysts whose task is to forecast future trends in company earnings over usually the next two or three years. This work is accomplished by close study of company reports, a mass of available statistics and by keeping in close touch with the Management of large companies.

The advent of the computer has also begun to have an effect on the work carried out in research and one Broker is well known for the extensive data bank that is available from its computer giving a mass of statistics on many of the leading U.K. companies. For example, the computer will answer the question, which twenty companies have past growth rates of more than 15% per annum, price earnings ratios not more than fifteen, say, and dividend yields greater than 4%.

This work is associated with the idea of making available as much information as possible for the institutional investment manager, but perhaps a more interesting and potentially valuable approach has been to use computers to try and help actually make the investment decisions and another Broker has applied the computer to evaluate the relative attractiveness of different companies in relation to their prospects and also to forecast the probable future trend for the U.K. stock market as a whole.

Another important topic, though not strictly in the field of investment research, is that of portfolio performance; and in the last two or three years a lot of work has been done in the U.S.A., and more recently in this country, in setting up systems to calculate portfolio performance figures so that investment managers and trustees can compare the progress of their funds one with another. It is interesting to notice that the result of this work may in fact be to place greater emphasis on the statistical and mathematical analysis being done on U.K. stock markets since it may be shown that the gains to be had from careful selection of shares are potentially small in relation to those that will come from investing in the best overall market. Thus, for example, the work already referred to which tries to forecast the possible trend of the U.K. market by relating the level of share prices to changes in company profits and money supply has great potential in terms of benefits to a pension fund, and of course this type of technique could readily be enlarged to include, for example, the markets in the Common Market countries and in the U.S. It is thus possible to argue that whilst no doubt the conventional analysis of companies will continue, we may soon be approaching the point when much more work will be done on analysis as applied to markets than to individual shares.

Quite recently votes have been taken by the members of the various Federal Exchanges and they have all unanimously voted to form one Stock Exchange. In 1973 therefore there will be *The* Stock Exchange and all Members will be Members of *The* Stock Exchange. The Stock Exchanges in Scotland, the Midlands and elsewhere will remain and be controlled by a Committee for local affairs and the Council of *The* Stock Exchange will have representatives on it from all these regional Exchanges. Its many advantages will take time to become apparent. First there will be a national compensation fund for all investors which will mean that any investor with a legitimate claim will be compensated should his Broker run into difficulties. At the present moment no Member of a Federal Stock Exchange can open up an office within twenty-five miles of another Stock Exchange. This really has been a ludicrous position because, as mentioned earlier, we have allowed Brokers to open up in Geneva, New York, Melbourne or Hong Kong but will not allow a firm in London to open in Manchester. However, this restriction is going and it will mean that London Firms if they so wish can open anywhere in the country and country broking Firms can come to Throgmorton Street. At the same time it will mean that a Jobber in London, for instance, will be able to deal with a Jobber in Cardiff. The speed of dealing should increase and prices will represent a kind of national price more than they do at the moment. Another result will be that all new issues being launched in the country will have to have the same high standards which have been set by London. Other advantages will be that as all Members will be Members of the one Exchange there will be common standards for all.

The Stock Exchange has not been slow to use and to adapt its techniques to the computer. But like so many others it ran into serious difficulties in the early stages. About four years ago the Council embarked on a project to cover all transactions and cash movements between Firms. This project was in some difficulty and it was then overtaken by decimalisation, so it had to be deferred until that problem was overcome.

There are two main areas where the computer is now being used. In the first place there is the dissemination of prices through the Market Price Display closed circuit. Prices are being continuously collected from the market and fed into the system, which is then relayed into television sets. Up to seven hundred prices are being brought up to date and a further fifty "feature stocks" may be relayed. Two channels are devoted to company news and news of more general interest. Originally the service was for Members, but there are now some fifty institutions and others in London who subscribe to the service. The development will be to extend the service to other institutions throughout the country and there is no technical reason why it should not be extended abroad.

There are restrictions on this service which will continue. In the first place the price that is shown is a "middle market" price and not the two-way price that is quoted by the Jobbers. Unlike America where there is no competition between specialists, Jobbers in the majority of stocks dealt have one or possibly more in competition with each other and so it would be unreasonable for a Jobber to disclose to all what business is being done. At the same time the service is a Market Price Display and is not there to give dividend yields or price earnings ratios which in most cases can be a matter of opinion. Information of this kind will continue to be given by a Broker to clients.

The other main area for the computer is that of accounting transactions between Members. For some years now the computer has been in use in the clearing office where it compiles lists of bargains in some two hundred active stocks (which account roughly for a third of all bargains) and matches up buyers and sellers for delivery of stock. It is also used to list and total deliveries between Members through the Central Stock Payment Office which on account-day may total some 40,000 cheques amounting to £50 million or more.

The Report of the Heasman Committee was published in May 1970 and this made many fundamental proposals for a complete change in the system of delivery and settlement between Member Firms and between the Stock Exchange and registrars. Generally the report has been accepted so far as it covers the handling of paper and the completion of the settlement but the proposal for altering the dealing cycle is more contentious.

It is not many years since the Stock Exchange first had its computer, but I think I can say that by the end of this decade a fully centralised system of settlement covering not only London but also all the country Stock Exchanges will have come into being.

Now finally, where is the London Stock Exchange in the Common Market? It seems that we have two alternatives. In the first place, no doubt, Jobbers could open up in Continental centres or else have arrangements with European banks. This, to me, would be to fragment the market and also I feel that the firms would have enormous problems not only of financial control for their commitments abroad but also over the delivery of stock. I would prefer that the Jobbers deal in European shares in London. To start off with, I do not suppose there would be more than forty or fifty companies where there is a large issue of capital and a reasonably good market, and anyhow about twenty of such companies from Europe are already quoted. European stock is already held by United Kingdom institutions and it seems possible that an extension of the stock-borrowing system which aids the liquidity of the equity market in London could in due course be extended to cover Continental shares. This could quite easily give a much better market in the shares than the domestic exchange of the European company. This is not new to London, as prior to the war the market in many American securities was in London. When the various restrictions on investment between the U.K. and the Continent go, as they must in due course, the large institutions in this country and no doubt on the Continent, will be looking on investments from a Common Market point of view and comparing a German chemical share with a French one as in this country one compares two companies in the same industry. Already Brokers are beginning to expand their research into European companies and analysts have been abroad to go over companies. Because of our remarkably sophisticated securities market, and in this case I extend this to include not only the Stock Exchange but the Merchant Banks and the large institutional shareholders such as insurance companies, pension funds, investment trusts and others, one would hope to see European companies coming here to raise capital in all forms. This was one of the old traditions of the City and it has only been post-war fiscal restrictions which have stopped it.

However, for a company to be dealt freely in London it will have to have a quotation. I am sure the standards which have been set here, which have taken many years to reach and are still being improved upon, may become a hurdle for many European companies. The kinds of standards I am thinking of, for instance, are the proportion of shares which will be available to the general public if a company goes public, and the question of disclosing at least a ten-year record of the company's profits. We would have to see fully consolidated accounts in the prospectus and this and a report made by the Board sent to the shareholders at regular intervals. There are many signs now that a move in this direction is being made and we will find our professional firms either in the accountancy or legal fields helping their counterparts in Europe in providing the requirements of London. This may take a little time but I hope not too long and I can see no reason why an Italian selling a French share to a Dutchman will not do this through London.

Chapter 9

THE FUTURE FOR BUILDING SOCIETIES

Andrew Breach
Chairman, Bristol & West Building Society

Any discussion of the future of building societies must begin by recognising their recent emergence as major financial institutions.

Although the societies have performed a valuable function for many years and have helped finance two big house-buying booms – the one between the wars and the one which started in the 1950s and is still in progress – it is only during the last decade that their remarkable asset growth has promoted them into the financial big league.

In 1960, the societies' assets stood at £3,180 million. In 1966, they had doubled to £6,350 million: even so, this was £2,000 million less than both National Savings and the London Clearing Banks. By 1971 total assets had grown to £13,000 million compared with figures for National Savings, including Trustee Savings Banks of £9,200 million. Building societies now control funds greater in aggregate than the combined net deposits of the London Clearing Banks and are second in size only to the insurance companies (see Tables 1 and 2, page 129).

In the mortgage market, building societies in 1971 advanced £2,700 million to house-buyers and provided approximately 90% of the total amount advanced by the three institutions which provide the great bulk of home-loan finance: building societies, local authorities and insurance companies (see Table 3).

Building societies were established about two hundred years ago as self-help organisations. They were literally *building* societies, groups of men combining to provide the capital and the labour to build houses on a co-operative basis. When each member had been housed, the societies were terminated.

128

TABLE 1 PERSONAL SAVINGS INSTITUTIONS – TOTAL LIABILITIES (£M.)

Year	Building Societies	All National Savings	T.S. Banks	Unit Trusts	London Clearing Banks (net deposits)	Insurance Companies	Private Superannuation Funds
1964	4,888	8,290	1,894	429	8,548	9,132	2,985
1965	5,577	8,366	2,030	522	8,652	9,866	3,293
1966	6,350	8,335	2,151	582	8,760	10,596	3,365
1967	7,523	8,472	2,272	854	9,412	11,802*	3,719
1968	8,357	8,547	2,365	1,482	9,898	13,164*	4,280
1969	9,336	8,452	2,411	1,412	9,801	14,201*	4,468
1970	10,940	8,589	2,542	1,398	9,997	15,452*	4,673
1971	13,067	9,220	2,797	1,953	11,859	17,100*	6,175

* Includes the holdings of Commonwealth Companies' life funds.

TABLE 2 PERSONAL SAVINGS INSTITUTIONS – NET INVESTMENT FROM PERSONAL SECTOR (£M.)

Year	Building Societies Shares and Deposits	Local Authorities (not quoted securities)	Banking Sector Deposits	H.P. Finance Companies**	Unit Trusts	Life Assurance and Superannuation Funds	All National Savings	T.S. Banks
1964	501	120	458	24	77	1,164	358	192
1965	657	217	512	30	59	1,187	74	137
1966	726	123	250	12	105	1,287	-35	121
1967	1,090	31	740	-10	84	1,474	125	121
1968	762	104	682	-1	258	1,508	75	93
1969	890	191	308	-2	186	1,505	-113	46
1970	1,484	-13	822	9	89	1,763	114	131
1971	1,961	-203	953	5	46	1,981	612	255

** Series rebased from 1966.

TABLE 3 MORTGAGE LENDING – AMOUNT ADVANCED (£M.)

Year		Building Societies		Local Authorities		Insurance Companies		Total	
		Gross	Net	Gross	Net	Gross	Net	Gross	Net
1960		558	240	78	42		68		350
1961		544	221	107	67		81		369
1962		618	276	94	47	118	61	830	384
1963		852	422	119	59	107	34	1,078	515
1964		1,052	546	195	121	132	53	1,379	720
1965		965	459	244	169	163	90	1,372	718
1966		1,245	667	134	54	147	60	1,526	781
1967		1,477	823	168	69	124	34	1,769	926
1968		1,587	860	111	9	168	72	1,866	941
1969		1,556	782	69	-30	180	83	1,805	835
1970		2,021	1,088	154	37	154	36	2,329	1,161
1971		2,741	1,576			147			
1970	1	384	201	26	1	33	11	443	213
	2	497	269	32	4	35	8	564	281
	3	568	310	44	12	45	9	657	331
	4	572	308	52	20	42	9	666	337
1971	1	506	286	42	10	32	7	580	303
	2	674	389	37	3	37	4	748	396
	3	780	459	46	11	41	3	867	473
	4	781	442			38			

From these primitive beginnings emerged, in the mid-nineteenth century, the permanent societies which formed the framework of the modern building society. Although the size and influence of building societies have grown out of all recognition the basic philosophy and, significantly, the legal framework within which the societies operate have changed very little over the years. It is perhaps time to question, particularly when most financial institutions are diversifying rapidly, whether the constraints placed upon building societies should be modified.

HOME OWNERSHIP

But first, we should understand that the growth of the building-society movement has been created by the home-ownership revolution. The societies' prime function is to provide finance for the private housing market and their interest rate-structure has been devised to attract a sufficient level of funds from investors to satisfy the demands of the house-buying public.

The relationship between our home-ownership function and the means of performing that function is explicitly if wordily set out in the first paragraph of the Building Societies Act, 1962, which, almost verbatim, first appeared in building-society legislation in 1874: "The purpose for which a building society may be established under this Act is that of raising, by the subscriptions of the members, a stock or fund for making advances to members out of the funds of the society upon security by way of mortgage of freehold or leasehold estate."

Given this emphasis on the provision of mortgage finance, it can be seen that the rôle of the building societies is social as much as economic. Hence, our operations, our interest rates, our ability to satisfy the mortgage demand, keep us in the public eye. It also brings us into the political arena: sometimes willingly, sometimes less so.

We co-operated with Government in its aim, through the House Purchase and Housing Act of 1959, to encourage by means of improvement grants and generous building-society loans the rehabilitation of the nation's ageing housing stock. Co-operation is also evidenced by the current N.H.B.R.C. and S.A.Y.E. schemes, the commitment to support housing societies under the aegis of the Housing Corporation, the Option Mortgage Scheme which was designed to broaden the base of home ownership, and the arrangements with New Towns to expand owner occupation as a socially desirable alternative to rented accommodation.

Less happily, we have been subjected to pressure to keep mortgage interest rates artificially depressed for political reasons and a few years ago found ourselves investigated, for political reasons, by the Prices and Incomes Board. Generally, however, the politicians, particularly when chastened by the responsibilities of office, have understood that if building societies are to play their part in the housing effort we must be allowed to pay and charge the market rate for our funds.

CURRENT SITUATION (1972)

We have now had a situation for at least twelve months in which the inflow of funds to building societies has been more than sufficient to satisfy the mortgage demand. We have, indeed, reduced the borrowers' rate from $8\frac{1}{2}\%$ to 8% and the simultaneous reduction in the investors' rates has not seriously affected inflow.

Societies' liquidity ratios now stand, on average, at about 19% of total assets: rather above the norm for the past ten years, when the average liquidity ratio for all societies has normally fluctuated between $15\frac{1}{2}\%$ and $17\frac{1}{2}\%$. There are good reasons for maintaining somewhat higher levels of fall-back funds at present: a larger proportion than usual of our funds may prove to be "hot money", savings tend to be more volatile in these more sophisticated days and there is the expectation of an expansion of consumer spending.

Having made this point, I must concede that at the turn of the year levels of liquidity were something of a minor embarrassment. This was on two scores: first, there was a feeling that we *ought* to have been lending the cash instead of pushing it into gilts or the local-authority market, and second, it is difficult to secure returns on our liquid funds to compare with the return on our mortgage assets unless we invest in maturities of a longer date than is really appropriate to building societies.

This raises an interesting dilemma. When there is a surplus of funds should we, as individual societies, seek further to relax our lending requirements in a competitive effort to secure a larger share of the available mortgage business, and in the process add to the house-price spiral? Or should we reduce interest rates and run the risk of choking off the ready flow of funds when, by all accounts, the private-sector building industry is gaining in confidence and is poised to turn in record post-war figures?

HOUSE BUILDING EFFORT

It is generally recognised that the construction industry is built on confidence and credit. It is no accident that the recession in private housing activity in the very late Sixties and from which the industry is only now emerging coincided with a period of credit restriction which hit both the builders' and their customers' ability to raise capital.

If building societies are to perform their social obligation they must seek constantly to have adequate funds available for the whole of the private housing market: to finance the purchase and, indirectly, the construction of new houses as well as lubricating the wheels of the second-hand market. The housing problem, stripped of the hysteria and the special pleadings, is basically one of matching supply with demand. We must build more houses, and if the demand manifests itself in the private sector, building societies must play their part as financial intermediaries in providing the resources efficiently, speedily and as economically as possible.

In the current period between recession and full production in the building industry, excess building-society funds are finding their way into the second-hand market, and increased liquidity. The ready supply of credit, when there are too many buyers chasing too few houses, has prompted the argument that building societies are adding fuel to house-price inflation. I must admit that there is a relationship. Our lending terms, generally, have been relaxed in response to the demand from our customers to an extent which we would not entertain in more stringent times.

I believe that this will be a relatively temporary phenomenon and that, through the interaction between incomes and house prices, the market will begin to settle down towards the end of 1972. Figure 1 illustrates the relationship between average earnings and and the index of new house prices and supports this probability.

CONSTRAINTS

Many of the criticisms of building societies stem from the legal restraints within which we operate. Our liquid funds are restricted to authorised investments consisting mainly of gilts, local-authority paper and bank deposits, and furthermore there are regulations governing the proportions which can be held in short-, medium- and long-dated stocks. We cannot invest in equities and our only hedge against inflation is the ownership of office premises which must be partly or wholly occupied for the conduct of our business.

We are closely circumscribed in how we deploy our mortgage

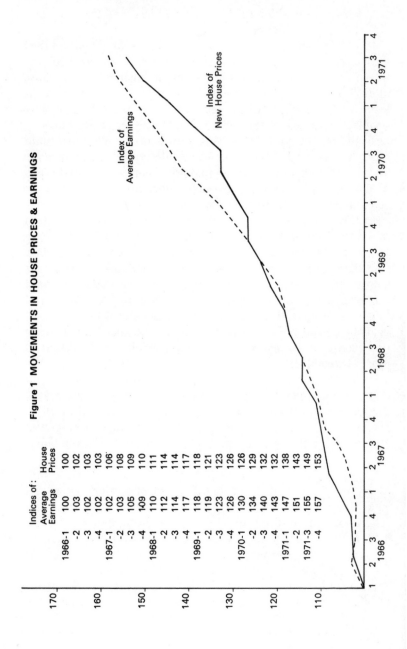

Figure 1 MOVEMENTS IN HOUSE PRICES & EARNINGS

	Indices of:	
	Average Earnings	House Prices
1966-1	100	100
-2	103	102
-3	102	103
-4	102	103
1967-1	102	106
-2	103	108
-3	105	109
-4	109	110
1968-1	110	111
-2	112	114
-3	114	114
-4	117	117
1969-1	118	118
-2	119	121
-3	123	123
-4	126	126
1970-1	130	126
-2	134	129
-3	140	132
-4	143	132
1971-1	147	138
-2	151	143
1971-3	155	149
-4	157	153

assets. The special advance regulations limit the amount of lending in any year (in very broad terms) in respect of loans of any size to corporate bodies and loans of more than £13,000 to any one individual to 10% of a society's total advances in that year. Given that £13,000 is a very modest sum in the South-East (and that even the suggested new limit of £20,000 is hardly less so), a substantial proportion of our special advance quota is spoken for in traditional house-purchase loans.

Our scope for lending on commercial developments or even financing house construction (which has been recently advocated) is even more severely limited than appears at first sight. This may not be a wholly bad thing, and I am not suggesting that we should discard our traditional virtues. But I am forced to ask whether the circumstances of the past year (1971/2) – admittedly exceptional – do not give grounds for believing that, by virtue of their size and economic power, building societies have outgrown the need for the severe limitations placed upon them.

Why, indeed, are we held in this tight legislative straight-jacket? First, because the public expect building societies to be literally as safe as houses. Second, because a handful of societies have in the past been used as vehicles for the business interests of their directors, and thirdly, because with over four hundred societies of varying size there is inevitably a wide gap between the best and the worst managements, no matter how conscientious. Commenting two years ago on the effect of the Building Societies Act of 1960, the Chief Registrar of Friendly Societies considered that "the new provisions covering special advances, authorised banks and the investment of surplus funds have helped to ensure that honestly-run societies avoid mistaken policies which brought difficulties to some societies in earlier years; policies which were nonetheless imprudent because they were honestly followed."

CASE FOR GREATER FREEDOM

But is it right that our largest societies – there are twenty or so with assets in excess of £100 million – the largest having assets in excess of £2,000 million – should be subject to the same restrictions as a small, locally-based society run by an estate agent or solicitor in his spare time? The time has surely come for some differentiation in the scope of activities allowed to societies of varying size. Larger societies – of, say, £250 million and upwards – could perhaps be allowed greater freedom of investment – at the present time they have not even the discretion allowed to ordinary trustees under the Trustee Investments Act, 1961.

The building-society movement is currently exercising its mind on the contribution it might make to urban renewal and the sought-after partnership between the public and private sectors. The scope for meaningful participation would be much greater if the societies were allowed to participate other than as mere mortgagees.

Might they not also be allowed to play a more active part in the provision of consumer credit? There is, ironically enough, nothing in the legislation to prevent building societies lending for any purpose provided their security is a first charge upon freehold or leasehold estate. It is widely known that, in the relaxed climate of the past twelve months, building societies have expanded their lending to existing customers and it has by no means been a prerequisite that the additional loans should be utilised for home improvement.

But tradition still discourages the societies from publicising their willingness, when they have surplus funds, to enter the consumer credit field. Perhaps because of this they have escaped the directions to which other financial intermediaries have at times been subjected – maybe also because of the social importance of their primary function.

I believe, however, that significant but logical diversifications of these kinds can be justified on social, economic and philosophical grounds. As far as *wider* diversification is concerned we cannot lose sight of our prime purpose in the housing market. There is no case for seeking powers which would divert our main energies away from the provision of finance for the house-buyer. In my view, the future growth of home ownership is assured at least until the end of this century.

FUTURE OF HOME OWNERSHIP

In the post-war period we have seen ownership rise from 26% of the total housing stock to a situation in which just over half the population own their own homes. Subject to the capital being available, I see the owner-occupation proportion rising to approximately 60% by 1980. Thereafter, the rate of growth may slow.

Even so, I do not foresee any significant decline in the demands for traditional building-society finance. Building for additions to stock will be increasingly supplemented by building for replacement. Improved standards of living, greater environmental pressures to replace the outworn styles and fabrics which we accept today can be expected to maintain the momentum. Underpinning all this have been constant inflationary pressures. It requires no mean skill to keep pace with inflation and I think that, for the average man, the house in which he lives provides as good a hedge against inflation as any.

In this climate, the major long-term problem for the building societies will be to attract and retain an increasing volume of personal savings. The recent surplus of funds, whilst it highlights the outdated restrictions placed on building societies and undoubtedly points the way to the need for wider powers to deploy our assets, may well prove exceptional. Our primary concern, possibly for four years out of every five, will be to maintain an adequate investment inflow.

GROWTH ORIENTATION

On this simple analysis alone, building societies will be justified, as they have been for two decades, in aiming to maximise their growth performance; indeed they may be forced to if they are to do the job expected of them.

But even without this justification I venture to argue that building societies have every right to be growth-orientated. They have shown their capacity for mobilising personal savings. I quoted some figures earlier to show the remarkable share of the savings market which the societies now command. Table 4 illustrates the growth in assets and accounts since 1945. On economic grounds, it seems to me that successful, efficient gatherers of savings should actively be encouraged to expand their sphere of activity. This accords with the official policy of encouraging more competition in the banking sector. And although we are currently being enjoined to spend rather than to save, the long-term needs of the economy require the encouragement of a high level of personal savings.

And on a philosophical level, is there any reason – provided they fulfil their home-ownership function – why building societies should be denied the freedom enjoyed by the insurance companies, the banks or indeed the many other financial inter-mediaries which have emerged and flourished in the post-war period?

Accordingly, I enter a second plea for building societies to be allowed to widen their range of activities. Already, in the face of competition, there have been minor marketing initiatives . . . the innovation of a life-assurance-linked scheme for regular savers, a building society-and-equities package, a property-bond link, but we have little room for manoeuvre. Building societies, with their twelve million investors and nearly four million borrowers, have an established access to a large proportion of the population. Their growth in recent years is evidence of the confidence which they have engendered among an ever-increasing number of people, and it is an anomaly that, alone among the established savings institutions in the private sector, they should be subjected to their existing narrow limit of activity.

TABLE 4   BUILDING SOCIETIES: POST-WAR GROWTH

	No. of Societies	No. of Investment and Mortgage Accounts	Total Assets
		'000	£m.
1945	890	4,150	824
1950	819	4,418	1,256
1955	783	5,580	2,065
1960	726	6,838	3,166
1965	605	9,299	5,532
1970	481	14,538	10,940
1971	467	16,119	13,011

DIVERSIFICATION

If societies were allowed (with proper control) to diversify into fund management or property bonds, their existing captive clientèle would not have to search the Sunday newspapers when they felt the time had come for them to diversify from the fixed interest of building society investment. There could be considerable economies in management, bearing in mind the existing network of building-society offices. I am sure the philosophical problems would be fewer than those which have beset other financial institutions with a long traditional rôle of independent advisers who now find themselves selling their own wide range of services in competition with others.

I believe the trend is firmly towards the all-round money-management concept and towards greater links between specialist institutions. At present, a legislative framework designed for the nineteenth century effectively debars building societies from even beginning to move in this direction.

Wider powers for societies of a certain minimum size might enable diversification which could transform the investment scene for the man-in-the-street.

I concede the danger that too much diversification and too quickly might blur the very image which has created the building society success-story – simplicity, safety, liquidity – but with proper safeguards, building societies could become financial supermarkets par excellence. They have the management, the administration, the outlets, the public confidence and the growth record . . . all they lack is the opportunity.

Chapter 10

BUILDING SOCIETIES

AND THE DEMAND FOR HOUSES

Brian H. Phillips
General Manager (*Finance*)
Nationwide Building Society

Any building-society executive must always be prepared to explain and, if necessary, defend building-society policies and the effect they have, or are assumed to have, on the housing market at any particular point of time. In my experience, criticisms fall into two categories – either that building societies have restricted lending to the extent that a mortgage "famine" has been created, resulting in a slowing down in the number of housing-starts and in a reaction in the prices and sales of second-hand houses; or, that the supply of mortgage funds is so plentiful that house prices have risen to the extent that only the high-income groups are able to meet the prices being asked. At the present time building societies are able to meet most requests for housing finance and as house prices have un-questionably risen appreciably during 1971/2 it is natural that societies are being urged by their critics to reduce lending in order to stabilise or reduce what are thought to be artificially high house prices. However, the situation can change so rapidly that I have little doubt that in the future, criticisms will again be voiced suggesting that societies should further increase lending in order to avoid a mortgage "famine".

Building societies are as conscious as their critics of the need to equate the supply of mortgage finance to the demand and do their very best to achieve this, and I am pleased to have this opportunity to explain the various economic factors which affect the supply of mortgage loans, the practical implementation of monetary theory to building-society operations and the methods which are used to balance the supply of savings to the demand for mortgage finance.

THE STRUCTURE OF THE MOVEMENT
AND HOW IT FITS INTO THE NATIONAL ECONOMY

Building societies are mutual organisations which have grown from very small beginnings. They are not profit-making concerns nor are they basically sophisticated or commercially-orientated institutions: any surplus arising on the difference between the interest rate charged on mortgages and that paid on investments is added to reserves in order to maintain them at or above the statutory requirement. Whether by accident or design societies have become big business in the 1970s and have now reached the stage where they are one of the nation's largest financial institutions. Table 1 illustrates the size of the movement at the end of 1971 and how it fits into the nation's economic structure. The total savings held by building societies appreciably exceed all forms of National Savings, are larger than the amount of personal bank deposits with all the Clearing Banks and are second only to the balances held by Life Assurance Companies. At present comparable rates of growth building societies will very soon become the largest single savings vehicle in this country. The significance of these figures is not merely their size but the very real responsibilities which flow from handling balances of this order and in servicing many millions of investors; for without investors there could be no borrowers, a seemingly obvious statement which is so often ignored when considering the economics of building societies and when making suggestions as to how societies should run their business. In particular it must always be acknowledged that due to the competitive climate which prevails in the savings market building societies must ensure that their investors receive a competitive rate of interest on savings deposited with them. Above all, it must be remembered that societies do not have access to vast and mysterious forms of cheap money.

On the lending side – Part B – it will be seen that nearly four million people are buying their own homes with the help of a building-society loan. Therefore, although building societies do not have a monopoly of the private-housing finance field they

TABLE 1

THE IMPORTANCE OF BUILDING SOCIETIES
IN THE NATION'S ECONOMIC STRUCTURE

Total population of Great Britain (1971 census) 53,821,364
(Figures relate to the position at the end of 1971)

(A) As Savings Institutions

	£2,607m	£2,816,m	£1,865m	£1,042m	£890m
NATIONAL SAVINGS	National Savings Certificate	Trustee Savings Bank	National Savings Bank	Savings Bonds etc .	Premium Bonds

Total £9,220 million

REGISTERED PROVIDENT SOCIETIES — £2,865m*

LIFE ASSURANCE COMPANIES — £14,680m*

PERSONAL BANK DEPOSITS — £11,016m

UNIT TRUSTS — £1,991m

BUILDING SOCIETIES (Shares & Deposits) — £12,186m

```
0   2,000   4,000   6,000   8,000  10,000  12,000  14,000  16,000
£ million
```

Total number of building-society investors & depositors 12,223,000
*Estimated figures.

(B) As Mortgage Lending Institutions

Total number of dwellings	18,967,000
Total number of owner occupied dwellings	9,508,000
Total number of building society borrowers	3,886,000

THE NATION'S HOUSING STOCK

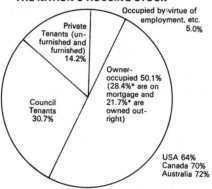

Private Tenants (unfurnished and furnished) 14.2%

Occupied by virtue of employment, etc. 5.0%

Owner-occupied 50.1% (28.4%* are on mortgage and 21.7%* are owned outright)

Council Tenants 30.7%

USA 64%
Canada 70%
Australia 72%

must, and indeed do by their actions and decisions, exert a considerable influence on the savings scene, the supply of money for the housing market and the price that must be paid for it.

Furthermore, the greatest influence is exerted by the largest building societies, of which the twelve with total assets exceeding £250m. account for nearly 70% of the movement's total assets, the other 30% being held by 455 societies. The smallest societies with assets of under £1m. account for 0.5% of the movement's total assets, although in terms of numbers they represent just under half of the total number of building societies. It is because the greatest influence is exerted by the largest societies that many of the smaller societies are able to, and do, charge a higher interest rate on mortgage loans and pay a higher interest rate on investment monies than the larger societies without measurably affecting either the savings or housing markets.

RELEVANT FACTORS AFFECTING INTEREST RATES

Mortgage loans are financed partly from capital repayments on existing loans (41.6%) but mainly from new savings, and although lending could be maintained on a restricted scale by applying capital repayments only, it is the flow of new savings into building societies which enables lending to be maintained at anything like the required level. Furthermore, as 85% of the savings balances held – almost all of which are repayable on demand – are lent on the security of mortgage loans for house purchase for periods of up to thirty-five years it is important that a realistic rate of interest should be paid on existing savings balances. The rate of interest paid on investment accounts is therefore a critical factor in ensuring the security of existing mortgages and in attracting sufficient funds to lend on new mortgages. This is why the Building Societies Association recommends the rates of interest payable on investments and chargeable on mortgages – recommendations which are accepted by the vast majority of building societies and certainly the large ones. The Building Societies Association meets each month and has before it up-to-date savings and mortgage statistical information and consciously reviews the need to adjust interest rates either upwards or downwards at every meeting. It is extremely important to appreciate that the building-society interest-rate structure is determined by the investment rate rather than the mortgage rate, although societies must, of course, be conscious of the acceptability of the mortgage rate and balance this consideration against the demand for mortgage loans. Once the rate of interest which it is necessary to pay on investments has been determined, then the mortgage rate is an arithmetical calculation on the following lines:

	£
Paid to Shareholders ($5\frac{1}{4}\%$ tax paid)	5·25
Income Tax payable thereon by Society at 30%	2·25
	7·50
Management expenses	0·72
Corporation tax at 40% on operating surplus	0·11
Operating surplus	0·17
Mortgage rate ($8\frac{1}{2}\%$)	8·50

BALANCING THE SUPPLY OF SAVINGS TO THE DEMAND FOR MORTGAGES

Due to the short-term nature of investment balances, building societies are required by statute to maintain adequate liquidity, the purpose of which is to meet withdrawals and, in the event of the supply of investment monies reducing appreciably, to finance mortgage loans previously approved. The amount of liquidity held is expressed as a percentage of total assets and the amount so calculated is known as the liquidity ratio. Liquidity may be increased at a time when the flow of new savings temporarily exceeds the demand for mortgages – resulting in an increase in the liquidity ratio – and reduced at a time when the reverse position applies, in order to maintain a more stable rate of lending. Mortgages take an average of three months to complete from the time an application is approved and therefore investments received at any given time are generally speaking utilised to finance mortgages agreed anything up to three months previously. At the end of 1971 Nationwide had nearly £70m. outstanding in this way.

The liquidity ratio is an important monetary device as, apart from its possible use in order to even out the supply of mortgage finance, prudence dictates that it needs to be higher if the economic outlook is considered to be doubtful and may be reduced if there is an abundance of confidence and the prospect for savings seems good in the months ahead. But it cannot be considered in isolation, as the achievement of a predetermined liquidity ratio is an integral part of financial planning. An explanation of financial planning techniques adopted by building societies does not fall within the subject matter of this chapter, but they cannot be ignored as they are a most relevant factor in establishing the level of mortgage finance. Nationwide's Chief General Manager, Mr. Leonard Williams, has been reported as saying that "Financial planning and control plays a crucial rôle in the Society's objectives which aim at bringing price stability into the housing industry". He went on to say that "annual cash-flow budgets and forecasts ensure that the supply of mortgage finance is kept at a high and stable level and building societies realise that this is their prime responsibility. Forward planning enables the society to maintain the confidence of builders who, in the past, suffered from the inhibiting effect of rising interest rates and credit shortage." Effective financial planning requires considerable thought and judgement, as the flow of investment monies is not even. All months are subject to seasonal fluctuations, some years are good, others not so good, and some days can even produce a net outflow, a position for which the Americans have coined the word "disintermediation". Similarly, mortgage demand varies from year to year, from month to month, and the rate of completions is affected by seasonal factors. It is the financial planners' job to bring all these factors together and as a result of short-, medium- and long-term budgeting processes to examine actual performance compared with budgeted projections and to take corrective action at frequent intervals in order to maintain an even flow of mortgage finance. This is vital if the confidence of builders and the housing industry is to be maintained, for it is quite purposeless to encourage builders to purchase land and to commence building if by the time those houses are completed there is a shortage of mortgage funds and the finished properties remain unsold for that reason.

In simple economic terms therefore the task of building societies is to pay an adequate rate of interest on investment accounts in order to meet the demand for mortgages for house purchase, and this is why the demand for housing finance must be known and the future researched. There are a number of bodies which research the housing market in order to assess building activity, some of which include building-society executives and others who do not but who make their findings available. Amongst these are NEDO, which forecasts the number of housing starts and completions and the value of output both for the private and public sectors and the Department of the Environment which sends periodical questionnaires to all large builders and property developers and to a sample of smaller firms who undertake speculative house building. Estimates are then made for the whole of the private sector. Building societies also carry out a great deal of research themselves through their surveyors and Branch Offices in order to ensure that the demand for housing finance is known and the appropriate action taken.

THE RELATIONSHIP BETWEEN BUILDING-SOCIETY LENDING AND THE DEMAND FOR AND THE PRICES OF HOUSES

Any organisation which finances 90% of the available supply of goods in an almost wholly credit market must undoubtedly exert influence over the demand for those goods. This position will prevail until other organisations move into the market to finance an increasing share and thereby reduce the degree of influence originally exerted. In the case of consumer spending, the pattern is for sales of motor cars, refrigerators, etc., to increase at times when credit is plentiful and to reduce during periods when credit is in short supply: indeed the introduction, tightening or relaxation of credit restrictions has in the post-war period been an economic regulator adopted by successive Governments. This is a logical and acceptable way of regulating demand and supply of consumer goods, as it can be achieved without necessarily resulting in increased prices as a result of increased demand. In many industries the opportunity to produce goods up to maximum output, without increasing overheads by further investment, should enable prices to be reduced or profits increased.

But the same considerations do not apply in the housing market. The supply of new houses cannot be increased as rapidly as the supply of new motor cars or new refrigerators. The purchase of suitable land, planning and legal procedures, the installation of services and the actual time involved in erection and final completion will span a period of about three years. Building land is a commodity which is strictly limited in supply and, in the absence of Government action to release land which is not at present available for building, the total supply of land with the requisite planning permission is strictly limited and the price inevitably expensive and increasingly so. Therefore the supply of new houses cannot be increased even marginally in the short term and can only be increased marginally in the medium term by the early implementation of carefully prepared plans.

This inevitably means that if the supply of mortgage finance is relatively plentiful at a time when the demand for owner-occupied housing is high, then the bulk of the demand must be satisfied by the second-hand market resulting in an increase, not only in the price of new but also of second-hand houses. But it is the demand which initiates and accelerates the increase in house prices. The supply of mortgage finance coinciding with substantial demand is a contributing factor.

The responsibilities of building societies at present are to ensure that sufficient housing finance is available in order to meet the demand, not to create it. This is a most important distinction which needs emphasising in view of the criticisms which have been levelled at societies as a result of the substantial increase in house prices during 1971/2. The part which societies play in satisfying demand is to offer loans to those whose incomes are such that they can meet the monthly outgoings. Building societies have not to my knowledge materially relaxed basic income requirements during recent years (although new schemes have been introduced by some societies to assist first-time purchasers) and it may be concluded therefore that the ability of house purchasers to pay present prices is as a result of either larger deposits being accumulated or wage and salary levels having risen to the extent that they enable larger loans to be financed. Were there any evidence that societies departed from their status requirements, as adjusted for present-day needs, then the argument that building societies were largely responsible for the increase in house prices would be more valid. Table 2 below shows the amount of building society advances during the eleven years to 1971, the increase in house prices and the increase in the index of average weekly wage earnings over the same period, together with the number of housing completions. From this it will be seen that in 1961, when building-society lending was reduced by 2·5% compared with the previous year, house prices rose on average by 9%; in 1965, when there was a reduction of 8·3% in the total advanced house prices rose by 7·59%, more than in 1966 when building – society lending increased by 29%. In drawing conclusions from this table it must of course be recognised that catching-up processes occur from year to year and this would seem to be particularly the case in 1971 when house prices rose by 21% following a year in which the increase in average weekly wage earnings was almost 14%. It is of significance also that the average increase in house prices during the last five years has been of the same order as the increase in average weekly wage earnings.

THE FUTURE

In order to assess the likely demand for housing over the next few years, Nationwide Building Society commissioned Colin Buchanan and Partners to carry out a research study, the results of which were published in 1971 under the title "The Prospect for Housing". The Society felt that in the last few years there had been so much comment in the Press and elsewhere to the effect that the housing shortage had been virtually overcome and the rate of housing constructions was likely to show a steady decline to a lower level of activity that it would be worth while commissioning consultants to assess on a factual basis future demand. It was felt at that time that the comments had not taken full account of the proportion of dwellings in this country which are unfit (one in four), nor did they take account of the grave deficiencies of the housing environment which many people now endure. Moreover, rising levels of income and mobility, educational attainment and leisure opportunities

TABLE 2

| YEAR | BUILDING SOCIETY ADVANCES (U.K.) | | INCREASE IN HOUSE PRICES (G.B.) | | | | AVERAGE WEEKLY WAGE EARNINGS ANNUAL INCREASES | HOUSING COMPLETIONS (PRIVATE SECTOR) (U.K.) |
	Amount	Increase over previous year	New	Modern	Older	Average		
	£m.	%	%	%	%	%	%	000's
1961	544	− 2·5	7·82	9·19	10·14	9·09	5·4	181
1962	618	13·6	6·05	4·05	5·93	5·02	3·2	178
1963	852	37·9	5·51	12·61	9·20	9·98	5·3	178
1964	1,052	23·5	7·88	8·47	7·47	8·07	8·3	221
1965	965	− 8·3	7·46	7·83	7·24	7·59	8·5	217
1966	1,245	29·0	6·29	3·75	4·87	4·67	4·2	209
1967	1,447	18·6	5·92	7·35	9·01	7·41	5·6	204
1968	1,587	7·4	7·26	6·18	6·82	6·61	7·8	226
1969	1,556	− 2·0	3·67	5·62	6·30	5·30	8·1	186
1970	2,021	29·9	6·40	5·20	7·92	6·18	13·7	174
1971	2,741	35·6	21·22	21·66	18·74	20·82	10·1	196

SOURCES

Building Society Advances (U.K.) – Building Societies' Association.

Increase in House Prices (G.B.) – Nationwide Building Society.

Increase in index of average weekly wage earnings – *Ministry of Employment Gazette*.

Housing Completions (Private Sector) (U.K.) – Housing and Construction Statistics.

would clearly give rise to demand for better environment and call for a reappraisal of policies in this field. Clearly these views were not supported by the Press and other commentators at that time and there was therefore a need to establish what the demand was likely to be. The report looks ahead to the end of the century, assesses how the form and character are likely to change as people become more affluent, better educated and more leisured. A short summary of the report under three headings is as under.

Environmental Poverty

"The Prospect for Housing" breaks new ground in that it looks not simply at the structure and condition of dwellings, but at the broad setting in which people live. It finds that four out of every ten persons living in Britain live in areas that do not meet present-day needs and that in many towns and cities housing, which may itself be in reasonable or even good condition, is spoiled by drab and poorly-designed surroundings. Detailed studies of housing areas in the North of England and the South-East revealed a disturbing picture of widespread environmental poverty and neglect. It is pointed out that this is a situation which cannot be left to heal itself and that the need to remedy these deficiencies is an urgent priority for both public and private investment.

Larger and More Adaptable Homes

What kind of houses will the coming generation demand, and how can those responsible for the Nation's housing ensure that new houses meet these demands? These are the two main questions which the consultants sought to answer. They point to the certainty that people will want houses which are larger, more adaptable, and allow greater privacy. Thus they anticipate that the average house in the year 2000 will be at least 1,100 square feet in area, or about a quarter as large again as today's average family house, and will have a more flexible interior plan as well as more outdoor space. These are conditions that can be provided more readily by detached houses than by semi-detached or terrace units and they correspond to the needs of families with young children, which are expected to remain the prime element in housing demand.

A larger proportion of present-day housing areas will be unable to offer a more generous allocation of space and relative lack of adaptability is likely to condemn even recently-built properties to an earlier obsolescence than might otherwise have been expected. In other words, many existing houses will become inadequate as living units far sooner than they suffer structural decay.

Building Rates

Raising the overall quality of housing to an acceptable standard and meeting the needs of the new households formed during the last quarter of this century will call for high rates of activity in the building industry. The consultants see grounds for optimism that these rates can be achieved and suggest that an annual completion rate of 500,000 houses is feasible. A high construction rate, however, would have to be sustained by Government policies which emphasise the needs for intensive clearance of unfit housing and the positive renewal of inadequate housing areas, and which define more generous standards of space and amenity as part of long-range objectives for housing development.

The results of this study indicate that the Society was justified to research into a field which at that time had not been dealt with by other research bodies and furthermore, in making the results available, performed a useful social function and confirmed the view that the demand for private housing finance will continue at a very high level for many years to come. This, then, covers the environmental aspects of future demand, but also it must be recognised that only 3·9 million out of 9·5 million owner-occupied houses are at present mortgaged to building societies, and a large proportion of the owner-occupied properties which are at present owned outright will be the subject of mortgage finance in the future. Many of these were acquired at prices substantially below today's levels and when they are put on the market, mortgage advances will be required in the future at future price levels. Much of the finance for this will be channelled into building societies by beneficiaries under wills who own their own homes and who will not therefore require to take over the family home. Another important factor is the desire for home ownership in this country – a difficult factor to quantify. Why do people wish to own property rather than rent it? Probably the most important reason is the pride of home ownership – satisfaction which derives from acquiring the family home rather than just a house; also the increasing realisation that property and certainly the right property is probably the best investment that most individuals can acquire without necessarily being people of great wealth. Government policy has encouraged home-ownership for some years – valuable tax concessions are given on interest payments (or the Government Option Mortgage Scheme) and with certain exceptions on the capital appreciation realised on sale. Faced with rising rents, which are not an allowable expense for tax purposes, many existing tenants can acquire houses or flats, even at today's levels, more cheaply than by paying rent. An example of this is in the new towns where properties are being offered at a 20% discount on relatively new and attractive developments in order to encourage tenants to purchase their own homes. Many local authorities are offering 100% advances to those who rent property and who wish to purchase it.

These, then, are the factors affecting demand which at the present time can only be seen as remaining buoyant for many years to come. This must mean that if inflation continues at anything like the rate experienced during recent years, societies will be financing a larger number of loans at higher prices, which is why the building society movement is gearing itself up for continued expansion. There are no other specialised mortgage finance institutions in this country and if the demand for housing finance is to be met then societies must continue to grow, not merely for the sake of expansion, but in order to satisfy what is a compelling social need.

Chapter 11

THE FUTURE FOR INSURANCE

Basil Robarts
Director and Chief General Manager, Norwich Union Insurance Group

In discussing the future of insurance in relation to the financial system, there are two aspects we need to consider. There are the changes likely to take place in the structures and sources of insurance business itself, and those likely in the external factors affecting the business.

There are many classes of insurance business, and the same prospects will not apply to them all. We can conveniently divide them into two categories having different characteristics, life and other long-term business on the one hand, and general or short-term business on the other. Life insurance, including pensions business, is a major channel for savings and investment, in addition to providing life-insurance cover; the essential feature of this class is that the proceeds of most contracts are payable on the happening of an event which is certain to arise at some time. General insurance provides for financial security against misfortune, indemnifying the insured on the happening of an uncertain event, so that for insurers there is a much larger risk element.

Insurance cover is offered by many companies, both proprietary and mutual, and also by Lloyd's. These different sections of the market might well have differing long-term aims because of their structure, and the way in which they market their business. Nevertheless, the aim of all sections of the insurance industry must be to continue to develop their business profitably in order to satisfy the investment requirements of their proprietors, be they shareholders in a limited liability company, the policyholders of a mutual company, or the members of syndicates at Lloyd's.

Some measure of the future prospects of the insurance industry as a whole may be found by comparing the movement of the share price index of, say, the composite insurance companies with indices in other sectors of the market. In 1970 and 1971 the composite insurance sector out-performed most other sectors of the stock market – from a common base figure of 150 at the beginning of 1970, the index figure for insurance composites at the end of 1971 was around the 240 mark, whereas the All Share index over the same period only rose to about 200. After a period of disenchantment with the performance of composite insurance companies, investors seem therefore to have become more optimistic about their future, in spite of the traumatic experience of the failure of several companies in the past few years.

STRATEGIC AIMS

Insurance business has always required strategic planning and the present strength of British insurance is largely due to the plans made by our predecessors in the last two hundred years. Recently, many insurance companies have been giving closer attention to their strategies for the future and have had to answer the question "What business are we in?" and "Where do we want to go?". Their answers reflect the fact that insurance companies regard themselves as being in the financial-services field as well as carrying on both traditional and new forms of insurance. It is also clear that other institutions, such as banks, have been asking themselves the same questions and have come up with similar answers. Consequently, it is likely that we shall see in the future a widening of the activities of many insurance companies in the financial field and an increase in the competition for available business, which should be of benefit to the customer, both private individual and business enterprise alike. This extension of activities can take a number of forms, depending upon the existing size and structure of individual companies and their long-term policy. Some of these developments could well be:

(a) The setting up of new financial centres where banks, insurance companies, building societies, finance houses, hire-purchase companies and others would have their own counters, and in this way maintain their own identities. The term "financial supermarket" has already been suggested for this type of development.

or (b) Other services being attached to an existing business without the latter actually buying, or merging with, other organisations. Most insurance companies have branch networks which cover the whole of the United Kingdom and many parts of the world. These branch offices are usually situated on prime sites and in order to maximise their use, insurance companies will be looking for ways of enlarging their activities. One can therefore visualise some branch offices eventually becoming financial centres offering facilities for current bank-account customers, deposits, loans of all types (both secured and unsecured), in addition to all the present insurance services.

or (c) A large financial group consisting of a holding company owning the shares of, say, a Clearing Bank, an insurance company and such other financial institutions as seem appropriate. This one group would be able to offer to the public a complete range of financial services under one roof.

LIFE INSURANCE

Life insurance has traditionally been at the long-term end of the savings industry and its rapid and continued growth through periods of wage freezes, unemployment, slumps and booms in the economy underlines the confidence of the public in this important form of saving. Between 1961/1970 the premium income from long-term business written by member companies of the British Insurance Association has virtually doubled. There are, however, still many families who do not have private life insurance policies and the figure has recently been put as high as over 20% of all households. We are always concerned to enlarge the insuring public with whom we deal and this has directed our attention towards wage earners who may well, traditionally, not be inclined towards Ordinary life insurance, although the Home Service Life Offices play an important part in attracting the savings of this section of the community. Business obtained from wage earners may be significantly increased in future, especially with the increase in the provision and scope of occupational pension and group life-insurance schemes.

There are several reasons why pension schemes should represent a growth area in the future. The present Government is committed to encourage occupational pension schemes as set out in the 1971 White Paper – "Strategy for Pensions". This envisages that only in the absence of an appropriate occupational pension scheme will the State reserve scheme provide a payment over and above the flat rate pension.

Another factor favouring expansion is the changing attitude of Trade Unions, who are beginning to appreciate the value of good pension benefits. We can expect this to become a much more important feature in wage negotiations in the future.

A further probable development is that more insurance companies will undertake the management of the pension funds of organisations which do not have insured schemes. In this way the pension funds will, for a fee, benefit from the investment skills of the institutions who will themselves benefit by earning an additional contribution to their fixed costs.

The market for life insurance is expanding rapidly and is very versatile and quick to react to opportunities for new and attractive contracts. Recently, companies have been issuing bonds for medium terms of, say, five–ten years, which guarantee the payment of a specific sum on maturity and in some cases of the provision of annual payments.

Unit Trusts have been popular for many years on the grounds that equities are a hedge against inflation and investors can see regularly how their fund is performing. Insurance companies recognised that the success of unit trusts in the 1950s could give rise to a demand for life insurance policies linked to equity-type investments, both ordinary share and property; consequently, attractive schemes were devised and these have now become an established source of new business. Nevertheless, the traditional with-profit policies continue to be remarkably successful and have been modified to fit the changing pattern in that capital appreciation of the funds, resulting from investment inequities and property, is reflected in the form of terminal bonuses. We expect these types of contract to continue to be a major source of business.

The Government has recently set up a committee under the chairmanship of Sir Hilary Scott to consider the workings of the Insurance Companies Act, 1958–1967 and Prevention of Fraud (Investments) Act, 1958, in relation to unit-linked contracts. The terms of reference of the committee are not very wide, and therefore, while it may be necessary to introduce some safeguards, it is hoped that legislation will not impose restrictions which stifle the devising of new forms of policy. In this connection, some thirty-five companies who are interested in linked contracts have formed a Linked Life Assurance Group, with the aim of acting as an informal consultative body and a forum of discussion for its members on matters of common concern in the conduct of this type of business.

GENERAL INSURANCE

General (or short-term) insurance has in recent years been regarded as the problem area of the insurance industry, because of the difficulty of calculating a rate of premium adequate to meet claims which may not be paid for some years, with the final settlement being affected by inflation in the meantime. While inflation continues, the insuring public must expect periodic revisions of premium rates to counteract its effects.

There have been signs recently that general insurance is entering a more profitable phase and the world-wide demand is rapidly growing. The premium income of British companies has been expanding at an average rate of about 10% per annum or more. This trend is likely to continue as higher standards of living are achieved and real wealth increases. The size of risks is increasing rapidly and some of the largest will stretch the capacity of the market, which must be sufficient to keep pace with world economic growth. For example, the value of jumbo jets and the new supertankers is much in excess of those previously placed on the market. Capacity depends on the confidence of insurers in their ability to trade at a profit and provided that profits, sufficient to yield the proprietors a reasonable return on their invested capital, can be made on the business underwritten, insurance facilities should be available and there should be no problem of capacity.

Industrial technology is continually introducing risks which are completely new to insurers and for which we have initially no reliable statistics on which to base our rates. Nevertheless, the insurance industry has been renowned for its willingness to accept new risks and this we shall continue to do. To help us in evaluating the effects on our business of such changes, we need to keep abreast of new technology and scientific changes being considered by industry, together with their associated safety aspects.

General insurance business involves the acceptance of large and, as I have said, sometimes unmeasured risks and companies need considerable reserves to support their business. They will each have differing views on suitable levels of reserve, above the statutory minimum, and each will follow its own corporate plan. Whatever their reserve ratio is, it is highly unlikely in an inflationary period that companies will be able to add sufficient to their reserves out of profit to maintain these ratios. We are therefore likely to see companies raising additional share capital.

In 1968 the Monopolies Commission was instructed to enquire into the supply of Fire Insurance services in the United Kingdom. The Public Interest Hearing was held in September 1970 and the Commission's Report and recommendations were at the time of writing not yet published. Strong arguments have been advanced in favour of the maintenance of the present method of operation in the fire-insurance market. Any other might materially change the present availability of cover in some sections of this market.

SERVICES TO INDUSTRY

It is, I think, fair to say that the insurance industry has been one of the leaders in the application of computer techniques to their business. A great deal has already been done and during the next five years much of the work of insurance companies will have been converted to computer operation. The highly qualified teams who have been instrumental in establishing the new computer systems will in part be available for other work. As the insurance companies have funds invested in computer equipment and the accompanying technology, it seems logical that they should offer a computer service to other industries. If, for example, they were to undertake accounting services, they could enter the factoring field by discounting the debts due to the companies for whom they were accounting.

Purchasing major items of equipment and leasing them to industrial users is a developing market and one in which insurance companies are likely to play an increasing part. Industry has recognised that there are savings to be gained from leasing equipment instead of owning it. The rent paid is usually a fixed sum per annum, and this is wholly allowable against tax. The tax allowances which are given on equipment may be of such a size that the industrial company – if it owned the equipment – could not take advantage to the fullest extent.

Financial institutions can, however, gear the amount of funds which they allocate to leasing to the extent to which they can claim these allowances against their profits.

One example of a likely field is that of purchasing and leasing aircraft, since the cost of aircraft used by airlines is high and the independent operators might find it difficult to raise funds direct, although well able to service the cost of leasing suitable aircraft. We shall face strong competition here from overseas aircraft manufacturers, who can offer finance at attractive subsidised rates of interest. Another suitable outlet is in the leasing of sprinkler equipment, which should assist in reducing national fire wastage.

EUROPEAN ECONOMIC COMMUNITY

Perhaps the most important challenge that appears to confront U.K. insurers in the entry of the United Kingdom into the European Economic Community. However, unlike some other industries, U.K. insurers have never been prevented from operating in the Community by any trade barriers whatsoever. They have always been able to compete on equal terms. The main difficulty has been the legislative requirements which have made entry relatively unattractive to all but a few U.K. insurers.

There are certain fundamental differences in the characteristics of the U.K. insurance market and the insurance markets of the E.E.C. countries. The British insurance industry has had a predominantly international character, whereas the domestic companies of the E.E.C. countries have been primarily concerned with their local markets. The British approach to the supervision of the insurance industry has generally been one of "freedom with publicity", whereas most of the E.E.C. countries have installed a strict system of control. These control systems vary in each country but can extend to such matters as rates, policy conditions, deposits, the disposition of reserves and restriction of choice of investments.

The problem presented by entry into the E.E.C. is therefore not one of increased opportunity but whether legislative restrictions will be imposed in the United Kingdom. The E.E.C. has for some time been attempting to develop a common set of rules which will govern insurance throughout the Community and has, naturally enough, been working on an extension of its control systems as the common basis for the enlarged Community. One of our aims has been to see that companies which can satisfy certain requirements as to standards of solvency could freely operate in other countries in the Community without the need to establish deposits. Such an aim would be the ideal basis and it is to be hoped that the U.K. will have sufficient influence to negotiate an agreement of this kind. If we do not succeed there could be a continuation of restrictions which, although designed to protect the policyholder, can so often operate to his disadvantage, particularly restrictions on investment of funds. In the United Kingdom the freedom which has been given to British insurers to invest has been greatly valued, and proved to be of the greatest benefit to all types of policyholders.

The British insurance industry has always been prepared to face the competition of foreign insurers in this country on equal terms, and we hope that insurance can benefit from the creation of a larger market, free of onerous legislative restrictions. One cannot stress too strongly that if life-assurance legislation within the enlarged Common Market were to lead to a limitation on the freedom of choice of investment, the attraction to the British public of life assurance as a means of savings could be seriously reduced. Bearing in mind that about one thousand million pounds of new savings is attracted each year in this way, there could well be repercussions on the British financial system and British industry.

OVERSEAS

British insurance derives a considerable proportion of its business from other parts of the world and makes a substantial contribution to our national economy, representing as it does over half the total invisibles. In countries overseas there has been – and one can anticipate that there will continue to be – increased nationalism with resulting restrictions on the activities of non-resident insurers. The trend is likely to be for U.K. and other foreign insurers to be forbidden to write direct business in more overseas territories. The nationalised or indigenous insurers in these territories will, however, require reinsurance by virtue of the fact that there will be insufficient capacity to absorb all the risks arising in a particular country. They will also want to spread their liabilities and be looking for business in exchange from overseas insurers. London is already the leading reinsurance market and it will continue to provide the facility for placing these additional reinsurance requirements.

RESPONSIBILITIES AS SHAREHOLDERS

The insurance industry is already responsible for the investment of very large sums of money and has the potential to handle much more. A considerable proportion, about 30%, of all insurance funds is invested in the ordinary shares of industrial companies – in 1970 the net new investment by B.I.A. members in such shares alone totalled £261,000,000.

In common with other institutions, insurance companies have sometimes been criticised for failing to shoulder their responsibilities as shareholders. The critics, however, tend to forget that the primary objective of investment decisions must be to act in the best interests of our policyholders and shareholders. We are certainly pleased if our actions, in discharging these responsibilities, prove to be of assistance to other shareholders, but this is very different from being expected to assume some form of general watch-dog rôle on their behalf – or indeed on behalf of any other section of the community.

The critics are probably also unaware of many occasions when insurance companies, in collaboration with other institutions, have spent much time and effort in encouraging managements of companies to overcome problems besetting them. On these occasions publicity is usually avoided – quiet diplomacy may often succeed when the conflict of public debate would not.

The possibility of further co-operation in this field between the various bodies representing the major institutional investors has been discussed. The difficulties and dangers of any move in this direction must not be underestimated. It is important, whether one is considering companies in which institutional investors have shareholdings, or investing companies themselves, that the directors and executive who manage a company should seek to fulfil their responsibilities to those whom they are appointed to serve, and should not be expected to subordinate this duty to external considerations.

CONCLUSION

I have tried to suggest some answers to the two questions to which I referred early in this chapter. I cannot, of course, speak for the whole industry, but I feel sure that my insurance colleagues would agree with me in saying that, looking to the economic growth which is likely to take place throughout the world in the years ahead, the future of insurance will be an expanding one.

We may well see a trend towards larger units in the industry, partly to achieve economies of scale, and partly because the needs of our customers will tend to become more diverse and international. One must also bear in mind that expansion appears to be necessary to high staff morale in any organisation. I am not, however, an advocate of size for the sake of size, and I believe that there is a bright future too in the industry for well-managed medium and smaller sized companies, some of whom may be of a more specialist character than the larger units.

Whatever else the future may hold in store, I feel certain that we shall be faced with many challenging problems, both by our customers and by our competitors, and I believe that, with the rapid development which has taken place during the past few years, the insurance industry is well equipped to meet them.

Chapter 12

THE FUNCTION OF

RISK CAPITAL IN INSURANCE

A. R. N. Ratcliff
Joint General Manager, Eagle Star Insurance Company

As someone who has spent his whole working life in insurance, I cannot be sure what the industrialist really means when he talks about risk capital. Like the giraffe, you know it when you see it – even if you cannot believe it – as many investors in undertakings as far removed as Rolls Royce and Mersey Docks and Harbours have found out to their cost.

Basically the textbook tells me that capital is raised to finance the provision of equipment, of stocks of raw materials, of labour, of stocks of finished goods and of credit to customers. Capital is, of course, at risk in the event of unexpected loss or deterioration of any of these factors and such loss can be covered by insurance. Insurance premiums and depreciation charges are thus part of the price of maintaining capital intact. Loss due to bad management, bad trading or sheer commercial bad luck cannot be insured against and these are, I suppose, the risks to which capital is normally exposed.

TIME LAG IN SETTLING CLAIMS

In insurance the concept of risk capital enters a different dimension. In relation to turnover – premium income – the capital required to set up offices, staff and credit to customers is infinitesimal. And once an insurer has put up his plate, the time lag between receiving premiums and settling claims (his product) is such that, providing he is trading profitably – and these words

163

beg the whole question of this chapter – his business is self-financing. (The special case of financing life assurance sales is considered later in this chapter.)

Under the Companies Act 1967, the Department of Trade and Industry required to see paid-up capital of £100,000 before licensing an Insurance Company to trade and then required that it should maintain a "solvency margin" of 20% of its premium income up to £$\frac{1}{4}$ million p.a. and 10% of premium income over and above that level after all liabilities have been provided for. It is, however, the intention of the 1973 Insurance Companies Bill to confer on the Secretary of State powers to raise these standards.

I have referred to the time lag in settling claims. Insurance Companies not only take a pride in serving their policyholders by quick claims settlements, but have good commercial reasons for doing so. The days when the claims assessor spread out pound notes on the table to clinch a cheap settlement may be behind us but claims costs are, by and large, governed by the general level of costs ruling at the date of settlement and cost inflation in recent years has been a strong spur to quick settlements. This has been sharpened by the Administration of Justice Act 1969, under which Courts are required to increase personal injury awards to cover interest for the period up to the date of settlement.

Whilst, therefore, there is every incentive on the insurer to settle claims quickly – and the majority of claims are settled quickly – the more complex and the more expensive claims are subject to long delays before settlement. In the case of personal-injury claims, national insurance and industrial-injury insurance provisions mean that a claimant is no longer forced by pressure of poverty to accept a settlement rather than prolong negotiations and in many cases solicitors and Trade Unions will advise against any negotiations taking place until the full extent of any injury and loss is known and this is all to the good.

The following figures exemplify the time lag in personal injury settlements: 50% of cases are settled within one year; 28% in second year; 12% in third year; 5% in fourth year; 5% after four years have elapsed – an average interval of nearly eighteen months. But if the cases are weighted by the amounts paid, the average interval extends to two years.

THE IMPACT ON PROFIT AND LOSS

In the case of an established Insurance Company, therefore, at the end of any calendar year a very considerable number of claims will be outstanding and the cost of settling these in due course will be above the average general level of current settlements. Whilst the key factor in the fortunes of an Insurance Company is the settlement of claims within the amount of premiums available after deduction of expenses and so as to provide maximum profit, the critical problem in the management of an Insurance Company is the correct assessment of the liability for these outstanding claims (including the expenses of settlement).

On an expanding account, consistent underestimation of the liability results in an apparent source of profit in the annual accounts year in, year out, so long as the expansion continues. But when the snowball stops rolling settlements catch up and the full extent of the damage inexorably emerges. The report of the V. & G. Tribunal shows this process in operation very clearly.

At the end of any year of account, in addition to the estimation of liability on known outstanding claims, Insurance Companies also have a liability for claims which have been incurred but not reported (I.B.N.R.) and in these days of decentralised claims-handling and computerised book-keeping "reported" can have a very extended meaning. In the past I.B.N.R. have generally been regarded as offset by savings on settled claims estimates but again, with an expanding account and in times of inflation, this would give rise to a further source of concealed loss carried forward indefinitely. The importance of I.B.N.R. provisions is only now becoming recognised and many companies still do not show any specific provision under this heading in their returns to the D.T.I.

On an expanding account consistent underestimating of outstanding claims can convert a real loss into an apparent profit. It did not need the V. & G. Tribunal of Enquiry to show us how it was done. It has been done time and again and each time the popular Press acclaims the adventurous newcomer and writes up his shares.

The converse is interesting: on an expanding account consistent overestimating of claims outstanding (whether reported or not) can convert a real profit into an apparent loss. When it is borne in mind that in the Fire and Accident Accounts the provision for outstanding claims is frequently of the order of 75% of the year's premiums, the knife-edge on which the accounts are balanced must be held very steady.

This assessment governs not only the published accounts, but also the company's own views on the current profitability of its business and the adequacy of its current rates. It is therefore pertinent to consider how this critical problem is tackled in practice.

The majority of cases can be disposed of satisfactorily. In cases of material damage – caused by fires or in motor accidents – estimates of the cost of repairs and replacements will have been submitted shortly after the event. In the case of fires at industrial premises with consequential loss of profits, each loss invariably is assessed by independent loss adjusters.

Difficulties arise, however, in the handling of liability claims. Liability insurance takes many forms: employers' liability to employees disabled or injured by industrial accidents or diseases; public liability to members of the public injured by the negligence of firms or private individuals (like motorists); products liability where injury is caused by defective products or workmanship (products-guarantee insurance even covers replacement of the defective products themselves, a risk which should really be the entrepreneurial risk of the producer); professional liability where damage or injury arises from acts of professional negligence; and combinations of these in multi-peril policies such as contractors' performance bonds, contractors' all-risks policies and engineering insurances.

ESTIMATING LONG-TERM CLAIMS

But these classes have one thing in common: they are all long-tail business, that is, as I have already illustrated for personal-injury settlements, it is a long time before the claims arising in any one year are finally disposed of – and only then does the insured really know how he fared on that year's business.

Traditionally, claims of this type are assessed periodically by a case-by-case examination in the light of the up-to-date knowledge of the circumstances of the claim and the claims official's experience of current levels of settlement. In other words, it is an assessment largely subjective to the outlook of the particular claims official concerned, and one which, in times of inflation, is particularly susceptible to the view he takes as to the future rate of increase in claims costs. This thought process (if it can be so dignified) is complicated by reason of the fact that it is founded, to a considerable extent, on another subjective factor, namely, the awards made in courts by judges for damages. The individual judge is considerably influenced by the awards his brethren have made in similar circumstances until there is a sudden break-through and one judge, for whatever reason, sets a new standard to which his brethren quickly adjust – under pressure from plaintiff's Counsel. The great majority of cases are settled out of court but legal advisers and others are, of course, equally influenced by published awards.

This produces a step-like effect in the progression of judicial awards and a similar step-like effect in the outlook of claims officials, probably with a time lag in between, and possibly then with a degree of over-reaction, for it is a matter for private un-dying shame for a claims official to have a claim settled at a figure above his last estimate.

This system can thus result in sickening lurches in the level of outstanding claims estimates, with the whole amount of the addition for past claims apparently falling into the cost of current claims and alarm and despondency all round. But, in a large organisation it is at least the product of the individual reactions of a large number of claims officials and the end result reflects the overall outlook rather than an individual outlook.

Because of the subjective nature of this traditional method, a great deal of thought and research has gone into producing an objective statistical system. Whilst this has resulted in much more satisfactory analysis of claims experience and the run-off of settlements, all the systems put forward inevitably rely at the end of the day on an inflation factor and, in practice, this factor will be decided by an individual claims manager (or, more probably, by a committee). Thus, instead of being based on a multitude of subjective judgements by a considerable number of individuals, the statistical system is based on the judgement of a small number of individuals. Its superiority will depend on whether their wisdom transcends the balance of errors of the claims officials.

Where a company is prepared to rely on a statistical system there can, of course, be a significant saving in the work of claims officials in examination of files, especially at the end of the year. But this may be counter-productive, as the examination yields useful by-products in the form of weeding out dead cases and waking up those that have gone to sleep.

My own personal view is that the best we can do today is to underpin the traditional method with a statistical check valuation – this can have the particular advantage of smoothing out the steps in the progression and so provide management with a more up-to-date picture of the underlying claims experience.

So far as incurred but not reported claims (I.B.N.R.) are concerned, the necessary provision should be determined by a statistical system which takes account of the pattern of late reported claims in earlier years adjusted to changes in the portfolio exposed to risk, and the average level of estimates on newly reported claims.

PROVISION FOR UNEARNED PREMIUMS

Apart from the provisions for incurred claims, a company must make also provision for the unexpired portion on all annual policies in force at the year end up to their next renewal dates. Traditionally the "unearned" premium provision has been set up as 40% of the total annual premiums – on the basis of 20% of the premium being absorbed in commission and expenses at the date of payment, leaving 80% for the year's cover, of which, on the average, one-half (i.e. 40% of the premiums) will be required to cover the period outstanding, assuming renewals are evenly spread over the year.

More recently, however, companies have been calculating the provision for unearned premiums month by month according to the weight of premiums each month, assuming an even spread over the month – hence the so-called "twenty-fourths" basis. Practice has, however, varied between offices as to whether the whole of the net premium, after payment of commission, should be brought into account, or whether a deduction for expenses is admissible. From the point of view of the company's solvency it may be argued that if it were to discontinue its business it would be liable for the expenses incurred in running of the existing portfolio of risks so that no such deduction is defensible.

In recent years we have seen a situation in the U.K. and elsewhere where the general level of motor insurance premiums has been below that of the claims and expenses incurred and this has resulted in substantial losses to most companies. In such a situation the net unearned premium carried forward at the end of the year would accordingly be insufficient to meet the cost of the unexpired risk and this would be a source of loss in the following year's accounts. In such a case the company should hold additional provisions to supplement the unearned premium provision up to the level required to run off the previous year's account without loss and the trading losses incurred in recent years have resulted in greater appreciation of the necessity for such provisions to be set up specifically so that each year's accounts properly reflect the results of the policies entered into or renewed in that year.

Even where the premiums on policies in force are reckoned to be marginally profitable, an unexpired risk provision, additional to the proportionate unearned premium provision, may be indicated if the cost of claims is expected to rise over the year, for example because of the impact of inflation or the incidence of new taxes (e.g. the imposition of VAT) affecting claims payments.

For an established company solvency depends, in the first instance, on the accurate establishment of these provisions to cover the liabilities for its non-life insurance business. Similarly, in the case of life assurance, where the liabilities are of considerably longer term and assets in the form of future contractual premiums must also be valued, the net liability will be established by the actuary at each periodical valuation. The need for risk capital over and above these provisions equates with the solvency margin and its significance depends on the maturity and the stability of the office.

BAD LUCK

The risks to which the capital is exposed are, as in the case of industry, bad management, bad trading and commercial bad luck and these are the factors to which regard should be had in determining the levels of solvency margin required. Bad management and bad trading are scarcely capable of statistical assessment and bad trading is a temptation to which insurers collectively seem particularly prone. The so-called insurance cycle arises in practice from the ease with which expansion of insurance capacity invariably occurs when the business appears to be profitable. The resultant buyers' market forces the cost of insurance down to a level only supportable on marginal cost assumptions and the overall losses emerging lead to a loss of market capacity before profitability returns and the cycle starts again. So long as the market continues to permit this state of affairs solvency margins must be sufficient to permit a company to survive cycles of unprofitable trading.

The risk of bad luck falls into two categories: fluctuations in the incidence of claims experience and loss of value of investments. The fluctuation risk can be guarded against by reinsurance, whilst the investment risk can be guarded against by matching assets to the emerging liabilities. A company may well decide to expose itself to a greater degree of risk than is necessary under both these headings. On the one hand, to build up its premium income by reducing the reinsurance protection, and on the other to increase the yield on invested funds (whether by way of income or capital appreciation) by taking a view on the investment situation and mismatching its assets accordingly. To the extent that a company does this there will be an additional need for a margin of solvency.

SOURCES OF RISK CAPITAL

It is important to note that as a company's premium income expands, its minimum level of risk capital must also be expanded. Even if no real growth of business occurs, inflation of insured values and premiums will require an increase in this minimum level, whilst real growth of business will give rise to a further increase. It is therefore relevant to consider the sources of risk capital.

The capital structure of insurance companies takes many different forms:

(i) *State-Owned-Insurance Offices.*

Offices owned by central or local governments exist not only in Communist countries but also, for example, in New Zealand, Australia and Germany. Such companies may have a monopoly of business or, as in Germany, a partial monopoly, or may be in competition with other types of office.

These offices can, in general, be said to have the unlimited financial resources of the State behind them.

(ii) *Corporation of Lloyd's.*

At the other extreme we have the unique example of Lloyd's of London, a collection of private individuals organised in underwriting syndicates, all of whom undertake unlimited personal liability for the risks they incur. Here again, because of the operation of guarantee funds, the financial resources collectively available are far in excess of any minimum solvency margin considerations.

(iii) *Proprietory Companies.*

It is in the case of proprietary companies, with limited-liability proprietors, that the establishment of an adequate solvency margin and its maintenance becomes a matter of significance. As the proprietors are entitled to expect a reward on their invested capital, the expansion of the minimum capital base, at any rate in so far as it does not arise from real growth of business, must be financed out of the trading profits before payment of dividends.

(iv) *Mutual Companies*

If the insured persons have come together to share their risks in a mutual insurance company, then they could philosophically share equally in the risk of failure of that company. In practice, however, they will wish to insure its viability and the same considerations as to solvency margin therefore arise as in the case of a proprietary company.

A special need for provision of capital arises where a company transacts life assurance because of the "front end" expense charge which usually arises in the sale of life policies. This can be coped with (partially) through modification of the reserve calculation basis ("Zillmerisation"), but, in practice, is often met out of capital resources being recouped eventually out of the expense loading in the premiums – the "new business strain". New business strain can be a very heavy item for a company expanding on orthodox lines but, because of the orthodox bonus structure, the capital of such a company is not exposed to risk of loss as such, and represents instead an initial investment which will be continuously turned over as successive branches of new business absorb the expense loadings released on the earlier branches. This funding operation – and methods of minimising or avoiding the problem – are matters of considerable technical difficulty and must be taken into account in the capital structure of a life office. This is, however, a separate consideration from the assessment of risk capital.

The responsibility for determination of the minimum solvency levels required falls on the Supervisory Authorities and all the factors mentioned above must be adequately covered if failures of insurance companies are to be guarded against in future. In the U.K. the powers conferred upon the D.T.I. by the new Insurance Companies legislation will enable them effectively to discharge these responsibilities in the future.

Chapter 13

DEVELOPMENTS

IN THE LONDON MONEY MARKET

Alistair J. Buchanan
Managing Director, Allen Harvey & Ross Ltd.

The London money market is (September 1972) approaching the first anniversary of the introduction by the Bank of England of its new monetary system to cover competition and credit control. The new system received a baptism of fire, having to contend first with the unfamiliar problems caused by a large surplus on the United Kingdom balance of payments, and then with the more familiar pressures of a deterioration in the balance of payments, an accelerating rate of inflation, and an out-flow of "hot money". A number of changes have been experienced by the market in this period.

Increased volatility of movements in short-term interest rates is likely to be a permanent feature of the new system. Under the previous system, there were a number of built-in stabilisers, which had the effect of keeping short-term interest rate movements within reasonable bounds. The Bank of England, for example, intervened actively in the gilt-edged market to preserve orderly price movements, particularly when prices were falling. The syndicated tender by members of the L.D.M.A. for Treasury Bills, and the agreed Fine Rate for first-class bank acceptances, had a moderating influence on interest-rate movements. These stabilisers are not to be found in the new system of competition and credit control. The effect of increased competition when interest rates are falling, and of a lack of stabilisers when they are rising, has produced a situation when, for example, in June and July 1972, some short-term interest rates doubled in six weeks – three month £ Certificates of Deposit rising from $4\frac{1}{2}\%$ to 9%. Such movements are likely to be characteristic of the new system unless the Bank of England chooses to intervene more effectively. The discount market cannot be expected to welcome such extreme movements because it becomes very difficult to deal in such volatile conditions. Turnover used to be the bread-and-butter business of the money market. Volatile prices discourage turnover because a trading portfolio becomes an investment portfolio and dealers cannot afford to trade against the market trend because the penalty for a mis-judgement is too great. Ideally, a balance should be found between the desirability for competition amongst dealers, on the one hand, and the maintenance of viable short-term markets on the other. So long as the Bank of England is in a mood of disengagement, it is difficult to see how such a balance can be found.

The Bank of England requires each discount house to hold at least 50% of its £ funds borrowed in what is described as "public-sector paper". The definition of "public-sector" assets includes Treasury Bills, Government stocks with less than five years to run to redemption, and local-authority bonds and bills. This requirement distorts the interest-rate yield-curve from time to time. When, for example, there is a small issue of Treasury Bills, competition for them drives the rate well below the rate on three-month commercial bills of exchange, particularly if short-dated Government stocks are not in favour at that moment. Likewise, when interest rates are rising, the discount rate for commercial bills rises unduly rapidly because the dealer quoting a buying rate knows that, if the commercial bill remains in portfolio, it must be matched by a corresponding holding of public-sector paper. In quoting a rate, therefore, the dealer has to bear in mind the possible loss on the public-sector paper as well as considering the potential profitability of the commercial bill itself. If the commercial bill is in the form of a bank acceptance eligible for re-discount at the Bank of England, it will command a significantly lower rate of discount than an ineligible bill because the commercial banks are allowed to hold up to 2% of their reserve assets in the form of eligible bills. This creates a better market for eligible than ineligible bills.

A redeeming feature of the new system has been the inclusion of money lent to a discount house against collateral as a reserve asset for U.K. banks. This has provided a pool of money for the discount houses which might not otherwise have been available. As there is no longer any restriction on discount houses taking deposits from non-banking institutions, the discount houses have been able to widen their source of funds and have been able to obtain funds with comparative ease even at the most difficult times.

The discount market continues to offer an expanding service, both directly and indirectly, to institutions dealing in the money market, as borrowers or as lenders. The markets in £ and Euro-dollar Certificates of Deposit provide opportunities for sophisticated institutions with funds to lend to enjoy the best market rates for their funds, without losing liquidity. The discount houses provide the secondary market in such paper, quoting buying and selling prices and thereby giving the certificates their negotiable character. These markets bring the discount houses directly into contact with financial institutions other than banks. Indirectly, the discount houses have also developed contact with financial institutions outside the banking system through money-broking subsidiaries and associates. These broking firms provide useful financial services to local authorities, banks and companies in the United Kingdom and abroad. Such services will continue to be developed to meet the changing requirements of the financial system. For borrowers, the discount market continues to provide a valuable source of working capital by discounting bank and trade bills at competitive rates.

An unexpected development in the organisation of the discount market has been the takeover of Clive Holdings Ltd. by Sime Darby Ltd. Before this takeover, it was generally assumed that the main scope for discount market rationalisation lay in mergers between existing houses. A new dimension has been introduced by the Bank of England's permission for this deal. It is unlikely that vertical integration will be encouraged, in the sense that the Clearing Banks or merchant banks will be allowed to add the functions of a discount house to their existing banking services. The prospect, however, of alliances being formed with non-banking institutions is an interesting development in the market's history.

The rôle of an independent discount house in an enlarged E.E.C. will depend on the type of monetary system which develops. The money-market function in London will continue, in that there will need to be an active money market to support all the other City markets and to facilitate the flow of funds between the public and private sectors of the U.K. economy. It will be for the Bank of England, or for a future European Central bank, to decide whether to operate in the future through specialist middlemen, such as the discount houses, rather than to deal direct with the banks themselves. A factor in this decision will be the quality and cost of the services to be provided by independent specialists. In the meantime, the discount houses are improving their contacts in Europe and the Far East and look forward to playing an active rôle in the international and domestic money markets.

PART II

Strategic Planning

Chapter 14

PENSION FUNDS AS INVESTORS

Michael Pilch
Director, Noble Lowndes & Partners Ltd.

I want to look at Pension-Fund Investment in the broadest possible sense and to do so under four headings:

1 The impact of pension funds on the market.
2 The effect of Government plans for reforming pension funds.
3 The effect of the new State Reserve Scheme.
4 Some reforms that I would like to see.

Before writing about the impact of pension funds on the market, it may be as well to define what I mean by pension funds. For this purpose I am not going to draw any distinction between privately invested funds and those which are based on insurance, because what we are concerned with is the effect they have on the market and it makes very little difference to this whether the schemes are insured or not. The real distinction is between schemes which are funded – that is, where real assets are set aside in advance to provide for future liabilities – and those which are unfunded. The latter are no more than promises to pay and, as such, can be ignored. Where a scheme is funded, however, it matters very little whether contributions are invested directly in the market by trustees or are paid by them as premiums to an insurance company which then makes the investment to match whatever liability it may have undertaken.

Table 1 shows the net growth of pension funds in the private sector during the five years to the end of 1970. It covers both insured and non-insured funds. One of the difficulties about making this kind of analysis is that none of the data is really 100% reliable – but even if they are a million or two out here and there it will not affect the general shape of the picture.

TABLE 1 ESTIMATED NEW INVESTMENT ARISING FROM
PENSION FUNDS IN PRIVATE SECTOR

Year	Contribution Income	Interest Earnings	Total Income	Total Outgo	Net Growth of Funds
	£m.	£m.	£m.	£m.	£m.
1966	634	323	957	397	560
1967	715	365	1,080	460	620
1968	835	429	1,264	546	718
1969	886	459	1,345	642	703
1970	1,028	525	1,553	769	784

TABLE 2 ESTIMATED NEW INVESTMENT ARISING FROM
PENSION FUNDS IN PUBLIC SECTOR

Year	Contribution Income	Interest Earnings	Total Income	Total Outgo	Net Growth of Funds
	£m.	£m.	£m.	£m.	£m.
1966	503	106	609	432	177
1967	550	115	665	475	190
1968	599	126	725	514	211
1969	664	137	801	559	242
1970	780	150	930	612	318

There are pension funds in the public sector (Table 2) which
are "notionally funded" and for such schemes the contribution
figure has been taken as the amount necessary to balance
income and outgo. This is why the figure for interest earnings
is relatively less significant than that for the private sector.

TABLE 3   ESTIMATED NEW MONEY FOR INVESTMENT
COMPARED WITH NEW ISSUES IN U.K. MARKET

Year	Net Growth of Private Sector	Net Growth of Public Sector	Total Growth	New Capital Raised in Market
	£m.	£m.	£m.	£m.
1966	560	177	737	701
1967	620	190	810	483
1968	718	211	929	638
1969	703	242	945	619
1970	784	318	1,102	276
			4,523	2,717

Table 3 takes the growth figures for private- and public-sector funds combined and compares them with the amounts of new money raised by U.K. quoted companies in the capital markets of this country during the same period. I am not suggesting that it is possible in any sense to equate the two. There are many additional factors that would have to be taken into account. There are, for example, other institutional investors – the unit trusts, the insurance companies in relation to their ordinary life and general business, and so on. Nor does all new money go into the market. A great deal nowadays, for instance, goes into property. Nevertheless, the broad picture is that over a five-year period more than £4,500 millions of new money has had to be invested by pension funds, compared with new capital of just over £2,700 millions raised by companies in the market.

There is, of course, no mystery about where the missing millions come from. Private investors are now believed to own about 46% of all U.K. equities and this figure has been reducing for some years at something between 0·5% and 1% a year. The steady transfer of shares from individual to institutional ownership is part of the answer.

Another factor is that not all pension-fund money by any means goes into the stock market. The Life Offices have recently published their figures for 1970, showing that $27\frac{1}{2}$% of their money was invested in ordinary shares, $18\frac{1}{2}$% in debentures, loan stocks and preference shares, 16% in British

Government and local authority securities, 17% in mortgages and 13½% in property with the remaining 7½% invested overseas and elsewhere. The interests of privately invested funds would be similarly dispersed, though possibly in somewhat different proportions. I.C.I., for example, recently published the accounts of their pension funds for the year ending 31st March 1971, which showed that they had about 51% in equities, 36% in fixed-interest and Government stocks, and 13% in mortgages and property.

I do not think it takes an economist to conclude from these figures that the continuing flow of new money from pension funds exerts a pressure on the market. Not, of course, a constant pressure. It would be a mistake to suppose that this steady build-up of funds predicates steadily rising share prices. You have only to look at the behaviour of the market over the last few years to see that this must be false. There could be many explanations for this – the most obvious being that investment managers who think that the market is going to fall can find other homes for their money, at any rate for a while. I have already mentioned property, but there are plenty of other possibilities. One manager bought silver bars and there is no theoretical reason why a long-term investment should not be made by a pension fund in a non-income-producing asset like, perhaps, an Old Master or even a cellar of port – though I do not believe this is what most trustees have in mind when they show liquid assets in their balance sheets!

In general, however, it must be true that the existence of pension funds and the continuing source of new money which they produce gives an underlying strength to the market, which is likely to result in an upward trend in prices over an extended period. Any sharp increase in the amounts that are channelled through pension funds could upset the balance of supply and demand for securities and result in disproportionate price changes.

Let us consider what other conclusions follow from the growing influence that pension funds exert on the market. Pension funds, after all, have their own special characteristics that differ markedly from those of other investors and it is to be expected that these will be reflected in corresponding changes in the market. There are four main ways in which pension funds differ from the private investor.

1 First, as we have already seen, they are steady net investors of new money.

2 Secondly, they are almost completely exempt from tax and are therefore likely to attach more significance to dividend income than the private investor, who may prefer capital growth in view of the lower tax rates payable.

3 Thirdly, pension funds are essentially long-term investors and can afford to take a patient view of prospects, though in practice this factor may be offset by the more active management of a pension fund portfolio.

4 Fourthly, the investments of pension funds tend to be handled by professionals and thus investment decisions are concentrated into fewer hands than is the case with private investors.

A broad picture is thus created of a gradual movement away from widely scattered, disparate individual shareholdings towards a much more concentrated, highly-organised and research-based, professional management of pension-fund portfolios. The new shareholders are likely to prove more demanding in the performance they require and *will want to measure*. It might be thought that the long-term nature of pension-fund objectives would lead to a stable investment policy with holdings being retained for long periods, but in most cases the search for maximum performance precludes such a policy, and one consequence of the concentration of investment in a small number of hands is that greater emphasis is placed on marketability. If you act as investment adviser to a number of pension funds and you become disenchanted with the performance of a particular company, you do not want to find yourself locked in. Where the aggregate holdings of the funds you manage are substantial, this could easily happen, unless the share is one that can be freely dealt in, and the consequence is likely to be a further widening between the ratings accorded to the leading shares in the market as compared with the remainder.

The Government intends to overhaul the whole of the present State Pension Scheme completely and introduce a new system which will start in April 1975. There will be two parts to this – a Basic Scheme and a Reserve Scheme which will provide additional benefits based on earnings. The intention of the Government is that this Reserve Scheme should be largely restricted to employees who are not covered by occupational schemes. They hope that employers will, wherever possible, seek exemption for their employees from the Reserve Scheme by setting up suitable schemes of their own, or, where such schemes are already in existence, by altering them to satisfy the Government's requirements.

These requirements can be summed up roughly as follows:

(a) A minimum level of personal pension benefit.

(b) A pension to the widow of a man who dies before or after reaching retirement age.

(c) Some protection against the erosion of the value of these pensions as a result of price changes.

(d) Preservation of benefits on changes of employment.

(e) Adequate financial provision for the funding of the benefits.

Will employers seek exemption from the Reserve Scheme? Nobody can be quite sure about this yet – a lot depends on the fine print – but first signs are that most of them will. The National Association of Pension Funds carried out a survey of its members a month or two ago, and 87% thought they were likely to apply for their funds to be recognised under the new legislation. Replies were received from nearly 500 funds with a total of about $3\frac{3}{4}$ million members, so the sample was a pretty good one.

What will be the main effects on funds which have to satisfy the rules for recognition?

The basic benefit test will not be an obstacle to many funds, except from an administrative angle, but there will be some funds – particularly those covering manual workers – which will have to increase their pension scales.

Death-in-service benefits likewise will present few problems. The widow's pension payable on death in retirement is another matter. Only 50% of the funds responding to the N.A.P.F. survey offer such a benefit at the present time. The rest will have to introduce it if they want to be recognised. The cost is anybody's guess, but could be 20% or more on top of what they are paying already.

Price protection is another unknown factor. Only about 5% of pension funds *guarantee* to increase pensions in retirement either on a stated scale or in proportion to a cost-of-living index. Another 40% or so give occasional increases when they feel like it – which usually means after an actuarial valuation – but whether this will be good enough to satisfy the Government requirements on this score remains to be seen. Once again the other 50% or 60% will have to comply with one or other of the alternative tests laid down. The cost of doing so is likely to add at least 20% to the cost of the basic benefit, whatever method is selected.

Preserving pensions when members change their jobs will add substantially to the costs of some pension funds and nothing at all to others – depending on what their practice is at present. About 70% of the funds taking part in the N.A.P.F. survey do already give the benefit to a member leaving service, either as of right, after some minimum period of service perhaps, or as a result of exercising a discretionary power by the trustees. Clearly, such funds will not be making any major changes and will not now incur much in the way of extra costs. Other funds which generally withhold the benefit from a member when he leaves, will not be free to do so in the future and their costs inevitably will be increased as a result.

The effects of Government supervision over funding rates are again imponderable, but are certainly not likely to reduce costs. This is a revolutionary new departure. In the past, Inland Revenue eyes have scrutinised the funding from the opposite point of view. They have been concerned only to make sure that you did not put *too much* into the kitty and thus get away with tax reliefs to which you were not entitled. Over-funding was the only crime. If you put in *too little* and your employees were, in consequence, deprived of pensions, nobody minded – except presumably the employees. Now one of the requirements for recognition will be a degree of security in the funding and, here and there, this must result in a higher rate of investment than in the past.

The combined effect of all these changes on the market as a whole is not at all easy to estimate, but I should be very surprised if the result is not to push up the annual costs of existing pension funds by at least £250 millions by 1975, over and above the normal increases that might have been expected to stem from salary rises and the like.

Next we must think about possible new schemes and the easiest way to look at this is to examine the shape of the Reserve Scheme. The intention is that it will be funded. Employers will pay 2½% and employees 1½% of earnings up to 1½ times the national average, and these contributions will be invested by a Board of Management to obtain the best return they can in the market. Given these facts, it is a fairly simple calculation to assess the flow of extra new money to the markets resulting from these arrangements as at least £510 millions a year.

The White Paper describing the new scheme estimates the initial contribution to the Reserve Scheme as being something like £250 millions a year. There is, in reality, no conflict between these figures because the Government Actuary has assumed that some new schemes will be set up to secure recognition, whereas I, being only interested in the effects on the investment market, have assumed that no new schemes are established. All employees not already covered by schemes would therefore have to join the Reserve Scheme, and my figure of £510 millions is arrived at by applying 4% to the earnings of such employees, assuming them to be earning the national average. If new schemes are set up to cover some of them, the cost of doing so is likely to exceed 4% of earnings and to that extent my figure will be an under-estimate.

The net result of the Government proposals, therefore, in my view, will be to raise total new investment through pension funds including the Reserve Scheme by a minimum of £760 millions a year by 1975. I would prefer not to speculate on who will benefit from this extra spending, except to say that I do not share Mr. Crossman's belief that the insurance companies will be major beneficiaries of the Conservative plan.

There is one other aspect of the Reserve Scheme that we might consider briefly. The fact that it will be funded, and the sheer size of it, have attracted some critical comment. In fact I do not share these fears at all. It is not the size of the Reserve Scheme itself that is going to create problems for the market, but the consequences that flow from it. As I have pointed out already, it makes little difference to the market whether money is invested directly through the Reserve Scheme or through occupational pension funds that are set up to replace it. I have absolutely no inside knowledge of how the Board of Management of the Reserve Scheme fund will go about their business, but I refuse to believe that they will contemplate for one moment channelling £250 million a year for investment through one pair of hands.

Put yourself in their shoes. The chances of beating the index, or producing really spectacular investment results with a fund of that size, must be so slim as to be almost non-existent. The best you could hope for is to match, or very slightly out-perform, the movement of the market. Indeed nothing less than this will do, because the Government will obviously try to appoint to this Board the leading, most highly respected financial brains in this country, and their performance is bound to come under critical public scrutiny. Seven million members of the Reserve Scheme will be dependent on the success of their efforts for the size of their pensions, and nothing much less than matching the performance of the markets is likely to preserve the hard-earned reputations of the members of the Board of Management. So what would you do in their place? Spread the risk, I suggest. Appoint at least four, and probably nearer ten, of the largest and most highly-regarded merchant banks or other financial institutions, each to handle a proportion of the investments for a stated period. Monitor performances and compare them, making changes as required in the advisers and perhaps in the share of new money allocated to them. Such a policy would not disrupt the normal working of the market.

I believe, too, that we can discount the likelihood of back-door nationalisation, which is another of the bogeys that we have been threatened with. Sir Keith Joseph has answered this question, quite effectively in my view, by making it clear that the legislation will bind the Board of Management to invest its funds in the best interests of the members of the Reserve Scheme, and these could hardly be construed to include nationalisation. I do confess to one lingering doubt in this connection. I think there is a danger, a more subtle one, that a situation might arise like Rolls Royce or Upper Clyde Shipbuilders where the Government wanted someone other than themselves to bail out a sinking ship (or aeroplane). I can imagine that they might convince themselves that it was in the interests of Reserve Scheme members, if enough of them were employed in the company or industry concerned, that the Board of Management should come to its rescue. I am not even completely sure that I would condemn such an approach, if it were restricted to a relatively small part of the total funds, though I recognise the difficulties that would arise if there were to be any departure from strict financial criteria as the yardstick for investment policy.

There are, in fact, some interesting moral issues that ought to be more widely discussed than they are among pension-fund trustees in general. For example, consider the dilemma which faces them if they have even a small holding in the employing company and there is a takeover bid. Let us suppose that the offer is financially attractive but would result in some redundancies among the staff. Should they accept the offer, which might enable them to raise the level of benefits for existing pensioners, or should they reject it in order to safeguard the jobs of members who are still at work? Should they lend money to the company to tide it over a lean spell – and if you are tempted to answer "No" to that one, what should be the attitude of the trustees if the employer wants to make a temporary reduction in the rate of funding (which comes to exactly the same thing)? How do you feel about trustees who allow a pension-fund holding in the company to be used deliberately to block any possibility of a bid and thus to protect the management when conceivably the staff might benefit from a change?

Nor are these problems confined to cases where shares are held in the employing company. There are wider issues to consider. One pension-fund manager, consulting a sociologist about the problems arising on early retirement of some of his fund members, was startled to be told that he must share the blame for much of the hardship and distress that can occur in such a situation. The argument was that the additional pressure on companies, created by the demands of pension funds and other institutional investors for ever-increasing profits, had compelled employers to give priority to financial over human considerations in the way they ran their businesses. I think that pension-fund investors should at least pause to consider what they are doing when they put their money to work.

My final heading is: reform that I would like to see. Not, I hasten to make clear, control of investment policy – though this is a reform that we are likely to have in any case, to the limited extent of restricting self-investment by the pension fund in the business of the employer, if nothing more. I am not a great believer in legislative reform, because I think you can often achieve better results in the long run by persuasion. Because, if a reform is truly progressive, you ought to be able to show people that it is in their own interests to introduce it voluntarily rather than rely upon compulsion. That has been my experience with pension schemes, with final salary benefits, with widows' pensions, with preservation of benefits on changes of employment, and it is certainly true of the reform that I would like to put forward now – the need for more information.

There has been a move in this direction, but it needs to go much further. The investment that an employee makes in a pension scheme is substantial – and I am not referring only to contributory schemes, his interest in a non-contributory scheme is just as great. There is no other kind of investment that he could be asked to make where so little information would be given about what happens to his money. Unit-trust holders expect, and receive, a statement at least once a year to show how they have fared: why not pension-fund members? Many of the larger pension funds do now publish their accounts, but few go as far as to give details of individual holdings, let alone a measure of performance.

The kind of thing that I would like to see is a quarterly report on the lines, for example, of that produced for the New Court Exempt Trust. This is a unit trust for pension funds and charities, run by Rothschild and Lowndes Management Ltd., of which I am a director, and once a quarter we publish a report by the managers on the investment outlook, a complete portfolio for the trust, highlighting the ten largest holdings, and a graph showing the performance of the trust since its inception measured against the *Financial Times* index.

There is nothing exceptional about this in a unit-trust context; but it is unusual in relation to pension funds, and one must ask the question, why? Quite apart from any basic right of the member to know what becomes of his money, it is surely in the best interest of the employer to stimulate interest among his employees in the pension fund and a regular factual report on its performance should be an excellent way to achieve this. I appreciate that this is by no means a simple reform to carry out.

I have perhaps chosen an unfair example by selecting an exempt unit trust with a portfolio of stocks and shares and no problems associated with property valuations and the like. The measurement of performance is a complex subject and some very sophisticated techniques are being devised to cope with it. One difficulty, therefore, is that any yardstick which is accurate enough to give a fair assessment is unlikely to be comprehensible to the average member of a pension fund. Another objection is that the successful management of a pension fund is a long-term business and ought to be measured over a period of years rather than months. All of this I accept, but I still feel that those who run pension funds should be accountable to members for the way in which their money is handled and that some attempt at least should be made to communicate to the members some idea of how they are doing.

The other reform I want to mention also relates to unit trusts. People can take many different views of unit trusts, some see them as an essential part of a share-owning democracy, others regard them as an expensive alternative to direct share ownership, and much the same division of opinion might arise over exempt trusts. Naturally, I am going to defend them on the grounds that they give to medium and smaller funds the same opportunities of professional management, spread of risk and measured performance that would otherwise be available only to larger funds. I would therefore go so far as to say that it is in the public interest that the growth of exempt trusts should be encouraged. At the moment they account for total assets of a tiny £75 millions or so, but they are growing fast. They would grow faster were it not for a minor tax disadvantage which I would like to bring to the notice of the Chancellor of the Exchequer.

The word "exempt" is a misnomer, because the so-called exempt trusts are not specifically exempt from anything except capital gains tax. Even though all the unit-holders are themselves exempt from tax, being registered charities or approved pension schemes, the trust must normally pay tax and unit-holders reclaim it. Worse than that, corporation tax is payable by the trust on unfranked income and cannot be reclaimed by unit-holders. It is patently absurd that pension funds which are themselves exempt should have to pay tax in some circumstances on an investment made through an exempt unit trust when they would not have paid tax had they made the same investment direct. What makes the situation even more ridiculous is that it is only an *authorised* unit trust that runs the risk of liability for corporation tax in the circumstances I have described. An *unauthorised* trust does not, because the Inland Revenue (as the expression is) "looks through" the unauthorised trust to the tax status of the individual unit-holder.

The effect is to discourage authorised exempt unit trusts from investing in certain types of fixed interest and convertible stocks and also, incidentally, Government securities – which can hardly, one imagines, have been the Treasury's intention.

This needs tidying up, and as it is so clearly not any part of the Government's intention at the present time to discriminate against authorised exempt unit trusts, I hope the Chancellor will find time to do something about it.

Chapter 15

CREATING AN EFFECTIVE

BUSINESS STRATEGY

C. H. Villiers
Chairman, Guinness Mahon & Co. Ltd.

I have chosen "Business" rather than "Financial" strategy because our thinking should not, in my view, be confined to the financial aspect. Finance is the pearl which pervades all business and business is its oyster. "Business strategy" is a rather high-faluting phrase and I have no doubt that it strikes you as something from the business schools – a phrase the whizz-kids use to persuade us that everything is different now and that the professionals have taken over from the amateurs. Dr. Johnson said, "Let fanciful men do as they will, depend upon it, it is difficult to disturb the system of life." The good doctor, of course, was right in his day and age, but we must admit that the system of life, particularly of business life, has been seriously disturbed in recent years. I judge this to be mainly due to the fantastic advance in technology which resulted from World War II.

Many of us were brought up in business on a much older philosophy, which can be put very shortly as – "suck it and see." I believe that this approach is far from outworn. The variants in any business situation are far too many to be sure of the results of any long-term objectives. So having set out upon a programmed course one must react quickly to changing environment.

My contribution to our thinking about business strategy is heavily conditioned by the need for flexibility as the strategy unfolds. My contribution will be broken down into three aspects of strategy: Structural, Managerial and Financial.

THE STRUCTURAL ASPECT

A business strategy, I think, must begin either by developing an existing situation or by identifying a new opportunity and cashing in on it. In most successful businesses you will find a bit of both. I have the greatest admiration for people who have created new businesses from absolutely nothing. They are very rare nowadays. The great entrepreneurs of today have, in fact, started with an existing business, however small, which they have acquired and developed. Those who start with a new process in a green field and nothing else seldom succeed, unless they have huge funds behind them to carry them over the early difficult years. But it is also true that those who acquire or inherit existing businesses and fail to develop their inherent strengths into new fields will also be likely to go down, since they will lack the dynamic to keep up with the competition.

So my first rule of business strategy is: take an existing business and develop its natural strengths. It may be that some of its activities are no longer profitable and have no future – these should be pruned back, hard and quick. It may be that other activities should be extended and developed – these should be cultivated but not beyond the managerial and financial resources available.

How big should a business be? This is the next strategy question. It was often said of us at the Industrial Reorganisation Corporation (I.R.C.) that we liked bigness for bigness' sake. This is quite wrong – we did not think or act on that mistaken principle. We did, however, from our rather uncomfortable perch between industry and the City, Westminster and Whitehall, see that in so many industries a process of mutual attrition was at work whereby British companies were destroying each other by intensive internal competition, while the external competition was laughing all the way. The case of G.E.C., A.E.I. and English Electric is the clearest example of what I mean.

The rule about size, I think, is that a business must be big enough to achieve its ambitions in view of the performance of the competition. It is no good being in business if you are hopelessly outgunned in the battle you choose to fight. If you cannot compete on price, design, delivery or credit with your rivals you will go down. So choose your battleground and create a business big enough to be successful. There are some industries where all the companies are small or smallish; much of light engineering and many service industries fall into this category. Heavy engineering, whether electrical or mechanical, is now for the big battalions. But there is a joker in this pack – the small, fast fish can often be a match for the Leviathan at scooping up succulent morsels, but note this: the premium on flexibility of management is then very high.

So, on size, settle what you want to do and be big enough to do it. Be too small and you may starve, be too big and you may become fat and flabby. The competition is changing all the time and you have to change with it. This means a restless, disturbed sort of life – not what Dr. Johnson would have liked – but I fear it is the price of success in the technology-dominated business world in which we live.

The third aspect of strategy is *diversification* and there is much perplexity about this. I take the liberty of suggesting that the principle should be: a multi-product or multi-service company is usually right, a conglomerate is usually wrong – there are exceptions to both which, I would claim, prove the rule. Companies succeed or fail because of management control. A single-product or service company is easy to control but vulnerable to market changes. A multi-product or service company is more difficult to control but still controllable if the same basic disciplines pervade the whole business.

A conglomerate, which covers a wide and incoherent spectrum of business activities, is extremely difficult to manage. It is often set up by one man at the height of his powers and reflects his ambitions and abilities. As these fail, and with the biological process they will fail, he may plunge on or in recession times become over-extended. He will cling to the reins and, by the time a successor is found, deep trouble is likely. A simple way of looking at it is to regard your hands. Down your arms into your ten fingers run bones, tissues, nerves, blood, which share a common discipline and can be articulated by a single management – and it is arguable that ten units is the manageable maximum. Try to graft other members – nose, ears or what-have-you on to this system and a natural rejection follows: the incompatibility is at once evident. An unnatural extension or addition to a business is often attempted and management persists long after rejection has become inevitable. It is the perception of what development is natural, which distinguishes the successful business.

THE MANAGERIAL ASPECT

Under my first heading we have considered how to start, how to grow, how much to diversify – the basic strategical concepts from the financial, industrial, and commercial viewpoint. I want now to take a look at the *strategy of management*.

No business can be better than its management. Good management can make a success of a poor business. Bad management can wreck a good business. What distinguishes good management? I shall now try to distil the strategical aspects into three:

1 The division of the supervisory from the day-to-day function.

2 The allotment of exact day-to-day functions.

3 The renewal of management.

The biggest flaw in management under the British arrangements of law and practice is that no distinction is made between the supervisory function and the function of day-to-day management. The result is that what the day-to-day side has got into a mess, as must and does so often happen, the non-executive directors (if there are any) are in there with them, involved in the mess and with no real standing in law or practice to make the necessary changes. I have seen literally dozens of cases where the non-executive directors, who should have a supervisory function, have become so involved in wrong decisions by the actual management that they cannot sack the unsuccessful managers and appoint new ones. In every case they knew what they ought to do but only in very exceptional cases do they have the courage and personality to stand up and be counted and insist on the necessary changes.

Now, we don't have the two-tier board system in Europe, nor the division of Board and Executive as in America, so we have to do our best in a pragmatic way. I think it is a matter of business strategy that the top board of any significant company should not include those with a "line" function. It should include a Chairman, who may or may not be executive, a Chief

Executive, with the functional directors responsible for finance, development, personnel, etc., and an equal number of non-executive directors who, ideally, would be Chief Executives of non-competing companies. A top board need not meet more than four times a year, and should have these functions:

1 Taking policy decisions and approving investment plans.

2 Appointing, remunerating and removing senior management.

3 Informing shareholders of the state of the business.

If you want an example of this in action look at the Board of the General Electric Company – the British one. There you will see just what I have described and, alongside the Board, the executives who actually run and manage the Company, set out with their function described.

And so to my *second point of management strategy*. The actual managers must know precisely what they are expected to manage, how they relate to other managers, what results they are expected to achieve and how variations can be effected quickly as operating conditions change. It all seems so obvious and yet how seldom is it done? The definition of tasks can, of course, cause embarrassment and friction, even resignations, but this is better than indecision and fuzzy edges where no one knows what to do. I have no doubt that in this matter we are behind the international competition from the U.S.A., Germany, Japan, Holland and, in some fields, we are behind the Latin countries as well. We still suffer from the old autocratic system of management. What we need are management teams, led by Chief Executives who allocate tasks, monitor results and initiate remedial action where necessary – he should be a beast but, as Stalky said, "a just beast".

Now, three very important points:

1 Organisation must reflect strategy; i.e. if you are building up one activity and running down another the status and remuneration of the people running the activities must reflect this process.

2 Within the Organisation push responsibility down the line as far as it will go. This is *Participation*. You need courage of conviction to trust the people in your Organisation structure.

Top controls strategy, monitors performance and delegates execution.

3 Motivation of Management – what makes it tick has been overly neglected in the U.K. We managers are no longer hired assassins of lordly owners, who deferentially pride themselves on such an association. We know that the owners, whether the general public or private people, lordly or otherwise, cannot do without us, or someone like us. And we will ply our trade where we can get two things:

(a) Job satisfaction.

(b) A chance to share in the financial success of our efforts.

In this way managers and entrepreneurs share their way of life. In this way managers can be induced to perform like the original capitalists, who have added so much to the world's wealth. I shall come in a moment to the renewal of management but, meanwhile, I underline that management taking over from the original capitalist, as it must do in due course, needs the joy, the delight of vigour in action which comes from being free to develop a business or part of a business, and fashion it in one's own way. But it must always be realised that failure means the sack and success a share in the profits. There was a heresy in circulation since the War that people had given up working for money – that is rubbish. Maybe it is wrong, antisocial, call it what you will, but many people – I would say most people – do work for money, and work better for more money. I know I do.

It is sad to work only for money, as many do; this leads to poverty of outlook and an incomplete person. I doubt if job satisfaction comes only from money: I believe it comes from a sense that one's efforts have some wider meaning and import-ance, that they affect the performance of other people, that they contribute towards the common good – this need not be a moral sense, but it is a sense most of us need. I have found that in nationalised industries, where remuneration tends to be lower than in the private sector, and where financial sharing of profits is virtually impossible, there are managers who are undoubtedly getting very great job satisfaction and take delight in their actions. I believe, however, that their cutting-edge is less sharp than properly motivated managers in the private sector. They are not, of course, so free as their opposite numbers to try their own ideas, they are essentially more bureaucratic. The national interest of full employment and low prices and wage restraint all bear much more heavily upon them than upon entrepreneurs.

This is the real problem of the mixed economy. How effectively to manage that part which the private sector has left behind as uninteresting for investment. This is not the place to dive into this subject, but I suggest that management motivation in the private sector can be very fully developed and you will not get much success without it. In the public sector it is just as necessary, but very much more difficult to arrange, and it is a continuing problem with which this and succeeding generations will continue to be occupied.

The last ingredient in this part of my recipe for a business strategy is *the renewal of management*. If there is one great need for success in business it is for arrangements to renew management before it is too late. This is immensely difficult. Compulsory retiring ages, pension schemes, all sorts of aids are required, but there is nothing more demoralising for a business than to see outworn managers clinging to the shreds of their job when their credibility is gone. When men are "past it" it is cheap for the company to part with them on generous terms. When men have clearly been promoted through their ceilings they must be reallocated. When no continuity is provided, men must be brought in from outside, however unpopular this may be with the local inhabitants. All this is disturbing to the rather cosy vision of business life, but we ignore it at our peril.

The rule is quite clear – only strong, unified managements will be successful and these will best be achieved by some directors having a supervisory function, by actual management having precise objectives, and by management renewal, where necessary, in good time.

THE FINANCIAL ASPECT

And so to my last strategical category – *Finance* itself. And, here, I consider only two aspects:

1 Profits.
2 Cash flow.

An enormous amount of sophistication has been applied to the financial aspects of business. But the great mass of it falls, in my judgement, into the tactical area and I am trying to stick to strategy and the consideration upon which major decisions in corporate life must be based. I find that if the structure and managerial set-up is right, finance seldom provokes a great problem, provided always that profits and cash flow are regarded as the strategical considerations; without positive flows here a company can do nothing.

It is extraordinary in how many businesses the *pursuit of profit* has given way to some other motivation, such as excellence of product or service, foreign earnings, employment, continuity, expansion, even environment. Family businesses are particularly prone to this, but all companies as they find profit earning becoming difficult are apt to find excuses for survival in one of these other fields. Whenever you hear it, you do, I am sure, become very suspicious.

It is true that we live in a mixed economy, but the private sector of our economy is capitalist and any part of it which does not behave in a capitalist way will go down. We have many examples now before us. If it becomes impossible for a sector of our economy to remain profitable it will either disappear or, if it is judged of great national importance – like the railways or coal mines or Rolls Royce – it will be nationalised. As we enter Europe this imperative of profit will become much more apparent. I have asked European industrialists how the Rome Treaty affected them in the early years, and they have told me that, for the successful, it was splendid, but for the inefficient it was disastrous. For example, the whole boot and shoe industry in Belgium disappeared in a couple of years. This test will hit all of us in Britain during the next few years as companies meet increasing competition; if they cannot remain profitable, and increasingly profitable, they will go down. This, perhaps, is the greatest strategical imperative of them all; and no excuse will be any good.

But closely allied with profitability is cash flow, a factor which in the relatively easy years of the Fifties and Sixties it was possible to ignore. Today not so. When companies were in real difficulties in 1968–70 they came, as a last resort, to the I.R.C. and it was always the same story – we cannot any longer pay the wages. And it was always the same answer – change the top management and the financial controls. Time and again the results of doing this were quite amazing. Tight, even rough, financial control can restore positive cash flows in an incredibly short space of time. Managers will always use the financial latitude that is given to them – remove the latitude and they have to cope in order to survive; it is amazing how the cash then begins to flow – managers are amazed themselves. I have seen it enough times to be sure of it. Unfortunately, in many cases it only happens in the face of disaster – how much better if rugged financial control was a normal part of company life. In the financial world this means, don't get locked-up with more of your resources than you objectively decide. Of course, a strategy of rapid growth eats up cash: often the financial planning shows a D.C.F. return of, say, 25% – but how often is the effect of this on the P. & L. Account or B/S considered? Unless this is thought through, the outside world will not be convinced that all is well, and the reception will be disappointing.

You will find no successful entrepreneur who does not know and practise this as a regular part of his business life. It is more difficult for hierarchical management teams to impose this on each other – what is sauce for the goose is sauce for the gander! The imposition of profit and cash flow disciplines on management is the job of the Chief Executive – no one else in the company has authority, and if he does not do it, it is no good hoping that others will – they can only supply the Chief Executive with the necessary material. Make no mistake, this is a strategical consideration of the highest order – it is much neglected under the current British business system – more's the pity!

You may ask *what should be the attitude of Government* to influence strategy and improve performance in business. After all, Government enormously depends upon successful business to provide the taxes, the foreign exchange, the import savers, which allow them to pursue their domestic and overseas policies.

The philosophy of the Left is to intervene actively, up to the point of nationalisation and then not to leave it alone.

The philosophy of the Right is to leave the forces of competition – the market – to get things right, and for Government to act only to stop abuses; i.e. the passive rôle.

As always, the Central position – the middle ground – is best.

Well-chosen intervention certainly has a place because:

1 We live in a mixed economy. In the U.K. investment now is 50/50 Private/Public sectors.
2 Advancing technology leaves some old businesses high and dry, and some new ones where investors simply cannot follow them; e.g. Shipyards; Concorde; I.C.L.; R.R.
3 Shareholders have opted out of management renewal.
4 Regional problems have become dominant.

We certainly had experience of all these at I.R.C. and today, in policy-making, the ghost of I.R.C. is present in all these areas. But the Government has swung back to the middle of the road after its loop to the right. The I.D.E. takes the place of I.R.C. The Governor of the Bank of England sets up machinery to try to concentrate shareholder action on bum managements. The C.B.I. studies the rôle and duties of directors. We have active intervention in the regions and in very many industrial situations. The truth is quite simple: if the market forces worked perfectly there would be no need for intervention by I.R.C., I.D.E., C.B.I., B.E., or anyone else. Successful managements would get all the money they needed; unsuccessful companies would go bust, releasing resources for others – this achieved by what Marshall called "the higgling and bargaining in the market-place".

But the market does not work perfectly – it probably never has except, perhaps, for a short time at the end of the nineteenth century. Managements don't like perfect markets – they are always seeking defensive arrangements on price, design, markets, etc., and most countries have Monopoly legislation to stop this. Governments don't like perfect markets – witness tariff arrangements, export subsidies and "dirty floating". Trades Unions don't like perfect markets; witness the biggest pay rises where unemployment is highest.

In business strategy there are three areas where market forces are often frustrated:

1 Structure. Desirable mergers or de-mergers held up because no one could break the log-jam.
2 Investment. Necessary investment missing because of market anxiety.

3 Management Change. No one willing to shift bad management.

These are strategical issues which Labour hoped intervention would influence – and it did. With the swing of the pendulum Conservative Government shied away and left it all to the market. Now there is a return to:

1 The concept of industrial logic.

2 Recognition of the management problem.

3 Anxiety about investment.

4 Real worry about the regions.

I would hazard a guess that intervention in business by Government would increase rather than diminish. We have developed business characteristics of resistance to change, self-protection, immunisation from external disturbance which, if left to themselves, will make us less competitive *vis-a-vis* our international rivals.

Intervention can be indirect via the Companies Act: this is the best way – disclosure etc. It can be via the Bank of England; e.g., the Take-over Panel, and the shareholder enquiry. It can be direct like I.D.E. in the regions or nationally. In my judgement, all these have a part to play, which we will see before this Government is finished.

Chapter 16

THE MARKETING OF FINANCIAL SERVICES

Deryk V. Weyer
General Manager, Barclays Bank

In this chapter we examine the application of marketing concepts to financial services, and suggest ways in which the special characteristics of services, as against products, and the structure of the service institutions, affect the way in which marketing evolves.

Discussions relating the marketing concept to financial services are still relatively rare in business writing, but in a work of this length one can attempt only a broad surface survey. Because the marketing concept is still quite new in financial business, we start with a description of terms.

WHAT IS MARKETING?

Marketing is:

1 Identifying the most profitable markets now and in the future.
2 Assessing the present and future needs of customers.
3 Setting business development goals and making plans to meet them.
4 Managing the various services and promoting them to achieve the plans.

FINANCIAL NEEDS AND SERVICES

Money is a store of value, an instrument of value transfer, and a criterion by which the value of all scarce economic real resources are measured. Humans therefore, acting personally or as corporate bodies, have certain needs in relation to the money commodity. These needs are met by those who offer financial services. Broadly, these services are:

1 Advice.	5 Investment.
2 Deposits and Savings.	6 Insurance.
3 Loans.	7 Payments and Debt settlement.
4 Leasing.	8 Factoring.

Those institutions which offer the various services are not segregated into distinct groups. The various banks, finance service companies and professional practitioners all overlap in competing to offer financial services, so that any one group of institutions, say the Hire-Purchase and Finance companies, are competing amongst themselves and with outside groups – say, the Clearing Banks.

THE DEVELOPMENT OF THE MARKETING CONCEPT
Growth of New Services and Markets.

Until the Second World War financial-service companies generally operated limited markets, dealing with a small range of trading customers and a middle or higher social class of personal clients. The resources employed were very flexible, being mainly money itself. Only more recently have much less flexible resources of people, premises and machines been deployed on a huge scale. Where a financial service consists of commodity trading in money with a clearly defined group of customers and competitors, marketing is so simple in concept as to be dealt with intuitively. Often the main element in the mix is price (and dealing skill).

Even where the retailing of financial services was developing traditionally, the broad strategy as to segmentation was intuitively settled and business development was, to some extent, a matter of personal and social contacts. In some small sections of the market this remains the position. There have, however, been major and far-reaching changes over the last fifty years.

First, there has been a gradual development of the range of financial needs of trading customers. This has partly arisen through a much more scientific approach by management to the optimising of the use of money resources in the business. There have been other structural changes; for example, a move from labour to capital intensiveness, which has changed the borrowing needs. The old-time customer had strong inhibitions on borrowing and lending, and a deep product orientation. His financial need was mainly to pay his labour each week. He was very different from the modern multi-national company treasurer who requires a very wide range of services.

Secondly, in the field of personal financial services the market has broadened. Every year larger numbers of people accept income payments in book-money rather than in cash, and adopt new methods of borrowing and investment. Partly this is due to greater financial education, and the growth of disposable income in new market segments.

The growth of the personal finance, saving, deposit and money transfer business is continual. In particular the cultural pattern of thrift for its own sake, coupled with moral inhibitions on borrowing, is not universally seen as relevant by the new generations, who observe that thrift in traditional savings produces a real value depleted by inflation, and they lean more heavily on consumer credit.

These broad historic trends have produced a new need for marketing expertise in the institutions that are catering for them. Moreover, since large and flexible resources of people, premises, machines and automated systems have now to be committed, particularly in those competing in the retail field, the need for a thought-out segmentation strategy becomes apparent. Once the strategy is settled, all elements in the marketing mix come into use. Price, in traditional money markets – and in wholesale banking today – the prime weapon, declines in importance in retail markets. Selling, advertising, channels, sites, all are more important.

Management of the mix on professional marketing lines becomes essential and both the strategy and the management must be based on objective analysis and market research, as an aid to, but not a replacement for, intuitive judgement.

These developments have produced a new emphasis on management, and challenged some very traditional management attitudes, particularly in the older institutions dealing mainly in credit.

In such institutions, a banker was a man who lent money at risk for profit. He still is, but he is having to learn other skills; the general management of resources and the marketing of services. From a product and technical orientation all institutions are moving to a stronger market and profit bias. This is the institutional change of the last few years, which has not been so revolutionary in the newer institutions (e.g. the finance houses, Unit Trust management), which were born into the retail business and the marketing era, as in the traditional institutions, for example the Clearing Banks, the insurance companies, where the development is dramatic.

Traditional Constraints.
Government. In the provision of all forms of credit there has been severe inhibition and distortion in marketing strategy which only in the last year has been removed.

It is impossible to disentangle the provision of private and commercial credit from the operation of the monetary system. The level of credit is one of many factors which influences demand and supply of goods, prices, imports, exports and the balance of payments. It is one factor in the inflation or deflation of the currency. Therefore, the monetary authorities have a proper interest in the volume of credit and such was the condition of the U.K. economy up to 1970 that marketing initiative was inhibited by restriction, and marketing strategy, in selecting areas of growth, was distorted from profit to community objectives. Consumer credit and property finance, prime sectors for marketing initiative, had low national priority. Exporters were favoured by the community as borrowers, but exporters are not necessarily those who will show their providers of financial services the greatest profit growth and market stability. Some may, some may not.

There have thus been times when the major providers of credit, particularly the Clearing Banks, have been unable to develop a marketing strategy worth the name. All this is ended, at least temporarily, and each institution can pursue its objectives with some freedom. Nevertheless, financial services are an area in which initiatives are more likely than most to be constrained by community considerations, because of the particular relationship between the volume of credit and the working of the monetary system.

Risk and Managerial Attitude. In any business which does not obtain cash for its products at the point of sale, there is a credit risk, and the leasing of money contains a special degree of risk. Goods sold or leased on credit can be recovered on default (in somewhat depreciated form no doubt), but money is so flexible and homogeneous as to be rapidly dispersed. The whole credit business therefore can be expressed as buying risks. Moreover, the profit on the deal comes from an extended time relationship, rather than at once at point of sale. Small wonder that Credit Managers, whether in branch banks or otherwise, find it hard to reconcile an aggressive marketing attitude with their rôle as buyers of risk. However, if the risk can be lowered or controlled, either by the provision of better information, or by the creation of disciplined formal loan schemes, the financial services manager will be prepared to market them more positively.

Apart from the question of risk, management attitude may be affected by the fact that many of the credit institutions straddle various markets. It is not easy for the manager in a bank dealing with the wholesale money markets, with very large individual customers, perhaps other international banks, to appreciate the marketing techniques needed in the retail field. To this extent, those institutions which supply all the various credit markets are having to stream their managements, so that those dealing with retail business for consumers are orientated specifically towards those markets, and not to the more specialist segments of, say, wholesale banking.

CHARACTERISTICS OF COMPANIES IN THE FINANCIAL SERVICES INDUSTRIES

The Nature of Services.

There are some characteristics of services as against products which relate to the nature of the services themselves.

The Intangibility and Non-visual Aspects of Services. Unlike most products, services are intangible, cannot easily be felt, seen or smelt. They are difficult to describe; they may embrace a quite complicated concept, e.g. a bank account, an insurance-linked unit-trust investment; they often involve a continuing relationship. Financial services therefore tend to have little visual appeal. This weakens the power of advertising and the other visual promotions. Financial services are less appealing to the senses and emotions than to reason, which is well known to be less powerful as a spur to human endeavour than appeals to warmth, security, sex, love and the family. Services therefore are less susceptible to impulse buying and there are many periods when demand for them is at a low level. All this reduces the part played in the mix of impulse-stimulating promotions, such as advertising and mail drops, and puts personal selling and commendation at a premium.

Non-standardisation of Product. Similarly, services are often in the form of completely non-standard "products". Not only does this inhibit description and concept advertising, it can reduce price comparability – and often price competition, putting weight on other parts of the marketing mix, personal representation and outlets.

Since the services are often so intangible, non-standard, and technical in content as compared with a basic consumer product, the emphasis in selling is not surprisingly on the seller's integrity and personal recommendation. The buyer has to have confidence in the seller's recommendation, since there is no way he can clearly check by demonstration that the "product" works. Indeed, in a sense the end product is manufactured at the point of sale.

Some services however (the credit card is one) are more tangible, more visual and reasonably standardised. Again consumer credit has a quite high basic demand, so some impulse promotion is viable in this field.

The non-standardisation of money services makes comparison between competing providers difficult, and this makes for a low propensity by buyers to shop around, and a high "brand loyalty" to one institution.

Risk Factors for the Buyer. In the case of some financial services, e.g. savings, deposit accounts, and other forms of investment, one must return to the risk factor, but from the buyer's point of view. In many of the retail institutions, selling ways of storing funds, the emphasis is not so much on price, though it has its importance, but very strongly on safety, liquidity and accessibility.

Industrial Structure.

Companies operating financial services may tend to have certain structural characteristics which affect their marketing.

Labour Intensiveness. They are usually labour-intensive, and their labour has tended to be inflexible, both as to terms of employment and adaptability. The pattern of the more traditional units, for example the Clearing Banks, is that their labour costs are partly long-term career people, who are industrially immobile, and whose numbers cannot much be varied with the volume of business. Some of the less traditional businesses, finance companies, unit trusts, are more flexible in labour usage, but all are characterised by high overheads, which tend to dictate a marketing strategy aimed at high volume. In retail banking and finance this is leading to a widening of services.

Capital Intensiveness. Some units in the sector providing financial services, particularly the retailers, are becoming also capital-intensive, particularly in handling money transfer. This again tends to lead to a volume-maximisation policy, to secure marginal income, since the greatest costs are those of automated installation, systems development and premises.

Size. Because of the capital input required, the complexity of money handling systems, and the very big individual risks, some financial-services industries tend towards an oligopolistic structure. Certainly in branch banking, retail insurance, and increasingly in the finance-company business, there are few suppliers and millions of buyers. In this situation price becomes a less important part of the mix; as between so few competitors economic forces prevent one from being out of line for long. The tendency is to compete by other means; service standards, convenience, accessibility and availability of credit. Of course, in wholesale banking, price is a major factor, but in the retail industries industrial structure and market pressures militate against price competition, and increase the importance of other marketing methods.

Pressures to Standardise. In spite of the traditional non-standardisation of financial services, the tendency at the retail end of the business – finance companies, branch banks – is towards some uniformity. In a process which employs automated systems "one off" products of a luxury nature (such as a hand-produced bank statement) are very expensive to provide. Only with specialised units, the wholesale and merchant banks, with small, highly flexible resources, can flourish on special products for a small range of customers with "one off" needs.

The Resources Mix. To understand how and why individual groups of institutions develop different marketing methods, it is necessary to examine the breakdown of resources they use. Wholesale banks use flexible but volatile and expensive time deposits, and comparatively small fixed resources of people, premises and systems. Clearing Banks use more stable and very cheap demand and short-term deposits and very large inputs of people, premises and computers. Their fixed overheads are very high, their variable costs comparatively low.

MARKETING STRATEGY

Research. In financial services valid research techniques into market selection, market needs, and customer attitudes, are still undeveloped. It is possible and helpful for a Clearing Bank or finance company to analyse the socio-economic characteristics of existing and new personal customers, and their relative growth and profitability. It is also worthwhile carefully to research into the best prospects for the siting of new branches, in relation to growth, customer habits, service usage, etc.

It is much more difficult to achieve any valid results from research in the corporate sector, on what services companies now use, what do they want and which institutions are they using. Even so, some work is possible and useful, and studies of the structural growth and decline of industries are valuable.

Generally in the corporate market one is dealing with tailor-made services for non-standard customers; and such research as there is tends therefore to be personal and intuitive, non-objective. Analytical research tends to be disappointing as a basis for strategic decisions.

Again, research into personal customers' or potential customers' attitudes to various institutions and their services tends to be a little barren as a decision base, partly because all attitude research on potential users is, in a sense, hypothetical, and partly because services are so intangible and have so low an emotional impact that the potential user finds it difficult to make judgements about his preferences.

Segmentation. In choosing its segmentation policy each institution must isolate its market strengths in particular customer groups, and its resources weaknesses.

The market strengths of a Clearing Bank are its wide retail penetration, its intelligence network and the standing of its branch managers, coupled with its commanding position in the money transfer business.

On the other hand, it may be badly equipped to deal with special individual financing problems by reason of the lack of special expertise, by the relative inflexibilities inseparable from size and by the standardisation of its procedures and systems.

A hire-purchase company's marketing strength is its penetration at point of sale in consumer financing, where it cannot yet be matched by the branch banks, and its skill in handling instalment credit.

Some segmentation trends can be discerned. The Clearing Banks are widening their segment, tackling users of a wider range of services. They are biting into the consumer-credit industry and into merchant banking. They are widening their international activities.

Finance companies and wholesale banks can, in turn, encroach into the Clearing Bank heartland of money transfer and general retail credit, but the capital resources and market penetration to succeed in the retail field are very great. No one is likely, in fact, to venture into automated money transfer, unless already established there.

Strategic Choices. One may sum up by defining the first strategic task. It is to make a choice between markets to attack. This choice will be governed by identified market needs and by:

(a) The company's market penetration.

(b) Growth potential.

(c) Short-term profit.

(d) Stability.

(e) Available skills and resources.

(f) Risk.

THE MANAGEMENT OF THE MARKETING MIX

Of What Does the Mix Consist?

(a) Pricing.

(b) Packaging, brand naming, etc.

(c) The service concept.

(d) Advertising and other promotions.

(e) Personal representatives (selling).

(f) Channels or outlets.

Individual Parts of the Mix.

Pricing. The importance of price in financial-service industries varies considerably. It is important in the international currency exchanges which are money commodity markets but, for instance, in consumer credit, price as reflected in the interest rate is less important than the required repayment. Users in the U.K. do not shop around much between banks for the cheapest rate. However, in corporate lending and wholesale banking price is clearly crucial. In certain highly specialised service fields such as the professions, in trust work, and perhaps in some aspects of merchant banking, the price of the service is one of the less important aspects.

There are pricing problems in service industries in terms of acceptability of the price to the buyer. In a mass market, where there is no face-to-face dialogue between buyer and seller, some form of tariff is desirable, as a means of communication.

But how does one fix a standard tariff for a non-standard product, particularly when there are also problems of product inter-relationship? The banking current account is a mixture of money custody and payment facilities, and it is not easy to find the right mixture of rebate of interest to cover transactions and actual charges. The trend, however, may be for a reduction in "trade-offs" between charges and balances.

Pricing is highly complex in service industries and is often a less important part of the mix than it is thought to be.

Packaging and Brand Naming. In the corporate market for financial services brand naming is of little importance; one is dealing with a sophisticated buyer in a non-standard product, and the deal is done between technicians who are not much interested in brand names.

In the personal market, however, brand naming and packaging can have great advantages. They help to provide visual stimuli and brand loyalty. The retail-service industries increasingly tend to use design themes, visual symbols, slogans, and to brand name their particular schemes. This is valid marketing, particularly where there is little other product differentiation.

An illustration of the use of brand names in a banking service that has more visual appeal than most is the Credit Card. When Barclaycard was launched in 1966, it posed for Barclays Bank a number of marketing problems including the attitude of managers to a very aggressive selling campaign, but the clearly identifiable blue and yellow plastic with the brand name was a great help to the launch. Since then Barclays has used its name to label a whole range of services, e.g. Barclaycard, Barclayloan, Barclaybond, and so on – a clear example of brand-naming policy in banking.

The Service Concept.   This is what the customer actually gets and the marketing man must match his concept precisely to his market. A highly professional advisory service can be tailored so as to meet the needs of the client. A merchant bank, with a small but flexible staff, can give an individual and specialised service to a narrow but profitable market. For a retail institution, say a Unit Trust management, a Clearing Bank in the personal market, a large insurance company with many branches, such an approach to the service concept is difficult in profit terms. Such an institution adopts a standardised approach to reach a mass market, and the service concept offered must match that market and live up to the terms of the offer. It need not be a luxury product, but at its level it must work efficiently.

Advertising and Other Promotional Methods.   We have mentioned that financial services lack visual and emotional appeal, and that basic demand is often low. Only at those times when it is high can stimulus be provided by advertising, to persuade buyers to use a particular institution. At other times advertising and other promotional efforts, such as direct mail, canvassing, are probably to some extent a waste of money. It is no surprise that at least two of the Clearing Banks devote the majority of their expenditure on media advertising to the student market and to the range of socio-economic groups, C1, C2, 16–25 years of age, who are at the point of entry to the banking system, and actually need accounts.

A further reason for concentrating at the point of entry is

that the buyer of services tends to be immobile, and does not switch easily his brand loyalty.

Another function in advertising is to cross-sell a wider range of services to existing customers, and to build the image of the integrity and authority of the institution in the market.

Except for those services in which a coupon response can. be measured (e.g. credit cards), the value of advertising remains difficult to quantify, and simply provides a backcloth for the more powerful efforts of the personal representative.

Representatives and Personal Selling. The prime part of the marketing mix in any service industry is personal activity by, say, the finance house representative, the bank manager, the unit trust representative, the insurance inspector, and major promotional effort should be directed to the attitude and training of these people. The rôle of the individual has to be accepted as a highly authoritative and technical form of salesmanship.

There are other problems of representation which one can briefly mention. One is the relationship between specialist and generalist. To what extent should a bank manager or an insurance manager be a generalist? To what extent should he specialise, either by market or by "product"? There has to be some balance between the retail point of sale and the specialised knowledge centre. Specialised knowledge centres cannot be housed at every retail point of sale and there has, in that sense, to be a two-tier system of service, in the longer term.

Another question is the extent to which the more traditional industries will follow others in calling on customers and non-customers. One can foresee that calling by bankers on customers and non-customers, already the practice of other financial industries, will develop, especially as banks are anxious to expand lending, but one prerequisite of the development of soliciting for credit business is a better public information service about individual and corporate creditworthiness. Cold calling is risky in businesses offering credit.

Retail Outlets and Channels.
Network Sizes. There are many units in the service industries that do not require a network of retail outlets. Merchant banks generally avoid them. The finance houses generally require small networks; the building societies ever-growing networks,

because that is their main method of competition in gathering deposits; the insurance companies have networks of varying size and, of course, the Clearing Banks, perhaps, have the largest networks of all.

Whatever the size of the network, its strategic distribution amongst areas of growth in the country is vital, and it must cover its rapidly increasing overheads. Turnover must, therefore, be maximised. The banks are meeting diversified needs by extending their range of services and competing more and more with the building societies and the finance companies to secure marginal income. It remains to be seen whether this new drive into the consumer field will make a number of branch banks profitable that are not viable now.

Design. It is through retail outlets that the main manifestation of a company's corporate image is seen, so design here is particularly important to marketing, and most of the retail financial institutions have moved their corporate designs away from the "Portland stone security image". Their difficulty is in finding a style attractive to all their varied customer groups.

Accessibility. Another aspect of retail financial outlets is the accessibility they offer in hours of business. It is arguable, for instance, that the Clearing Banks offer hours of accessibility unreleated to their markets. It was thought traditionally that the Clearing Bank customer market was professional and clerical; office hours were appropriate. Latterly it has become clear that the only customers really concerned about the opening hours of the banks are the personal customers, since others are satisfied generally with the existing pattern.

For the personal customer a bank is a money shop and a pattern of shop hours might be more appropriate.

SUMMARY

In this short survey, one has tried only to pose the fundamental questions about how a service industry directs itself to its market.

Every institution has marketing strengths and weaknesses. It seeks to avoid those situations where it has fundamental weaknesses and develop those situations where it is strong. The strengths of a retail institution are essentially market penetration; the strengths of a specialised wholesale organisation are probably a high degree of technical expertise in a narrow field.

Undoubtedly, the concept of marketing in relation to financial services is valid, yet it is different in application to the marketing of more tangible products.

Chapter 17

THE FINANCIAL INSTITUTIONS

AND THE CONSUMER

Andreas Whittam Smith
Editor, "The Investors' Chronicle"

Today the consumer feels a pressing need for advice in the financial sphere. The situation is, I think, very serious. It is, indeed, a crisis. With 270 unit trusts to choose from, with innumerable life policies to assess, with a multitude of national-savings schemes to consider, with the building societies complicating matters by offering products which have an insurance link, with this and that bank-borrowing plan, the consumer desperately needs guidance. Otherwise he can so easily buy the wrong product, take on more or less life assurance than he needs, buy the wrong type of unit trusts for his children, earn less than he could on surplus funds, blunder into a property-bond scheme which turns into a Gramco-type debacle. Now that sort of situation is clearly in nobody's interests. The last development the financial institutions want is one where customers feel vaguely cheated, vaguely oversold, get the feeling they have made an expensive and possibly irreversible mistake. The reaction could be very savage.

So what I want to discuss in this chapter is the way the need for financial advice has grown because more and more people have had the resources to buy financial products, because those products have become more complex and because the financial markets have become, in intensity of sales pitch, much more like the markets for soap flakes or breakfast foods than they used to be. I then want to look at the traditional sources of advice, finding that for a variety of reasons they are badly equipped to cope. I refer here to bank managers, solicitors, accountants, stockbrokers and insurance brokers. Finally, I would like to suggest some ways in which the vacuum could be filled.

The figures which plot the growth in business transacted by ordinary consumers with the financial institutions are pretty startling. You can look at the amounts of money lodged with various kinds of financial institutions or – which I find more interesting – the increase in the number of transactions. First of all the monetary figures. The total premium income of the life-assurance companies in 1966 was some £610 million. In 1970 it was over £800 million. Deposit accounts with the building societies show a similar growth with just over £1,000 million inflow during 1967 compared with nearly £1,500 million in 1971. The National Savings figures are not so good but still impressive: the general public had lodged £8,360 million with the National Savings movement at the end of 1965, £9,200 million at the end of 1971. As far as current accounts or deposit accounts with the Clearing Banks go, the growth has been from roughly £7,500 million in 1966 to nearly £11,000 million at the end of last year. Net new investment with the unit trusts fluctuates in line with stock-market conditions, but the average monthly intake was running at £6 million in 1964, reaching over £40 million per month in the early part of 1969 and was still running at over £10 million per month recently.

I have also looked at transactions. There were just under one million life-insurance policies in force, not including industrial branch contracts, at the end of 1960. That figure was 60% higher by the end of 1970. The number of deposit accounts with the building societies multiplied from around four million in 1960 to over ten million at the end of 1970. The rise in the number of individual unit-trust accounts was from one million to two and a half million over the 1960s. And the number of private bank accounts has been expanding by about 5% per annum pretty steadily over the past decade. It is estimated that fifteen million people have bank accounts at the present time. Let nobody, therefore, underestimate either the size of the need for financial advice or the rapidity with which it has grown.

If the sheer number of people involved in the savings market has increased many times in the past decade or so, so has the complexity of the products which are on sale. It is quite an effort of mind, indeed, to think back to, say, 1960 and consider what developments there have been since then. Looking at the life-assurance and unit-trust fields together, notable developments have been the emergence of the unit-linked policy, the discovery that property could form the entire basis of a savings proposition and more recently, as people have come to realise the merits of the widest possible flexibility, the concept of the managed fund. In 1966, for instance, only 2% of new life premium-income was represented by unit-linked policies. Within just two years that figure had risen to 15%. Now over seventy life offices offer equity-linked contracts. The first property bond appeared on the scene in 1966. But it was not really until 1969 that property bonds began to feature strongly in the savings market. On occasions since then they have actually outsold conventional unit trusts.

In the national-savings field the biggest development for many years was the introduction of Save as You Earn schemes in the 1969 Budget. These provide a very attractive rate of interest – if you are a standard taxpayer and if you complete the whole five to seven-year course. Most readers are very familiar now with the S.A.Y.E. idea. But consider how relatively sophisticated a concept it is. Now let us consider the building societies and banks.

Once upon a time, of course, you simply left money on deposit with your local building society or bank at the going rate, which bore a reasonably close relationship with bank rate. It was really very simple. But today your building society will be trying to sell you a dauntingly wide range of products. They offer you Save as You Earn schemes, they offer links with insurance companies, they offer products described as growth bonds. The latter appear in the promotional literature in terms more appropriate to Ordinary shares than to traditional building-society products with their emphasis on high immediate income. As for the banks, the customer must now accustom himself to think in terms of a base rate, to realise that banks may not in future change their deposit rates by the same amount, in the same direction, on the same day. And if you want to borrow, no longer should you add two or three points to Bank rate in order to calculate what you will be charged. Now the rate of interest has to be worked out by sophisticated mathematics which tells you the true rate of interest. And the ordinary consumer of financial products is bound to want to do the sums again because the answers come out so high.

So far I have argued that the consumer rather desperately needs good financial advice today. This need has grown as more and more people have reached a position in which they can afford to buy financial products and because the products themselves have become much more sophisticated. Later on I am going to argue that what is needed is not only specialists able to say which are the best products in certain areas but advisers who can look across the whole field; who can, in the modern phrase, provide a financial planning service. The latter is still found very rarely and only then for wealthy people.

Meanwhile I would like to add a further three reasons why the poor consumer so much needs guidance. In the first place, the savings market has the unusual characteristic that it is often hard to find the price tag on the product. It is notorious how secretive the Clearing Banks are about the way in which their charges are calculated. Newspapers have actually had to put teams of top investigative journalists on to the problem. But there are many other examples. The returns available on various national-savings schemes are expressed in terms which appear simple to the consumer. For instance, I find the following guidance in some notes on National Savings Certificates issued by the authorities. It says that the decimal Savings Certificate, costing £1 a unit, will be worth £1·25 in four years and is free of income, surtax and capital gains tax. There follow details of what the certificate is worth at the end of each of years one to four. But how many people could rapidly translate this information in terms of grossed-up redemption yields, which is, at least, one basis upon which you should compare returns from various fixed-interest media. I am not suggesting that school curricula should be redesigned so that every citizen can do such sums. But there is a need for sources of advice where the significance of such calculations is recognised.

To take an example from the unit-trust movement: how do the charges which one trust makes compare with those of another? If you read the small print and do a few back-of-the-envelope calculations you can find out. But how do the charges which life assurance companies make compare? How much commission do they concede on particular policies? What is the front-end loading? Of course, as these questions reveal, the whole idea of a price for a product begins to lose all meaning with insurance policies; it is not really an appropriate concept. It is not a question of looking hard for the price tag and you will find it. There isn't one. This characteristic seems to me to make the savings market a particularly difficult one for the consumer.

Second, potential buyers of certain savings products are forced into making a forecast about the future. If you are buying a unit trust, or a with-profits life policy, or a property bond, one question which has to be asked is whether Institution A is likely to prove more adept at managing one's funds over the next five years, ten years, twenty years, perhaps even over a life time, than Institution B. We all know that such a question cannot be answered satisfactorily, and yet the choice between institutions has to be made. The poor consumer is not equipped to do this on his own.

Thirdly, I must mention the enormous effort which is made to persuade consumers into buying particular financial products. The cold figures of how much money is spent by financial institutions in advertising are startling enough – indeed they pay my salary as a journalist.

Last year nearly £22 million was spent on financial advertising by local authorities looking for deposits, by building societies after the same commodity, by companies extolling their virtues to shareholders, by finance houses also looking for deposits, by insurance companies selling policies, by all varieties of bank seeking business, by unit trusts, by credit-card companies, by the sponsors of new issues. Some of this is not precisely saving-market promotion. But even if you refine these figures you are left with an enormous total. Here are some more figures. In January and February 1972 alone, the unit trusts spent £600,000 selling their wares. The insurance companies spent nearly £900,000. Altogether financial advertising was running 77% higher in January and February 1972 compared with the same period of 1971.

A more graphic way of seeing what is involved is to take any recent issue of a daily newspaper. In the one I picked the first page advertised an income plan returning 26·62% interest in three years. What's that in terms of real money, it asks? Turn to the next page and you are told that "the managed bond is a great investment concept". Another tells you to watch your money grow in one of Britain's leading building societies. Then there is the sobering thought from one life-assurance company that "you may not be around for tomorrow's sobering thought". Then there is a master plan for making money. And so it goes on, page after page. Three cheers we say in the publishing business, but spare a thought for the bewildered consumer. Indeed, as I said at the beginning, the savings market is not so much different from the market for soap powders or breakfast foods. There is the same high spending on promotion, the same false differentiation of product, the same liking for gimmicks, the same extensive research into consumer preferences.

Against this background, then, how do the traditional providers of financial advice measure up? I would like to start with the Clearing Banks because it is to the local branch manager that many people first turn when they have a financial decision to make. I think it is fair to say that until very recently advice about the savings market was provided in a very haphazard way. What you got varied from manager to manager. If it was an enquiry about shares to buy or sell, then the bank simply acted as a go-between linking the customer with a stockbroker. In many cases the result was a distressingly thin opinion, scarcely related to the customer's needs or hopes. Where other expertises were required, then experts outside the bank were suggested. Even now bank managers get very little formal training in assessing the savings market, though the subject does get covered from time to time on management courses. But I must stress that I do not want to write down the banks' older way of doing savings business too far. There have always been a lot of bank managers who have educated themselves into giving all-round sound advice.

Now the situation is changing. The talk is about financial supermarkets and one-stop banking. The banks' trustee departments have been revamped and now provide an investment advice service which is considerably better than it was. Similarly the banks handle tax problems with aplomb. More dramatic, though, has been their move into insurance broking, which provides the bank manager with independent competitive advice and competitive quotations which can be passed on to the customer.

All of this is impressive and why should anyone find these developments less than satisfactory? The trouble is that the bank manager is having to become something of a salesman. It seems sensible, of course, if you are always being asked about stocks and shares to set up your own unit trust. But is the big British public much better off if the bank manger turns from being a staging post for stockbrokers' advice to being a salesman for his own bank's unit trusts? Will we not see the same logic being applied to insurance? The Clearing Banks might quite easily decide not only to engage in insurance broking but also in writing insurance business themselves. Then the bank manager will find himself selling with-profits insurance policies as well as unit trusts. One can put the same point a different way. There is a sense in which the bank manager is becoming something like a modern general practitioner. In both cases the emphasis is upon handing anything out of the ordinary over to specialists. I would not presume to argue the pros and cons of this in medical terms but it leaves me with the feeling that the banks will not in fact prove to be a prime source of independent advice for consumers in the savings field over the coming years; rather they will be found largely in the ranks of those with products to sell. As the Clearing Banks, with their huge networks, are quite easily the best-placed organisation in the country to provide the sort of independent advice I think is needed, I find this prospect dispiriting.

I turn more briefly to two other sources of financial advice – solicitors and accountants. My whole feeling about the solicitors' rôle in this market is summed up by an opinion expressed recently in the *New Law Journal*. They wrote – "It is impossible to gauge how much money solicitors are responsible for or how they go about investing it, but no one would be surprised if the sum exceeded £1,000 million. The methods they employ in handling it are often rudimentary. To say this", the article went on, "is not uncomplimentary: investment developed a degree of sophistication in the Sixties that put anybody handling money as a by-product of his professional practice at a considerable disadvantage." There it all is – solicitors *are* much used to provide financial advice but they are no longer equipped to perform the rôle adequately. Of course some firms of solicitors have allowed members of their staff to specialise in the investment

area and one or two City firms have actually appointed investment managers. But the law is a full-time business, itself changing all the time and requiring very full-time attention from its
practitioners. I cannot believe that lawyers can or should aim
to provide a proper financial advice and planning service. They
do not, indeed, seem likely to fill the vacuum which I have
described.

The accountancy profession is, on the face of it, more
promising. In the booklet published by the Institute of Chartered
Accountants there is a section entitled "financial advice",
where it is stated that "many people need help and guidance in
planning their personal affairs, whether or not they also have
business problems. A chartered accountant who knows about
your finances, taxation position and family problems is well
placed to give such advice" – an excellent beginning, though it
is amusing that family circumstances should be described as
"problems". The booklet goes on to promise that accountants
can help with estate-duty planning, with investments and
insurance. The chartered accountant may advise you to employ
insurance brokers, it says, "but you would be wise to consult
him first before you commit yourself to any insurance policy if
a knowledge of your capital, income or taxation position is
relevant". Again, most excellent sentiments are expressed here.
The trouble is that one knows that many firms of accountants
have neglected to provide financial-planning services of the
type I have just described. The Institute admits this, commenting
in another booklet on the subject: "much financial-planning
work that might well have been undertaken by chartered
accountants has passed into other hands." Quite so. Indeed, I
believe that accountants are in somewhat the same situation as
solicitors. You cannot run financial-planning facilities as a side-
line unless you are a very big firm indeed. And then the charges
will make sense only for reasonably substantial private
customers.

I must next tackle the insurance brokers, or more specifically
the life-insurance brokers. They operate in the middle of the
savings market, selling not products but advice. They operate
at all levels of sophistication all over the country. They should
be exactly what I am looking for – but they are not. They are,
first of all, specialists, and quite often particularly narrow

specialists. One should make a distinction between the good insurance brokers and the less than good ones. Some idea of what I mean by this distinction can be gauged from the fact that whereas 1,600 firms belong to the well-established bodies of insurance brokers, with another 350 in a new grouping, many, many firms belong to no professional body at all. They come into the field with a minimum of training. Even the senior professional bodies do not insist on examination qualifications, though it is fair to say that entrants are rigorously screened. Now the good firms, which is practically the same thing as saying the bigger firms, offer personal financial-planning services, covering the whole savings field. And they avoid the criticism that can be levelled at the smaller firms – that is, they do genuinely assess the whole of the life-insurance market for their customers, even going to the lengths of using computers to make comparisons between a wide range of products at any one time. The smaller firms, however, are driven by commission-rate structures, and by habit and background, into using only a segment of the life-assurance market for their customers.

This brings me to one of the weaknesses of the insurance brokers as a sector from whom independent financial advice can be expected. The fact is that the insurance broker looks largely, often entirely, to the insurance company whose products he sells for his remuneration. It would be unfair to call him a salesman. He is indeed less of a salesman than the bank manager. But he has a closer relationship with the sellers than one would like.

You cannot level this criticism against the stockbroker so easily, though while he takes commission from his clients for the Stock-Exchange business which he transacts on their behalf, he may well receive commission from insurance companies or unit trusts for any of their products which he sells.

Again, though, the stockbroker is specialised, reckoning to devote the great bulk of his talents to Stock-Exchange business. Most firms will give advice on other financial matters, particularly those which have devoted a good deal of attention to constructing an effective private clients' department. But unfortunately the main fact about stock-broking in general is that, as far as member firms of the London Stock Exchange go as opposed to country broking firms, private-client business is *not* attractive business. Costs, particularly City rents, have risen so fast that the private clients get much less in the way of personal attention than used to be the case ten or fifteen years ago. And the likelihood is that matters will get worse. This is because commission rates on institutional business look bound to fall, as they have in New York. As big business subsidises little business, it is clear that the final result will be that the economics of stockbroking will move further against the smaller private client. Luckily, this trend is not so pronounced outside London, but everywhere the threat is the same.

It is time to recap. I have tried to show that the consumer needs a great deal of guidance in his dealings with the financial institutions. Their products are complex and sophisticated and they are sold hard. The consumer, however, cannot easily find all the guidance which he needs under a single roof. Where he can, it is either not independent enough, as in the case of the banks which sell products as well as advice, or it is expensive, as in the case where a professional firm offers a specific financial-planning service. Moreover, I think that the financial institutions should think carefully about the implications of this situation. As the Clearing Banks have found in the public's reaction to Saturday closing and increased banking charges, it is possible to attract hostility from one's customers. Perhaps the very high redemptions recently of unit-trusts holdings are part of an increasing disenchantment.

There is therefore a vacuum and it needs to be filled. I can only offer the briefest suggestions on how. I believe that of the five types of financial adviser I have mentioned the best equipped to widen their range of expertise and so organise themselves that they can advise ordinary people economically are life insurance brokers and stockbrokers. Should they each invade the other's territory or should they be allowed to merge and form firms which are more broadly based than at present? The technical difficulties confronting such a course are real but not insurmountable, given goodwill by official bodies on both sides. Something along these lines at least ought to be considered.

Chapter 18

THE FINANCIAL INSTITUTIONS
AND SMALL FIRMS

John E. Bolton

Chairman and Managing Director,
Solartron Electronic Group

The findings of the Committee of Inquiry on Small Firms high-
lighted the vital importance of the small-firm sector, in both
economic and social terms, and the dangers to the future of free
enterprise in Britain inherent in the sector's present state of
decline. In this chapter I would like to summarise the findings
of the research work which was commissioned to provide a
basis for a discussion of the key contribution needed from the
financial institutions in ensuring the future viability of the small-
firm sector.

THE IMPORTANCE OF SMALL FIRMS

In economic terms, the main findings of the research programme undertaken for the Committee of Inquiry on Small
Firms are as follows:

1 There are more than $1\frac{1}{4}$ million small firms in the United
   Kingdom, i.e. more than 95% of all firms. *N.B.* – Low-size
   cut-off point for statistics.

2 They create 19% of Gross National Product or, put another
   way, Gross National Product has to be created – by enterprise – out of sweat, toil and tears, 24% of the output of the
   private sector.

3 They employ 29% of the entire working population, i.e. they
   employ over seven million people, or more than the whole of
   the public sector.

4 Yet they are almost wholly unresearched and devoid of stat-

istical information – eighteen Research Reports necessary to fill the gap even partially.

5 Contrary to some folklore, they are at least as efficient as large firms in the use of total resources: less efficient utilisation of labour, more efficient use of capital, plus important rôle as specialist suppliers in virtually all industries; essential part of total U.K. production effort; most efficient size of operation where optimum small and requiring flexibility and speed of decisions. Moreover, they make a vital contribution, both directly and indirectly, to exports and the balance of payments. (*N.B.* – Study of the Department of Trade and Industry in North-West.)

6 They are an important source of innovation and of new industries. Innovation stems from small groups, e.g. the Hovercraft, printed circuits, the Moulton bicycle, the miniskirt were all produced by small businesses.

Finally, small firms provide necessary competition for the established order and ensure a more balanced industrial structure, thus contributing most importantly to the efficiency and vitality of the free-enterprise system.

Mr. N. Ridley, a former Minister for Small Firms, referred to the problem of technological unemployment and the need for small firms to take up the slack, rather than force workers back into service industries out of which S.E.T. was supposed to squeeze them! The unemployment problem would be largely solved if half of $1\frac{1}{4}$ million small firms or even the top one-quarter of them each took on one extra person.

In social terms, small businessmen are usually the pillars of local community life, making a vital contribution to local government and voluntary bodies. Also they improve the quality of life by ensuring adequate consumer choice, providing service and preserving the spirit of independence so important to the British way of life.

Then, small firms provide stable and satisfying employment for the large individualistic sector of our population, and their lower labour turnover acts as a stabiliser in an increasingly volatile occupational climate.

Finally, they are a means of entry and a training ground for new entrepreneurial talent.

But the small-firm sector is steadily declining both in numbers and in share of national output and employment – further than in other industrial countries. This decline may have reached serious proportions and if it continues unabated a point will undoubtedly be reached at which the small-firm sector will be unable to fulfil the essential functions I have mentioned.

However, it is impossible to be clear about this yet, because the statistics do not exist to enable effective measurements to be made and also because of the time lags involved, e.g. in new tax measures taking effect. Death duties involve a time lag of up to a generation.

MAJOR PROBLEMS

The major problems facing small firms as a whole are:

1 A hostile environment, resulting largely from the "benign", i.e. not intentional neglect of successive Governments.

2 The impact of inflation and progressive taxation leading to a very tight cash position – in old type of squeeze, small firms bottom of pile – especially true in 1969.

3 There are unfair burdens imposed by a wide range of legislation and by Government paperwork, both affecting small firms differentially more than large firms, e.g. paperwork load on small firms four times that on large firms.

4 Growing and often unfair competition – particularly monopoly buying power and the extraction by large customers of lengthy credit.

5 The problem was that of hitherto having no focal point in Government, or effective co-ordinated lobby outside, to represent their legitimate interests.

6 A serious "information gap" in spite of the plethora of advisory services available, a confusion of sources – with small firms not knowing where to turn for the most appropriate advice.

RECOMMENDATIONS

Our main areas of recommendations were aimed at:

1 Closing the Policy Gap via a new Small-Firms Division of the Department of Trade and Industry, reporting to a Minister

for Small Firms, plus a small-firms specialist in every other Department of Government, together able to ensure that the health of the sector could be systematically monitored, industry by industry, and as between different geographical areas of the country and to enable effective co-ordination of all Government policy affecting small firms – a watchdog rôle to ensure that the legitimate interests of small firms never again go by default. Also, we suggested a review of Government purchasing policy, and of the effects of entering the E.E.C.

2 Closing the information gap by means of a network of Small Firms Advisory Bureaux, located in each major town and providing a "sign-posting and referral" information service. Really "information bureaux", complementary to existing facilities and essential as "fibre roots" to provide real contact between new Small Firms Division and small firms at ground level.

In addition, our lengthy Report, plus the eighteen accompanying Research Reports, dealing with specific industries or areas of problems, together provide a much needed basic source of information about the small-firm sector. Nevertheless, much research still remains to be done; we could only scratch the surface.

Finally, we sought to relieve many of the unfair burdens via sixty or more recommendations aimed at solving specific problems, i.e. putting to rights the neglect of small firms in the past. There were nine in the area of organisation in Government, a further six relating to management skills and advisory services, thirteen covering the vital area of taxation, one major recommendation on industrial training, fifteen concerning form-filling and statistical and administrative returns, five related to the Monopolies and Restrictive Trade Practices Legislation, two covering the Disclosure provisions of the Companies Act and finally seven on Development and Planning Controls.

FOLLOW-UP ACTION

Now I would like to turn to follow-up action. The Government has taken immediate and positive action to implement the main recommendations. A new division has been established in the Department of Trade and Industry and some action has been taken in recent budgets and on the problem of paperwork. But active and sustained follow-up is needed by many interested parties and this is spelled out in some detail in the Report. The Committee having reported now has no status. My task now is to encourage others to act.

Follow-up action by:

1 The small firms themselves by way of self-help. Chapter 10 of the Report details some eight areas in which the general consensus of opinion suggested that small firms could improve their performance and earn higher profits and/or improve their cash position. Their major suppliers and customers also have a rôle here, e.g. Marks and Spencer – c.f. U.S.A. practice.

2 Action by their professional advisers in giving more effective services to management; accountants, bank managers and consultants providing tailor-made services to meet the specific requirements of small firms.

3 Action by the financial world to ensure the availability of adequate resources for short-, medium- and long-term needs. No direct Government intervention was suggested; rather we hoped to encourage a new climate of competition and recognition that cash *and management advice* is needed.

4 Greater involvement in small-firm sector by academics in research, teaching and consulting, more of what Aston University and Sheffield Polytechnic are doing.

5 Action by the Press and other communications media in creating an informed public opinion. Our Report was a non-event in the British popular media. The climate of opinion in Britain is very different from that in the U.S.A., Japan and France, where there are 230 Deputies in the Small-Firms Lobby.

6 Finally, action by trade associations and other representative bodies in ensuring that the legitimate interests of small firms are fully and effectively presented to Whitehall. British Trade associations must become more marketing-orientated like the Swiss Watchmakers' Federation. They need to serve the old defensive rôle plus common front and lobby on major

common issues, e.g. VAT, Corporation Tax, E.E.C., etc. A Confederation of small firms' representative organisations is needed for these basic issues.

Small-firm proprietors insisted time and time again that they did not seek subsidy or feather-bedding. Rather that they wanted a "fair crack of the whip" from Government and the freedom to stand or fall by their own efforts in fair competition with their larger brethren. We accepted this basic philosophy which underlies our whole report.

However, we did add an important proviso and I would like to quote from Chapter 19, "Conclusions and Summary of Recommendations", paragraph 8:

> To reject discrimination in favour of small firms is not, of course, the end of the matter. It is still necessary for the ring to be held if they are to have a fair chance to compete effectively. For the small-firm sector to flourish without subsidy requires that the following conditions be met:
>
> 1 A good general economic climate. It is impossible to isolate so wide a sector from general economic conditions and a real improvement in the growth rate of the national economy would probably contribute more than anything else to the health of the sector, and particularly of its livelier elements.
>
> 2 The elimination, so far as possible, of the disincentive effects of the fiscal system. This again is a general point, but we have no doubt that the small firm sector would respond to fiscal incentives at least as positively as any other contributors to the economy.
>
> 3. The encouragement of more effective and fair competition throughout the economy. Although we have commented adversely on some aspects of competition policy as it affects small firms, we are convinced that in the last analysis the sector must benefit from any measures taken to promote opportunities as nearly equal, and markets as nearly perfect as can be achieved.
>
> 4 Effective equality of treatment in every aspect of legislation and Government policy.

THE FINANCIAL PROBLEMS OF SMALL FIRMS

So much for the general background. Now as a basis for perhaps more detailed discussion on financial and manage-ment problems, I would like to quote from the relevant passages from our Report. We dealt with finance in Chapter 12 and in Research Reports No. 4, Financial Facilities for Small Firms, and in No. 5, Problems in Raising External Finance.

We said: We have found that small firms have suffered and still suffer a number of genuine disabilities, by comparison with larger firms, in seeking finance from external sources. First, they have suffered differentially from the official ceilings on bank lending. Second, some institutional facilities avail-able to large firms are not available to small ones. Third, for those facilities which are available, small borrowers must generally pay rather more than large ones – this is true of overdrafts, of term loans, of hire-purchase finance and even of equity raised by public floatation. Fourth, many small firms are prevented by lack of information, and by prejudice borrowing, from making use of the full range of facilities available to them.

However, most of these disabilities reflect the higher cost of lending in small amounts or the higher risk of lending to small borrowers – they do not result from imperfections in the supply of finance. Indeed the ability and readiness of the financial institutions to exploit every new legitimate demand for funds is one of the greatest strengths of our financial system. We believe that the new freedom to be extended to the banking system (helped we hope by our discussions with the Board of Trade and the Treasury) will improve this still further. (See Research Report No. 5.)

We therefore do not recommend the creation of a new institution for the provision of finance to small firms. Nor do we support the provision of finance at subsidised rates, whether through a new official institution, through existing commercial ones or direct to small firms themselves. We believe that small firms in general should be and are capable of paying the economic or going rate for the finance they need, provided they make full use of the resources, including net trade credit, available to them. As I mentioned above there is evidence of a higher return on capital employed in small firms than in large firms.

If, at some future time, it is thought necessary to subsidise the provision of finance to small firms, we strongly recommend that this should be done within the existing financial system – the creation of an official body for this purpose would, in our view, distort the market in highly undesirable ways. Moreover, what is required above all for the health of the sector is an economic and taxation system which will enable individuals to acquire or establish new businesses out of personal resources and to develop these on the basis of retained profits. Without this no institutional financing arrangements can preserve the small-firm sector.

SUMMARY

Finally, by way of a summary, I would emphasise that the small-firm sector I have been describing is:

One-fifth of Gross National Product and 30% of the employed population.

A fundamental part of the British way of life.

Essential to the vitality of the economy – to a healthy industrial structure and to the stability of employment.

The seedbed of free enterprise and perhaps vital to the long term survival of free enterprise in Britain.

For thirty years or more the small-firm sector has felt neglected, misunderstood, even discriminated against – an appendage to the cult of bigness. Now it has its champions at Court in the Minister for Small Firms, in the Small-Firms Division, and meaningful co-ordination with other departments in Government. Seven million voters working in small businesses (plus their spouses?) really are worth taking notice of and now the facts are clearly known. But equally essential is the follow-up action, which I have outlined, by small firms themselves and everyone vitally interested in their future, to ensure that never again will the legitimate interests of so large and creative a sector of our national life go by default – to ensure, in fact, the future of competitive free enterprise in Britain and the preservation of our democratic society. We must resolve to act now – time is not on our side.

Chapter 19

THE ROLE OF THE COMPUTER

M. G. Kendall
Chairman, Scicon (Holdings) Limited

I will assume that most readers have encountered the computer in some aspect or other of their work, and that I need not take up space describing it. There are, however, one or two points to make as a preliminary to a discussion of its powers. It works at a fantastic speed – nowadays we reckon unit operations on a large machine in a unit called a nano-second, a thousand millionth of a second, which is the time it takes light to go about a foot. However, the speed, important though it is, is not the only feature, perhaps not the most important feature, of a computer installation. The two things which make it so useful in commercial operations are, first of all, its memory and, secondly, the possibility of interrogating it from a distance. A large machine will have built in a memory capable of holding items of information numbering hundreds of thousands, and in addition will have peripheral equipment in the form of tape decks or rotating discs which extend its memory almost without limit. The consequence is that we cannot only store an immense amount of information, but can also feed into the machine or have permanently on store in it programmes of instructions so that it can perform complicated operations without human intervention.

Computers, devices for data storage and programmes, have been with us for a number of years. The other feature I mentioned, that of communication with the computer, is of more recent growth and the situation is changing very rapidly. Post Office technology has now advanced to the point where there is an experimental line transmitting information at the rate of 48,000 bits a second, which means, for instance, that you could transmit the whole of the Bible, Old and New Testaments, in about ten minutes. We must, therefore, conceive of a computer installation, not as a geographically centralised machine to which one takes one's work like clothes to a laundry, but as service which can be consulted from a distance in all kinds of ways: by ordinary teletype, by visual display units, even by little computers. A few years ago there grew up the concept of a central computer like a gigantic power-house, which we could all tap for computer facilities in the way that we obtain electricity, water or gas. I doubt whether the computer will ever become a public utility. There will always be a rôle for the relatively small dedicated machine which spends its whole life doing specialised tasks, such as payrolls and invoicing. But these modern developments, coupled with the relatively low cost of using bureau facilities, have made it economic for many consumers either to dispense with their own computers or to supplement existing data-processing facilities with terminals, particularly in research departments where there is an intermittent requirement for powerful facilities.

The introduction of any new technology, especially one as expensive as computerisation has been up to now, does not take place without some false starts, some blind alleys, some systems crashes and a few other mixed metaphors which reflect the imperfection of human prevision. I am well aware that the transfer of much of the City's work from quill pen to computer has not been trouble-free. But the problems are being solved and I do not think that anyone can seriously doubt that the computer has not only a great and growing contribution to make, but that it is becoming essential.

We already see the computer at work on portfolio records, contract notes, stock transfers, statements of accounts, ledgers and journals and a whole range of clerical jobs. One may fairly claim that the computer arrived just in time to make it possible for the City to get its transactions completed in real time without becoming choked by paper. Time, for the City, is the essence of much of its work, and like air-traffic controls and seat-reservation systems, rapidity of service is essential – and is now available.

All this, however, amounts to saying that with the aid of the computer we can do much more quickly and easily what has already been done in the past by hand. The more important impact of the computer is in the capabilities which it opens up of doing things that have hitherto been impracticable. We are, for example, currently engaged on a system of Unit-Trust Management which not only does all the clerical work – registration, production of certificates, distributions, agents' commissions, but can handle up to a hundred trusts simultaneously. Or again, automatic investment appraisal and the establishment of criteria by which an acquisition target (in the jargon of the trade) may be judged as a sound investment are now possible, again, within a time-span which makes for quick and profitable decisions. I do not mean that the computer makes the ultimate decision; what I do mean is that it does most of the preliminary work on which a human being can base an objective decision.

One further example will illustrate the use of the computer in sensitive and competitive markets. Oil-tanker broking is highly competitive and literally a few seconds can determine whether a broker is successful in arranging a fixture. A tanker broker's armoury consists of a position list which indicates the position and time of availability of each of the 4,500 tankers currently on commission, the type of cargo it can carry, and other details. When an oil company goes to the market for a charter a telex is wired simultaneously to all brokers and the first to come up with a suitable vessel at an acceptable price receives the fixture. However, the oil companies sometimes telephone a favoured broker and give him about half a minute's warning that a telex is to be sent out. An instantaneous computerised consultation of an up-dated information bank could neutralise this advantage. All of which enables me to make one comment of general application. The computer is going to take a lot of the chores out of commercial life, but it is not going to make management any easier. Probably the contrary is true, for it will speed up management information, increase its volume and present the manager with a much wider spectrum of choice within which his decisions must be made.

For many reasons people are somewhat nervous about the computer and there are two respects in particular in which it is distrusted. One is that it may make mistakes; the other that it can disclose confidential information.

In actual fact the hardware of a computer, once bedded in, is very free from error. The mistakes are almost entirely due to errors on the part of the human beings who operate it. To say that a computer makes errors is rather like saying that a motor car drives dangerously – it is the human being, not the machine, which is at fault.

Admittedly, when a computer off-print results in a silly error the machine, as a rule, will not know it for such, whereas a human operator might. But you have to remember three things about computer errors: first of all, if it makes a mistake it admits the fact; secondly, it does not try to lay the blame elsewhere; and thirdly, once the error is corrected it never makes the same mistake again. And in all these respects, I think, it compares favourably with human beings.

It is no part of my present purpose to defend the computer, but somebody must speak up for the poor dumb beast and I should like to interject at this point something in its favour. The computer is becoming a kind of whipping boy for all kinds of human error. Those of us who get invoices for things we never ordered, or bills multiplied by a factor of ten, or accounts which we have already paid or the wrong spare part for a machine, and duly complain about this are, nine times in ten, told that it is due to a computer error. I hope that you will receive such excuses with scepticism. No one yet, so far as I am aware, has compared the frequency of computer errors with those which would be committed by human beings doing the same job in comparable circumstances; but my money would be on the computer.

A more serious fear concerns the risk of losing information or of revealing it to unauthorised access. There have to be security precautions to safeguard information whether held in mass-storage catalogued files, magnetic tape files, temporarily in the computer, or on punched cards or other forms of documentation. They are very extensive and for obvious reasons, apart from the risk of boring you, I do not want to describe them. Some of them are very sophisticated and involve, for example, the use of scrambler mechanisms to prevent wire tapping or accidentally crossed lines; or the use of key instructions which are necessary before a programme will operate – the client has his own personal electronic key just as he might have a physical key to a deposit box or safe. No system in the world, I suppose, is completely impenetrable, given enough time and effort, but there are fewer people that one has to trust in a computer installation than in a manually-operated one, although each has, theoretically, access to a much greater amount of information. And this reminds me of another feature of the computer – you cannot bribe it.

Any manager who requires information has to keep in mind the time and cost involved in getting it. One of the main features of the computer is that it can carry instructions to perform its work in a very flexible way, so that, for the same degree of input it can provide a much wider range of analytical output than any reasonably-sized clerical staff. And it does so in a matter of minutes at a marginal cost. We have, perhaps, tended to think of the machine as doing numerical chores quickly and replacing a lot of tedious manual work. More important, perhaps, is the amount of work it can do for which no clerical staff would ever be found. A little time ago someone in the U.S.A. calculated that if all the cheques written in 1970 had to be handled in the traditional way, the whole of the U.S. population of women from 15 to 45 would be required. I do not guarantee this calculation, but it makes the point.

The subjects I have mentioned so far are ones in which the industry dictates the needs and the computer merely tries to fulfil them – it does not, so to speak, itself generate new financial methods or a new kind of managerial financial technique. I now pass to two areas where the computer (or rather, the people who operate it) is no longer a high-powered amanuensis but has something of its own to contribute: forecasting and model building.

There are various ways of classifying forecasting methods, but for present purposes the most effective is by the time ahead for which the forecast is made. Let me say at once that in my opinion the computer has little to contribute to long-term forecasting; that is to say, to the prediction of actual values of economic variables more than five years ahead. There are some exceptions to this rule: for example, we know a good deal about the demand for teen-age education in ten years' time because the individuals concerned are already with us. And both business and Government, of course, have to look further ahead in regard to capital expenditure on long-term projects. But the computer contribution in this area comes from model building and simulation, not from numerical forecasting.

For short- and medium-term work, however, the computer

has effected a complete transformation of the methods which were employed in the old days – the old days meaning about ten years ago. This has come about in three ways: first of all, the speed with which computations can be carried out means that forecasts from week to week or month to month can be carried out in an hour or two for several thousand products, as instanced by the monthly forecasts carried out in the Pharmaceutical Division of I.C.I. Secondly, a number of new methods have been developed by statisticians for up-dating short-term forecasts – what is known as adaptive forecasts – and although they sometimes involve considerable arithmetic and not all of them are yet fully validated, enough evidence has accumulated to show that they are a substantial improvement on methods formerly in use. And all this can be done at low cost and very quickly. Thirdly, methods of tracking aircraft, guided missiles or satellites, which have to give practically instantaneous prediction, are being adapted to economics and business where speed is essential. Again let me make it plain, if such a thing is necessary, that nobody puts complete reliance on a purely mechanical forecasting method, especially in the context of this symposium. It is too easy for a Government to alter the rules of the game, both here and abroad, for one to be able to lean too heavily on methods which, essentially, depend on the momentum of the economic system. Forecasting, like architecture, must remain partly an art, but it now get the same kind of support from the computer that architecture gets from the bulldozer and the concrete mixer.

Model building has now become a science in its own right. Rather than write in generalities I should have liked to build a detailed financial model to illustrate what a model is and what can be done with it. In the space available I can only sketch it in the simplest possible terms.

All accounts can be resolved into two components, stocks or levels achieved at the end of a period, and flows which have taken place within the period. Figure 1 shows a highly simplified set of flows which take place within a company during one time period. The main differences, apart from pure detail, between the flow diagram and a real accounting system are that there is no provision to accommodate the lags in tax payments and receipts, and no mention of holdings in other companies.

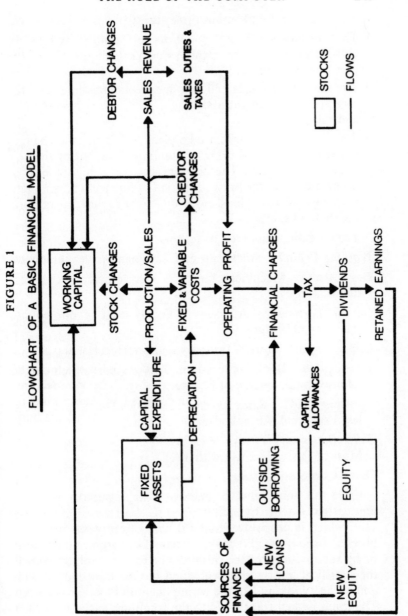

FIGURE 1

FLOWCHART OF A BASIC FINANCIAL MODEL

The flowchart builds up in three stages:

1 The four Balance Sheet items, Working Capital, Fixed Assets, Outside Borrowing and Equity, which are inherited from the previous time period.

2 The changes in stocks and non-finance indebtedness, and the revenue flows brought about by a given level of production and sales.

3 The financial flows which take place to balance the changes in fixed assets and working capital brought about by the new level of production. The diagram assumes a higher level of production than the previous period as finance is flowing into working capital and fixed assets to pay for capital expenditure, higher stocks, etc.

The definitions used are as follows:

Working Capital.   Stock plus cash plus debtors, less creditors.

Fixed Assets.   Machinery, buildings, vehicles, etc., at cost, less depreciation.

Outside Borrowing.   All outside finance that is not equity, including debentures.

Equity.   Issued value of ordinary and preference shares.

Depreciation.   Book depreciation. This is a cost which can be itemised and a source of finance.

Operating Profit.   Sales Revenue, less Sales Duties and Taxes, less Fixed and Variable Costs.

Sales Duties and Taxes.   Purchase Tax plus Excise Duties. Most of this will vanish with VAT.

Tax.   Corporation Tax.

From this point onwards one can disaggregate the model to any desired extent: by splitting it into shorter periods than a year, which is probably better for control purposes but raises problems about the allocation of items like corporate taxation; or by sub-divisions of the business; or by geographical area if the statistical information will stand it. One may end up with a flow sheet looking like the wiring diagram of a television set. The result is then transferred to the computer in the sense that it will store the inventory items and trace the effect of given flows through the system.

It is a fair question to ask what is new about all this? The novelties of the situation are as follows:

1 Based on the model the machine can print out at any moment the balance sheet and profit and loss account on any number of different assumptions. The reader may have sat on a board or committee at which the results of some costing exercise has been presented. Questions are then asked; for example, what happens if we postpone building for six months? What happens if interest rates fall? What happens if market demand has been underestimated? and so on. In the old days somebody had either to guess or go away and spend days or weeks reworking the arithmetic. With a model the answer is available in seconds.

2 However, even this is only condensing on the machine operations which could be carried out by hand. The more important contribution, in my opinion, is that the computerised model can do things which have hitherto been virtually impossible. Suppose, for example, that we chain a lot of models of the aforementioned type together in series, so as to follow the business over a course of years, the output of the model of one year being the input to the next. And suppose that we can decide by what criteria the concern is to operate, which is not always easy but could, for example, be defined as maximising the benefits to shareholders. The model can then be made to decide how the concern should be run to achieve that optimum. Instead of putting in the decisions and seeing what would happen, we settle on what we want to happen and derive from the computerised model the decisions which are necessary to achieve it.

There is much more to be said about the man-machine interface than this very brief account. No technology of any complexity is free from difficulties and dangers, but I think that the historians of the future will look back to computerisation, whether in the City or more generally, as the major technological advance of the late twentieth century.

Chapter 20

FINANCIAL PLANNING IN BRITISH INDUSTRY

P. G. Neild

Economist, Phillips & Drew, London

A gap in the literature on financial planning is detailed information on the extent to which computerised models are operational in the United Kingdom. This chapter attempts to supply such information, together with comments on the structure and type of model being used. It discusses a survey of 150 organisations, of which twenty-six were found to have financial planning models.

Financial modelling seems to be a fairly novel exercise begun around 1969. The most extensively used technique is deterministic simulation, but the general level of technical sophistication is not high, with the facility for backward iteration uncommon. The modular approach to model design is the most frequent, while interactive characteristics are rare, the models usually being run on in-house computers using batch processing. There has been some management resistance to the models. This and data-collection difficulties are seen as potentially the greatest constraints to further expansion of the systems.

The chapter, then, attempts to assess the current state of financial modelling in British industry, particularly in respect of the extent to which it is used and the techniques utilised to evaluate alternative financial strategies. It is also interesting to discover the problems that have arisen with the installation of such routines and the effect on management's attitudes towards systematising the decision process.

The chapter is in four parts. The first discusses the procedures used in surveying British companies, together with definitions of what is meant here by financial modelling and model type. In the second the results of the survey are presented, including technical characteristics, output and class. Thirdly, an examination is made of management's experience with the planning project, and inferences drawn regarding likely future reactions to complicating or extending the modelling system. Lastly, some of the main conclusions are mentioned.

I. PROCEDURES AND DEFINITIONS
Definitions.

The survey was aimed solely at the U.K. and tried to provide information supplementary to that of previous inquiries such as Taylor and Irving[1] and Boulden.[2] To do this it was thought necessary to specify exactly what a financial model is.

Strictly speaking, a financial model is any system of written statements, mathematical or merely qualitative, which relates to the money flows rather than the physical flows of all or part of an organisation's activities. This is not to say that physical flows, such as investments and output, are ignored by a financial model. On the contrary, a good financial model will relate all financial flows to the actual physical operations of the business, to the flow of goods being purchased, stored, processed and sold. However, the main emphasis is placed on the financial aspect of operations.

In this report a rather more limited definition is used in that the term financial model will be applied only to mathematical models which are capable of assessing the effects of changes in the organisation's operations on the Balance Sheet, Profit and Loss Account, Budget, Cash Flow or Funds Flow of the company or one of its divisions. Usually, these models will be computerised. As an illustration, a simple sequence of equations might be:

Trading Profit $= $ Trading Revenue $\times$ (Trading Margin/100)

Profit after Depreciation $=$ Trading Profit $-$ Depreciation

Total Profit $=$ Profit after Depreciation $+$ Investment Income

Corporation Tax $= 0.40 \times$ Total Profit

Post-Tax Profit $=$ Total Profit $-$ Corporation Tax

Available for Equity $=$ Post-Tax Profit $-$ Prior Charges

In the above sequence, the trading margin might depend upon capacity utilisation, which in turn depends upon demand for the company's products, and so on.

Where several of the company's operations are modelled the structure of the company might be expressed as in Figure 1.

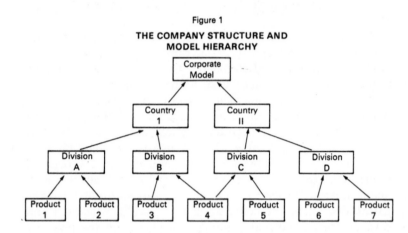

Figure 1

THE COMPANY STRUCTURE AND MODEL HIERARCHY

In addition to a definition of a financial model, it is necessary for clarity to classify the various types of model which this definition might encompass. Unfortunately, there is no generally accepted classification and ours follows that of Carruthers and Greggains,[3] though is not necessarily identical to it. Five classes are distinguished: (1) the full modelling system, (2) the report generator, (3) the project evaluation system, (4) the pre-defined system, and (5) the adapted package.

1 **The Full Modelling System.** This class has at least two distinctive features. The first is that the model is operated with a particular company specifically in mind. The sequence of equations which form the model's structure refer to the company's operations and its own accounting practices. However, usually the structure is sufficiently flexible that with only slight modifications other companies having similar activities and practices would be able to operate it usefully. The second feature is that rather than having a single model, the company has developed a system of models which can be linked together.

Each model within the system mirrors one or more aspects of the company's activities, and it can be plugged into the main system or eliminated as required. Sometimes, the input to one model will be the output of another, but even where this is not so there will be a linking mechanism which allows the effects of decisions in one division on another division to be assessed. This linking is undertaken automatically within the system and does not require the intervention of the user.

2 **The Report Generator.** This is distinct from the full modelling system in that the facility to link models is not available. There may be a series of models each depicting a set of the company's activities, but intervention by the user is required in order to study inter-model effects. Hence in this sense each model is a separate entity, but its structure still refers to the particular company for which it is being operated. Normally, the report generator is a less sophisticated model than the full system, although some generators do allow "consolidation". Thus a single model could be used to investigate the behaviour of several divisions, the results for each division then saved in a file and the files "consolidated" to provide a total picture.

3 **The Project Evaluation System.** These systems have been designed for specialist applications. The sequence of equations included in them refers specifically to the company, and to the assessment of the profitability or otherwise of particular projects and activities. Frequently they compute rates of return, discounted cash flows and net present values. However, they can be modified into simple financial planning systems with no model interlinking facility. The form in which results appear is restricted, e.g. Profit and Loss Account *or* Cash Flow, but this extension of the system to financial statements must have been adopted for them to lie properly within our definition of a financial model.

4 **The Pre-Defined System.** These are modelling systems which have been developed by computer service organisations for general use. Consequently, the structure of the model does not refer to any particular company. This bars the user from writing his own model and often requires him to conform to

some standardised set of accounting practices. The pre-defined system may be flexible enough to be used for several activities of the company, but failing this the system can only be adapted at considerable cost. If the adaptation is carried out the model enters class 5.

5 **The Adapted Package.** Because the cost of adaption is often high this class occurs infrequently. In this class, some of the equations within a pre-defined system have been modified to conform to the company's own activities or accounting requirements, but most have not. As with the pre-defined system the aim of the adapted package is "to provide standard reports containing all items and ratios which a wide spectrum of users might require".

Survey Procedures.

Selection Criteria. A preliminary investigation into the likely extent of financial modelling in British industry was made in early December 1971 by asking the opinion of prominent writers in the field and by scrutinising the *Computer Survey*[4] publication. The *Computer Survey* gives a list of 3,000 companies which have purchased computers in the U.K., the type of computer, the delivery date and a description of the current applications. If the description of applications seemed to be fairly analytically orientated (not merely routine) and specific reference was made to accounting, financial or advanced mathematical techniques such as programming or simulation, the computer type was checked to determine whether it had the ability to run a fairly sophisticated financial modelling pro-gramme. If it had, the company was sent a questionnaire. Naturally, these criteria were by no means exact, but they did seem to provide some basis for selection.

To the *Computer Survey* selections were added companies which were either known to have financial models (either through publications or from talks with individuals), or were thought very likely to have them. A list of six firms were known to have financial models, but only two of these completed the questionnaire.

Sample Characteristics. 150 companies were asked to par-ticipate. The industrial coverage of the original selection and the respondents is shown in Table 1, classified according to the *Financial Times* share subsectors.

TABLE I
INDUSTRIAL COVERAGE

Financial Times *Sector*	*Selected*	*Contributed*
Banks and Hire Purchase	5	–
Beers, Wines and Spirits	6	–
Building Industry	8	3
Chemicals, Plastics, etc.	9	2
Drapery and Stores	3	–
Electrical and Radio	8	2
Engineering and Metal	21	4
Food, Groceries, etc.	11	1
Hotels and Caterers	2	–
Industrials (Miscellaneous)	44	6
Insurance	3	–
Machine Tools	1	–
Mines: Finance	1	–
Mines: Miscellaneous	1	1
Motor, Aircraft Trades	7	–
Newspapers and Publishers	2	–
Oils	5	–
Paper, Printing and Advertising	3	–
Property	1	–
Shipping	1	–
Textiles	2	–
Tobaccos	2	1
Trusts, Finance, Land	4	2
Sector not named	–	4
	150	26

Because of the selection criteria the list of 150 companies cannot be considered random with respect to British industry as a whole, but rather a list within which the British population of financial models might be covered. Comments in this chapter should therefore be interpreted as properly applying only to the participants rather than to British industry in general. However, in so far as it is thought the respondents comprise a high proportion of British companies actually having financial models, their replies could indicate the present state of financial model-building in the U.K. There are at least two reasons for thinking that this proportion is rather high. The first is that the selection process covered a very large number of companies, while the second is that the number of individual replies was greater than our *a priori* notions of the number of models in existence.

As with all surveys there is some risk of bias in the replies. Companies with sophisticated models may be reluctant to divulge information which may help competitors, while some companies may have financial models but not run them on computers. The former is to some extent obviated by the option to reply anonymously, while the latter is a highly unlikely circumstance for an extensive model. Nevertheless, it is not claimed that this survey is free from reply bias, and the extent of this bias is one of the imponderables which need to be appreciated in interpreting the results.

Response. Of the 150 companies circularised, thirty-eight replied and twenty-six had financial models of various classes. Two concerns had two financial models, making the total number of models studied twenty-eight. In such a delicate field, our researches had not led us to expect above a 10% response, so we were quite pleased with the outcome. The number of companies having financial models was even more surprising as our initial researches put the likely figure at around fourteen and some of these did not reply.

II. MODEL CHARACTERISTICS

It seems most convenient to represent the results of the survey in chart form. This has the advantages of clarity, brevity and accuracy, since the respondents were asked to tick the alternatives under each question heading applicable to them. Hence the charts give the answers actually received and the reader may form his own impression of them, while the comments in the text relate to this investigator's interpretation of the results pattern. It should be noted that the alternatives are often not mutually exclusive.

Chart 1   Model Uses.

This shows that 64% of the models are used for long-term planning, and 57% for short-term, nine models being used for both long- and short-term planning. The proportions shown in Chart 1 suggest that the typical model is used for a purpose other than production control, security analysis, portfolio selection and internal management control. This supports the contention that the questionnaire answers refer to financial models rather than any other of the above types, and is in itself encouraging since one of the major problems of sending out an impersonal questionnaire is that the respondent may have misunderstood the type of model the exercise is aimed at. This misunderstanding does not seem to have occurred, a submission confirmed by the fact that 90% of the models print out a Profit and Loss Account.

From this evidence it may be concluded that the survey answers do indeed refer to financial planning models, though the term for which planning is undertaken is indeterminate. A proportion of the models are used for both long- and short-term planning, but this is not generally the case.

Chart 2   Model Class.

Here, 46% of respondents said they have a full modelling system, while 36% have a report generator. Fortunately, no respondent ticked both boxes. Hence four out of every five models studied have a set of equations showing the interrelationships of financial flows within the business, which refers specifically to the individual company. The firms have usually not taken full advantage of the packaged systems supplied by service bureaux (a list of those available is shown in Carruthers and Greggains[3]), but have "grown their own".

Another point worth mentioning is that the great majority of models given in the survey are not simply project-evaluation systems, involving relatively elementary calculations such as net present values and discounted cash flows. It seems safe to conclude that the financial models are mainly in the full-system or report-generator classes, that there is little difference in extent of use between these classes, that their construction has been directed specifically at the individual company, and that

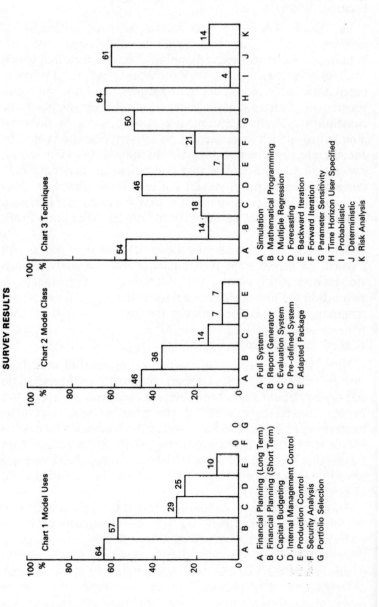

SURVEY RESULTS

Chart 1 Model Uses

A Financial Planning (Long Term)
B Financial Planning (Short Term)
C Capital Budgeting
D Internal Management Control
E Production Control
F Security Analysis
G Portfolio Selection

Chart 2 Model Class

A Full System
B Report Generator
C Evaluation System
D Pre-defined System
E Adapted Package

Chart 3 Techniques

A Simulation
B Mathematical Programming
C Multiple Regression
D Forecasting
E Backward Iteration
F Forward Iteration
G Parameter Sensitivity
H Time Horizon User Specified
I Probabilistic
J Deterministic
K Risk Analysis

their level of sophistication is somewhat higher than the elementary calculations needed for project evaluation.

Chart 3   Techniques.

Simulation techniques are employed to a far greater extent than mathematical programming, fifteen respondents using simulation and only four programming. Despite this relatively greater use of simulation, in absolute terms it still accounts for only fifteen of the twenty-eight models studied. In addition, the simulation models are themselves relatively straightforward. None use multiple regression techniques in an attempt to reduce the data base, 85% are deterministic rather than probablistic, none have statistical sub-routines, there is no tendency for them to include parameter sensitivity, and only two have a backward iteration facility. On the other hand, 80% of simulation models have the feature of allowing the user to vary the time-span over which simulations can be made.

As regards the form in which results are shown by the simulation models, all print out a Profit and Loss Account, and all but two a Balance Sheet. Cash flow is obtainable in thirteen of the fifteen models, and a source and use of funds analysis in twelve. Thus generally speaking the simulation models provide a great deal of financial information. A major limitation of the information flow is, however, its discontinuity. In only three cases is an interactive simulation system used, the tendency being for the work to be undertaken as separate jobs (in "batches"). This makes it harder for management to realise exactly what effect data changes are having on the results, by lengthening the time lag between the questions and the answers.

Almost three out of four simulation models in the survey use the modular approach to model design. This indicates the prevalence of a series of rather elementary models, or a simple model which is flexible enough to mirror several company activities, the information from which can be fed up through a pyramidal structure to the model which prints the company's balance sheet. The previous comment on the simplicity of the techniques used in the simulations is consistent with this finding.

To summarise, simulation is used more extensively than programming, but is not yet so prevalent as to dominate the

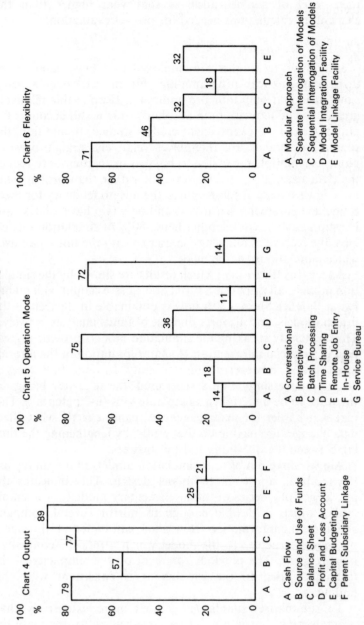

SURVEY RESULTS

Chart 4 Output

A Cash Flow
B Source and Use of Funds
C Balance Sheet
D Profit and Loss Account
E Capital Budgeting
F Parent Subsidiary Linkage

Chart 5 Operation Mode

A Conversational
B Interactive
C Batch Processing
D Time Sharing
E Remote Job Entry
F In-House
G Service Bureau

Chart 6 Flexibility

A Modular Approach
B Separate Interrogation of Models
C Sequential Interrogation of Models
D Model Integration Facility
E Model Linkage Facility

technical field. The simulation models themselves are usually comparatively simple and deterministic in construction. Most are modular in design, each simulation carried out being used as a supplier of information to other models higher up the company structure. An interactive system is generally not used, rather answers are obtained from the computer and reactions to these answers require a re-run of the model. However, the models do provide extensive financial information usually including a Balance Sheet and a Profit and Loss Account. Finally, it seems fair comment that in respect of simulation techniques and interactive facilities, British companies have not yet opted decisively in favour of either.

Chart 4   Output.

This shows that 89% of all the survey models assess the effects on the Profit and Loss Account of changes in the data, while nearly 80% also analyse the cash flow and the Balance Sheet positions. Therefore, regardless of the techniques used, the models provide information over a wide range of the financial spectrum and do not concentrate on any one particular aspect. Since the actual computational techniques are not of the highest order of sophistication, one implication appears to be that it is not difficult to formulate a financial model capable of yielding extensive information: given one type of financial flow, it seems technically relatively easy to obtain many more. Further, companies, or more probably company technicians, have thought it unnecessary to derive the initial flow in a highly complex manner.

Chart 5   Operation Mode.

The vast majority of models are run on the company's own computer using batch processing. The difficulties imposed by such methods have already been discussed under "Techniques".

Chart 6   Flexibility.

The modular approach to model design is used extensively, while models can be interrogated either separately or sequentially. Few have a model integration facility. Comments as regards flexibility but specific to simulation models are given under "Techniques".

III. MANAGEMENT AND THE MODEL

Experience.

The principal hazard involved in asking a question to which optional answers are not specified is that replies will be so woolly as to form no consistent pattern. It was felt necessary, therefore, to keep the questions brief and at the same time provide the respondent with a guide as to the lines along which we would like the questions answered. A measure of success seems to have been achieved in this respect, and some interesting points emerge. However, since the comments come mainly from the technician rather than the management, it is only human to expect bias particularly towards a more optimistic appraisal of the model's prominence in the company organisation than it properly deserves.

Four respondents made no comment regarding experience. Of the remaining twenty-four, sixteen have been using a financial model for around one year, and five for between two and three years. The longest time for which a model has been operational is seven years, but this is certainly exceptional. Hence it is quite easy to date the real beginnings of financial modelling usage in the U.K.: 1969. The recent upsurge of interest is unmistakable. A telling comment is provided by one of the contributors: "We have developed our system over the past fifteen months and used it for the first time last week."

As for simulation models, ten of the fifteen have been used for less than eighteen months, and another three for only three years. Because of their inexperience in handling the model, many respondents did not feel able to comment usefully on their technical difficulties. Five, however, felt that gathering the information to feed into the model had proved a problem, though some thought that the demand for such information had itself resulted in a more rigorous and disciplined attitude to the monitoring of statistics within the company's various divisions. Three mentioned that management resistance was apparent, primarily because of lack of understanding of how the model worked and what it could be used for. Two said they had encountered no technical difficulties, but one commented that increasing the sophistication of the model had led to such a decrease in its value that the company was thinking of reverting to manual methods.

Decision-Making.

This is the area in which most bias would be expected. However, surprisingly enough, of the twenty-two who answered the question only two went so far as to claim that the information given by the financial model is sufficiently important to merit greater management attention than non-model factors. The two comments that follow are not atypical and illustrate the cautionary, probably realistic, attitude of the modellers.

"The model is used as an aid rather than as a basis for decision-making."

"The model forms part of the *total* decision-making process in the areas where it is used." (Contributor's emphasis.)

On the other side, the following contribution is enlightening:

"The model forecasts are circulated to the directors, and sales and marketing managers are required to explain any significant differences between the model forecasts and their views of what demand will be."

However, this dominance of the model is rare, a much more prevalent state being the (proper?) subordination of the model to management.

Constraints.

The most frequently mentioned constraint on expanding the usefulness of the financial model was management:

"Lack of awareness on the part of users of the model's capabilities and appropriateness."

"The constraints and difficulties are due to human beings rather than the machinery."

"User involvement will be the crux of the matter."

"Convincing potential users of the advantages of the model, and quantifying the benefits to justify the development expense."

Few companies consider that technical constraints will be a problem, nor will computer hardware. Rather the cost involved in collecting sufficient data for more sophisticated systems may be prohibitive. Two contributors expressed the fear that management would become more sceptical if the complexity of the system increased. On the whole, then, the modellers have recognised that the human element may be even more active in the future if attempts are made to extend the models.

IV. SUMMARY AND CONCLUSIONS

It is very often difficult to form a clearly-defined picture of a "typical" answer in a survey of this kind, and our survey is no exception. However, it is possible to discern at least an outline of the present state of financial modelling in this sample of British industry. Although the technical characteristics of the models comprise very much a mixed bag, the most extensively used basic technique is simulation. Models incorporating this facility have developed mainly since 1969, with clear signs of a growing interest more recently. Indeed, financial modelling as a whole is a comparatively novel exercise, usually having commenced after 1969. Simulation is not so extensively used as to be the dominant technique, however, and many respondents rely on programming or statistical systems. The technical proficiency of the modelling art is of a higher order than that required for project evaluation, but is still some way below the sophistication possible.

As regards the model design, the most common is the modular approach in which a set of elementary models or a flexible single model is used to mirror individual activities of the company, information being fed from one activity to another higher up the company structure. Problems have been encountered in the collection of data to feed into the model, but the greater potential constraint is given as management's resistance to additional expenditure, an attitude encouraged by their inability to appreciate more sophisticated procedures.

The usual financial system in this sample has the following characteristics. It is either a full modelling system or a report generator; it is a deterministic simulation model, modular in design, which incorporates only simple testing routines. The model is run on the company's own computer and cannot be manipulated interactively. At the very least the system provides information on the Profit and Loss Account and the Balance Sheet, and this information acts as an aid to decision-making by management who are still the decision-takers. However, management is not convinced of the model's usefulness and it is likely that any attempt to complicate the model further would be resisted.

NOTES TO CHAPTER 20

[1] B. Taylor and P. Irving, "Organised Planning in Major U.K. Companies: A Survey", *Long Range Planning*, Vol. 3, No. 4, June 1971.

[2] J. B. Boulden, "Computerized Corporate Planning", *Long Range Planning*, Vol. 3, No. 4, June 1971.

[3] J. A. Carruthers and D. J. K. Greggains, "Simulation Under Focus", *Computer Management*, September 1971.

[4] "Computer Survey", November/December 1970, United Trade Press Ltd., M. Moseley, editor.

Chapter 21

RECENT DEVELOPMENTS

IN INVESTMENT RESEARCH

John M. Brew
Chairman, Society of Investment Analysts

The most obvious "recent development in investment research" is that there are more people doing it than there used to be. Though we have by no means a monopoly, I think it is fair to say that a majority of those professionally engaged in investment research belong to the Society of Investment Analysts, whose membership has been growing steadily over the years and now exceeds 1,300. This is a symptom of a general increase in resources being devoted to research in the investment field. I shall try to give a general idea of what has been going on recently, and a particular indication of the areas in which research is having, or is likely to have, a new impact on the practical business of investment management.

An unsurprising but most noticeable result of increasing numbers has been a much greater degree of specialisation. I think it was Walter Bagehot who was described as "specialising in omniscience", which is what most investment analysts used to have to try to do. But now very many firms have research departments large enough to permit labour to be divided extensively. This has clearly led to an increase in efficiency and to changes in the way research is done, but specialisation beyond a certain point can be counter-productive. An American firm used to advertise a large research department which included an analyst who specialised in "toys, conglomerates, and oceanography".

More investment research means fairly naturally more visits by analysts to companies, and more specialisation means that they want to visit a company often enough, and for long enough, to find out a good deal more than they used to. This means that company executives are being asked to give more time to an activity which many of them do not classify as productive; and in the end the process will tend to be self-correcting as more and more analysts see executives with less and less knowledge of the important parts of the business. I shall say only two things about that. The first is that no analyst expects to be given information which would not be available to any shareholder who asked for it. The second is that I believe that it is economically useful to have company securities valued in the market as correctly and as logically as possible, and if investment research helps this process (which I firmly believe it does) it should be encouraged. Some company managements may want their shares to be as high as possible, but most seem to realise that a *fair* valuation is a more realistic objective. To achieve this it must help to see investment researchers in good times and in bad and to give them whatever assistance can reasonably be given within the obvious restrictions of ethics and equity.

I hope that a good number of readers have bought Dennis Weaver's excellent textbook on Investment Analysis which has been published by Longmans in association with the Society of Investment Analysts. It is becoming increasingly difficult to pick up the knowledge necessary for modern investment research just by being "thrown in at the deep end", and this book will fill a large gap in many training programmes. I want to quote from it five factors which Mr. Weaver believes have encouraged the development of new techniques of share evaluation.

1 Much more informative accounts (and we hope even more informative ones in the future).

2 More market information available from the Stock Exchange and private sources.

3 Regular publication by the Government and industrial associations of statistics which enable the performance of individual industries to be followed.

4 Increasing professionalism in the investment industry.

5 Availability of computers to handle large masses of data.

I have not the space, even if I were competent to do it, to give a comprehensive survey of analytical techniques, but I shall try to tell you the areas into which increasing effort is being put, and then I shall say a little about where all this is getting us, whether investment techniques really are improving, and whether we are doing a useful job anyway. I have tried to arrange my remarks in the same sort of order as the thought process which should be involved in reaching an investment decision.

Any logical method of share evaluation, to my mind, can be divided into two consecutive operations – assessing the prospects (which involves forecasting) and evaluating the share in relation to these prospects. Opinions differ as to which is the more important, and also as to how much weight should be given to the opinion of the analyst in each part of the decision. My own view is that the analyst's opinion will, and should, usually predominate in the assessment of the prospects because it is very difficult for an outsider to do more than help in the argument and every now and then inject some new ideas. But in the present state of the science I think the share or industry specialist is only one among many in the final evaluation decision. Quite a lot of research effort has been going on into methods of evaluation, but before I turn to that I have two very short comments on the first part of the investment decision – the assessment of the prospects. I am not going to say much more than will give you an idea of the sort of areas which are receiving greater attention than they used to.

A slightly paradoxical result of the better flow of information about companies has been a greater awareness on the part of analysts that things are often not quite as they seem in the accounts. The distorting effect of inflation has brought this home particularly strongly. Whether or not we shall be given accounts in constant purchasing-power terms (and following the recent discussion document from the Institute of Chartered Accountants, we might be), the analyst is having to sharpen up his methods in this area. Such studies as have been published quantifying the effect of inflation on profits make very interesting reading.

Another analytical technique which is being used more is the preparation of a Financing Table. You see this in some company accounts as a statement of the Sources and Application of Funds. It shows how the company generated its funds and how it used them during the year, and it often gives a good indication, not obvious elsewhere in the accounts, of where the company is going. This is particularly true when the direction in which the company is going happens to be downwards. There is some interest in the application of computers to this type of analysis, to show, for instance, what the analyst's assumptions mean in terms of future cash flow.

The remainder of this chapter will be mainly about attempts which are being made to improve techniques in what I designated as the second part of the investment decision, namely the evaluation of the security and the construction of portfolios once the prospects have been assessed. The reason I am going to emphasise this is that it is the area which is currently attracting a lot of attention, which is not to say that it is the most important area or to say that the new techniques will prove to be useful.

Investment Analysis left its infancy in 1934 with the publication in America of the classic textbook by Graham and Dodd. One of the authors gave it as his opinion, and I am paraphrasing, that investment research could be successfully conducted without the use of any mathematical techniques more complicated than fairly simple arithmetic and possibly some reasonably easy algebra. So far he has been, broadly speaking, proved to be right. At any rate it is my view that so far the really important money-making investment ideas have been explainable to a non-technician in fairly simple terms. This is true even in that most mathematical of markets, the gilt-edged market.

But there is evidence that the future may in this respect be different. For some ten years now we have seen an increasing flow of academic work, mainly from economists, on investment subjects. So far this has had precious little impact on the way large portfolios were managed in practice, and I am bound to give my own opinion that the practical man's distrust of the academic work was well founded, even though in many cases this distrust was a rationalisation of the fact that he could not understand it anyway.

But it seems quite likely that academic research into the theory of investment will have an important practical impact fairly soon.

The big academic topic is the assessment of risk. You can argue for a long time about what is the best measure of risk and whether there is anything from the past which can be used as an indicator of the future risk level. The earliest, and still the most important, work on the subject was by Markowitz on Portfolio Selection. There has been an enormous amount of discussion about Markowitz's ideas. His fundamental idea is that an investment management cannot properly assess the merits of a particular investment policy by an estimate of the likely return alone. He must also assess the level of risk, and his objective should be to achieve the maximum likely return at each level of risk, and to choose the combination of return and risk which suits him best. This sounds all very logical and has proved a fruitful concept for discussion and argument, but practical application has been slow to materialise. The main practical result so far has been to give respectable logical and statistical backing to the belief that most portfolios have more holdings than they need if the purpose of diversification is to spread the risk. Markowitz's ideas, fairly well supported by subsequent statistical analysis, seem to show that beyond about twenty holdings there is not much reduction in risk to be achieved by further diversification. I hasten to add that in practice such a small number of holdings would give many funds severe marketability problems.

But the investment future is jolly difficult to forecast anyway even in the simplest terms and Markowitz's methods need the estimation of the future levels of a large number of parameters which designate the returns, the variabilities, and the co-variabilities for the securities involved and the practical difficulties are obviously formidable.

The potentially fruitful way of bringing the element of risk into share evaluation seems to be by means of a mathematical model which describes how a security is likely to behave relative to the market as a whole. The model is usually called the Sharpe Model, after Professor Sharpe, who has written famous papers on the subject. This is all the rage in Wall Street at the moment and is commonly called "The Beta Revolution", or rather it would be if they pronounced Greek letters the same way as I do. Beta is supposed to show, for a security or for a whole portfolio, the degree of volatility relative to the market as a whole. For instance, if we measured the market by the F.T.A. All-Share Index a Beta of 2 would mean that a 10% rise in the

Index would probably be accompanied by a 20% rise in the security concerned, which we could say was twice as volatile as the market. I have no space to say much about this except that my own assessment of the confused body of evidence and argument is that for individual securities it won't help much but that for portfolios the Sharpe Model says some quite interesting and meaningful things.

In the event I think that the main practical impact of the work on risk will be on the assessment of performance, because the real difficulty with the assessment of investment performance is to relate the results in some meaningful way to the risks which have been run to achieve them. You will have noticed in Wall Street how quickly the glamour faded from a lot of the managers who had beaten the rising market by really big margins. On the way down the gains melted away like snow off a dyke. In Professor Sharpe's terms they had had high Beta portfolios. The U.S. evidence is that Beta is reasonably constant in time for individual portfolios, and though the U.K. evidence is not nearly so solid I think some of you ought to be brushing up your Greek alphabet.

A very good, simple and readable account of this was recently produced by the American Broking firm Smith Barney and Co. It is called Risk-Adjusted Portfolio Performance: Its Investment Implications. To quote one of its more hair-raising sentences, they say that "Some academicians have gone so far as to forecast the eventual demise of the security analyst and the portfolio manager as a result of their studies of investment performances." But it will be a long time, I think, before that happens. For those who wish to dig a little deeper I recommend the book by Richard Brealey called Risk and Return from Common Stocks. It does not require any deep mathematical knowledge.

There has also been a lot going on in what are called Valuation Models. Broadly speaking, these take as given forecasts of future profits and dividends, and give a mathematical expression for the way each security will be priced in the market. The best known on either side of the Atlantic is the one run by Phillips & Drew. My impression is that such a model is useful in two ways. First of all it provides a better than random method of pricing and does so in a way which refreshingly ignores subjective likes and dislikes. And secondly, it gives a good insight into the way the market is valuing shares; how much weight it gives, for instance, to such factors as past growth, dividend cover, dividend yield or past variability. If these weights change it is quite an interesting thing to know how they are changing.

Another area of activity has been the investigation into the predictability of future price movements. Most of you will have heard about the Random Walk hypothesis. In very, very rough terms it says that future price movements do not depend in any way on past price movements. Statisticians have worked for years on the time series represented by Stock Exchange prices, and generally speaking have found the changes to behave as if they were randomly generated. The odd thing is that at the same time as the evidence in favour of Random Walk has been getting stronger, more investment managers have been making use of charts in arriving at their decisions. This increasing use of what is called Technical Analysis has been a feature of the last two or three years.

Technical Analysis is so called to distinguish it from Fundamental Analysis. It extends beyond the use of charts to include such ideas as Relative Strength and the statistical, rather than graphical, analysis of past trends. But the main emphasis is on the use of charts. My own position is neutral veering towards scepticism, but I think nearly everybody now admits that charts are useful even if they only serve as a sort of dealer's memory to which one can turn to see what has been going on in the market. But the chartists seem to find them much more positive use than this, the motto of the more extreme being commonly parodied as "Don't confuse me with facts".

Just as statistical analysis of price movements has been supposedly eating away at the foundations of technical analysis, but so far doing little harm to the superstructure, there has been a good deal of work published which seems to indicate that investment managers and investment analysts are not really very good at their jobs. Two papers were published by Ian Little on what he called Higgledy Piggledy Growth, which seemed to show that it was nearly impossible to identify growth companies (by which I mean ones whose future earnings were likely to grow at an above-average rate) by an examination of the record. Apart from the fact that this kind of statistical analysis is notoriously full of pitfalls, the difficulty with this type of study is that it imputes to the analyst a forecasting method which relies entirely on objective analysis of past figures. What should be checked are the forecasts analysts actually make. Such evidence as there is is more encouraging than Mr. Little's studies would indicate. On the investment management side the question is also being asked – "If you chaps are so professional and so expert why don't you beat the averages by a bigger margin?" A most comprehensive study by Professor Jensen of the American mutual fund industry showed that over a long period the industry as a whole equalled the performance of the market indices with uncanny precision.

I do not get as worried about this as some people do. First of all the institutions are now themselves a big part of the average and can only beat it at the expense of the dwindling band of outsiders, who though they are non-professional are often neither stupid nor lacking in inside information. But there is another explanation, I think. There are three situations in which we should not expect to beat the indices. The first is one of complete uncertainty when everybody is equally at a loss. The second is one of complete certainty when securities will tend to be correctly priced, each discounting its own prospects. The third is one in which even though the future is uncertain market prices accurately reflect the probabilities. The nearer we get to a world in which the relevant information is freely available and plenty of people are working on it, the more difficult it will be to beat the indices, for the simple reason that the future will tend to be more correctly discounted. In this situation you can, of course, stick the proverbial pin into the next-to-back page of our leading financial newspaper and do as well as the average professional, but that is a bit like saying that you don't need to be vaccinated against smallpox as long as the rest of the population doesn't follow suit. In any case I shall still back the professional side of the industry to come out on top. Even if they are only just on top I can still say that this is because securities are more correctly priced than they used to be, which is surely to the economic benefit of everybody.

The Society of Investment Analysts is a founder member of the European Federation of Financial Analysts Societies and we have for ten years now endeavoured to co-ordinate our research efforts and to identify fruitful areas for co-operation. If we have succeeded we can say that we have anticipated the work which would otherwise have been necessary after the enlargement of the European Community.

But I am conscious that I have written nothing so far about the effect our entry to Europe will have on investment research. I think the answer is that it will be vastly stimulated by the prospect of free capital movement, but that integration has been proceeding well for some years now. The enlargement of the Community will only speed this up if there is a prospect of more all-embracing legislation affecting all Community companies and of a move towards a genuinely European capital market.

There will be great opportunities in Europe for both investment managers and investment analysts, and I am confident they will take advantage of them.

Chapter 22

INVESTMENT STRATEGIES

FOR PENSION FUNDS

J. Derek Skelton
Fellow of the Chartered Institute of Secretaries

The implications of continuous inflation are awesome. An apparently innocuous example will suffice to illustrate its terrors.

Suppose a man of twenty has a wage of £20 a week (rounded off to £1,000 per annum) now. He receives no promotion or merit payments for the rest of his working life to age sixty-five, but he does have the benefit of a Cost-of-Living (C.O.L.) payment every year. If inflation is a steady 5% p.a. throughout that period his wages will be very nearly £9,000 p.a. when he retires forty-five years later.

If a good modern pension scheme promises him a two thirds of final salary pension plus a C.O.L. uplift every year (taking 5% p.a. again) a capital sum in the region of £90,000 will be needed in forty-five years' time.

Suppose he pays 5% of wages into the pension scheme each year and his employer does the same, what return must the pension fund earn on the contributions? Those unused to compound interest may be surprised that 10% p.a. will do it with little (or alternatively a few years) to spare. Nevertheless, experience in the last few years leads many people to accept inflation of 5% p.a. as a fairly modest, "bearable" rate of inflation without thinking of the implications of a nine-fold increase in wages in a man's working lifetime – in spite of no promotion or merit wage increases. Similarly, few pension-fund trustees realise that their fund must earn 10% p.a. if the promised benefits are to be forthcoming. The figures are even more staggering if inflation were to be 8% p.a. The £1,000 p.a. would then reach £31,900 p.a. after forty-five years and the fund would have to earn nearly $12\frac{1}{2}\%$ p.a. to provide the scale of benefits mentioned above.

Inflation has been averaging nearly 8% p.a. for a few years now. How many pension funds have increased their net worth (allowing for cash flows in and out) by $12\frac{1}{2}\%$ p.a.? How many, indeed, even have a minimum target of $12\frac{1}{2}\%$ p.a. on average (which may require well over 20% in a bull market year) and, for those who do aim high, what investment strategies are required to produce the necessary performance?

The measurement of performance is obviously important. It is also surprisingly difficult. Even so, too many fund managers still rely on old-fashioned methods which worked quite well in the pre-War period but which are unsatisfactory in an age of inflation. I am, of course, referring to the type of calculation which ignored changes in the capital value of securities and merely divided the investment income by the average of the book value of the fund during the course of the year in question. Some of the calculations used are more sophisticated but in essence are based on this type of approach. It is now much more important to consider the difference in net worth at the beginning and end of a year (using market values), allowing for net cash injections into the fund. This implies a measurement of "total return" comprised of both interest and dividends on the one hand and capital gains and losses on the other (whether realised or not), e.g. a fund wholly (and newly) invested in gilt-edged a year ago would have had an interest yield of over $8\frac{1}{2}\%$ but capital losses exceeding 11% so that the total return was negative. In a normal set of pension fund accounts the revenue account would show a healthy interest yield, whereas the capital losses (assuming for this illustration that the holdings were all sold at the end of the year or were re-valued downwards) would be tucked away in the Balance Sheet as a deduction from the "Superannuation Fund Account". If we further assume that pension and other benefits equalled the joint contributions that year, the balance representing the excess income over expenditure is transferred to the Superannuation Fund Account and could then be deducted from the loss on sales or revaluation to indicate in the Balance Sheet that a net loss had been sustained. More sophisticated calulations are needed in more realistic circumstances and a useful summary of objectives and methods can be found in the paper by John Brew.[1] Mention of two more recent approaches is made later in this article.

This is a type of approach which has not been favoured for pension funds and too few trustees look at their accounts in this way. They have been encouraged in the past to think that it is income which provides pension benefits and that capital only becomes important in the very long run (when nearly all of us are dead), i.e. when the fund becomes a closed one with no new entrants. Unfortunately, as some funds are still finding out, the old-fashioned approach can lead to disastrous consequences. There are still funds wholly invested in gilt-edged, and who can deny that the running and redemption yields look very attractive until capital losses and inflation are taken into account and adjusted total return is calculated. An adjustment for the inflation in the last twelve months alone indicates a further loss in real terms of nearly 10% which can never be revealed by conventional book-keeping.

The assets of Pension Funds are growing very rapidly and their composition is changing. This can be readily seen in the figures published in "Financial Statistics".[2] At the beginning of 1966 total assets in the private sector (private self-administered pension funds excluding the Co-operative Societies) amounted to £3,175m. and by the end of 1971 the figure had risen to £6,120m., i.e. it had almost doubled in six years. When it is borne in mind that book values are referred to in both cases, it is highly likely that the market values have more than doubled.

The changing composition of the Investments is also interesting, as the table shows.[2] Only in 1971, most of it in the trough between the bear market of 1969/70 and the new bull market of 1971/72, was there any substantial buying of Government Securities and this was concentrated in the dated long end of the market – £181m. in "over fifteen years to maturity" category. On the other hand, net additions of Industrial Debentures were fairly steady over the whole period, with a peak in 1969, preference shares were unpopular especially in 1967 (partly due perhaps to the exchanges for debenture and loan issues organised by some companies after the change to corporation tax), and ordinary shares were by far the most popular purchase. Nearly 50% of net additions were represented by ordinary shares – except in 1969 when the equity market suffered a steep decline. The other significant investments were in land and property, in ground rents and in property investment trusts.

These figures indicate that private self-administered funds are gradually increasing the proportion of equities in their portfolios and the tables for insurance-company investments suggest that a similar process is taking place in insured schemes.[3] The trend is hardly surprising. The financial press have emphasised again and again over the last twenty years that equity dividends and share prices have, on average, more or less kept pace with inflation, whereas gilt-edged and other fixed interest stocks have not and cannot. Since the Trustee Investments Act of 1961 gave powers to all trustees to invest part of the funds under their control in equity shares (subject to the detailed limitations regarding size of companies, regularity of dividends for five years, etc.) the question in most cases has been "how much" (to invest in equities) rather than "whether" and many schemes now invest 100% in equities and property with only rare incursions into the fixed interest market. (Most trustees have wider powers under their Trust Deeds.)

Inflation in the U.K. which helped to bring about the Trustee Investments Act of 1961 has been the main-spring of the changed outlook, but it is fair to say that the more sophisticated analyses of growth have been of considerable importance in many instances also. Once the decision has been made to enter the equity market on a large scale, the next problem is to find shares whose price and dividends taken together will grow faster than inflation. This more sophisticated analysis has parted from the legal notions of life-tenants and remainder-men and the strict actuarial divisions between income and unrealised capital gains (and losses)[4] and is allowing the aim of a portfolio to be based on the total improvement of net worth between two points in time – the "total return".

The actuarial profession is unlikely to be willing to take unrealised capital gains into account[5] when making the triennial or quinquennial valuations. Income received on the one hand and book values (written down if need be in a disastrous case), on the other, are still of first importance. As a consequence, it can be worth while to look for "good" opportunities to realise some capital gains before rather than after an actuarial valuation. This is, however, anticipating part of the argument and will be referred to later.

What were the views of the Sixties? The consensus seemed to be to venture more and more into the equity market but to keep a firm foothold in the gilt-edged market.[6] This is reflected by (or is a reflection of) the 1961 Act. How then should decisions regarding proportions be reached in the Seventies?

In pre-War conditions, when inflation was thought to refer to Germany of the early 1920s, most actuaries based their calculations on the assumption that investments would yield about 4%. This rate proved quite difficult for many funds to achieve during the period of artificially low interest rates, viz.: the depression of the 1930s, the 1939–45 war and the "Dalton" era. After the return of the Tories in 1951, the equity market had a remarkable period of growth and the "reverse yield gap" and the "cult of the equity" were well written up in the financial press. The old text-book explanations that equities provided a higher yield than fixed-interest stock so to give the investor a "risk premium" seemed to have been scrapped and forgotten, only to reappear again in a more sophisticated form. Equities provided a lower dividend yield, it was argued, because they "grew", more or less keeping pace with inflation. It was the fixed-interest stocks which had now become risky – the value of both income and capital were bound to fall in real terms in a period of inflation. So it has come about that Government Stocks which yielded 3% or less during the Dalton era have fallen in price in the last twenty years so that the yield has risen to 4%, 5%, 6%, 7%, 8%, 9% and more. The result has been disastrous for pension (and other) funds wholly or mainly invested in gilt-edged. In real terms the value of stocks dropped by about 80% between 1951 and 1971, most of it due to the very different interest-rate structure which, in turn, had come about because of inflation.[7] Much higher fixed-interest yields were essential, it was now argued, to compensate for inflation: e.g., if inflation is 3% per annum a 6% or 7% yield rather than the old 3% or 4% under stable conditions is called for and if inflation is averaging 6% or 7% p.a., 9% or even 10% p.a. is needed to ensure a "reasonable" net return in real terms.

Now that most trustees have even wider powers than the minima provided in the 1961 Act, the market has to provide the "fixed-interest premium" if stocks are to be sold. How then should Pension Fund trustees view the total investment market now? Has the gilt-edged market, for instance, gone as low as it will ever go and how high can we expect equity indices to climb in the future?

Pension Funds are "gross" funds, they do not have to bear any deductions for income or capital gains tax (they may have to bear income-tax deductions initially but can recover them from the Exchequer). In other words, the operations of a pension fund portfolio (compared to an individual one) is simplified by not having to do any tax planning, or make any adjustments for the differential tax rates applicable to income and to capital gains. It is open to enquire therefore:

1 What is the future trend of the "fixed-interest premium" likely to be? As indicated previously, this will depend largely on changes in the rate of inflation in the longer term, with smaller fluctuations caused by short-run changes in the money supply – and other Government actions. It is still possible that if inflation were to average 10% p.a. for a considerable number of years, gilt-edged stocks in the medium- and long-term markets could fall to prices at which the redemption yields were 13% or 14% p.a. Further substantial losses would then be sustained by pension funds with large holdings of gilt-edged. There seems little doubt that there are considerable risks involved in keeping large holdings in the gilt-edged market for long periods whilst inflation shows no signs of being brought under control.

2 At what rate are share prices of and dividends on equities likely to grow? This is dependent on two factors. Inflation appears as before because fixed costs in industry, etc., are eroded and, even without physical expansion, money profits increase as inflation continues. Secondly, the level of activity and the profitability of companies generally has to be taken into account. Managers, like other human beings, are fallible when operating in conditions of risk and uncertainty and the Exchequer is prone to interfere with the economy in ways which have a considerable influence on corporate activity and profitability. The rate of Corporation Tax is one important aspect of this "interference" but may be less important than

deliberate attempts to reduce the pace of the economy – "squeezes and freezes", when most companies find their liquidity position deteriorating and take remedial steps which, in turn, apply pressure at some other point in the economic system.

In the most vulnerable areas, companies have to go into liquidation, not always because they are "inefficient"; the single most frequent problem is that of liquidity – an inability to pay for raw materials or for next week's wages. This illiquidity may indicate a special form of inefficiency, a lack of financial management, but it is difficult for the smaller company to survive if sales drop off and/or it has difficulty in obtaining prompt payment for its products whilst having to pay for purchases if it is not to be "blacklisted" by suppliers. The construction industry is particularly prone to these liquidity problems.

Even without any special adjustments for gearing ratios, the earnings applicable to equity shares will tend then to fluctuate over time. Furthermore, equity share-prices tend to exaggerate the changes in earnings, so that prices fluctuate far more than fixed-interest stocks.

Even if it has been decided to invest wholly or mainly in the equity market, pension funds must have a contingency plan, maintaining emergency liquid elements in its portfolio, so as to avoid having to sell equity shares at depressed prices, e.g. to raise extra funds because the death rate of its contributing members and annuitants is higher than usual around some point in time – say, a 'flu epidemic one winter. So it will be wise to have some proportion of gilt-edged, preferably spread through the short, the medium and the long-term markets to maximise yield whilst compensating for the reducing chances of a forced sale in unexpected circumstances which occurs at a time when the equity market is depressed. The size of this contingency will vary with the size of the fund (the laws of large numbers cannot be expected to apply to a fund with only fifty members but are likely to work quite well if there are two thousand or more members spread around the country). It will also vary with the future expected net cash flow of the fund and, ironically perhaps, inflation helps future liquidity – contributions are increased in proportion to increased wages and salaries, whereas few pensions as yet increase annually after retirement to compensate for inflation. Again, the size of the contingency can also be varied with the buoyancy or otherwise of the equity market. It is important for trustees to budget well ahead and to prepare cash-flow estimates for at least two or three years into the future. In the absence of such estimates they cannot know what the contingency plan should be and I suspect that many funds have holdings of gilt-edged stocks far higher than will ever be needed for contingency reasons because the trustees have not asked for these simple estimates to be made.

It has been recalled above that equity share-prices swing upwards and downwards more than changes in corporate earnings and dividends and far more than the prices of fixed-interest stocks. This can be readily confirmed by looking at the "highs" and "lows" of almost any share quoted on the stock exchange in any year taken at random. The reasons for these exaggerations are interesting but beyond the scope of this chapter. Here we must content ourselves with the fact that the "highs" and "lows" occur, that the scope of some of them can be predicted in advance by expert investment consultants with a fair degree of accuracy so that it is possible to say at a particular point in time whether a particular share is "cheap", "dear" or "fairly valued". It follows that timing of purchases and sales is "of the essence" and that, with some exceptions in the case of "true-growth"[8] shares, fairly regular sales as well as purchases should occur[9]. This is a far cry from the days when only gilt-edged stocks were bought and virtually none were sold.[10]

This brings us back to the earlier comment that capital gains should, in suitable cases, be taken before a valuation – i.e. shares should be sold when they are "dear", and it should be stressed that they should be sold whether it is one, two or three years before the next valuation. It must also be emphasised that "cheap" shares should *not* be sold, whether or not they show a healthy increase above book-value. The criterion now has to be the maximisation of "total return" which in turn calls for maximum capital gains per quinquennium, not merely the occasional realisation of gains if they turn up. Furthermore, the capital gains will almost always be far greater than dividend yields. It is the capital gains, therefore, to which most time and attention must be given even if it involves the purchase of low-payout shares with dividend yields of 0·5% to, say, 2% p.a.[11]

It has to be borne in mind that most equities vary between 10% to 50% (some much more) between the "highs" and "lows" each year, and that there is enormous scope for the expert. An even more interesting comparison is between the "low" of one year and the "high" of the next – or better still to watch the share chart. This is not a plea for "chartism" which seems to ignore the fundamentals unnecessarily and which frequently misses worthwhile gains before a "signal" appears. It is a plea for a strategy of "active" investment based on truly expert and independent guidance, yet avoiding ill-considered switching from one equity to another as brokers' circulars appear. Some large funds now split their resources into two or more sections[12] and compare the performances of the two (or more) investment consultants to which the sections are entrusted. Joint stock banks as well as merchant banks have sharpened up their know-how quite markedly in the last few years and smaller funds are gradually finding good independent investment consultants who will take an interest in their portfolios (which are too small for the large institutions which usually like a fund to have assets of at least £500,000 and preferably £5m.). The charges are low compared to the improved results – usually a minimum of £500 p.a. or so, but only 0·2% falling to 0·1% p.a. of the market value of the fund in the case of large and very large funds.

The quotations and performance of the large insurance companies is an interesting comparison. Whilst the insured schemes provide a fairly painless way to start a pension fund, especially for small- and even medium-sized companies, it should not be assumed that insured funds are "best buys". Current quotations seem to estimate future "total yields" as averaging 8% to 9% p.a. for the next three to five years. This is a modest aim when inflation is serious. On the other hand, the funds which large insurance companies have to invest are so large that they cannot buy worthwhile equity holdings in any but the top thousand companies. Any sizeable purchase in, say, a medium-sized company will push up the price against the buyer[13] and, having bought (over a few months, perhaps), any large sale will, at best, push down the price[14] and, at worst, be impossible to achieve unless spread over several months. In other words, there is a real danger of being "locked in", even though the share is a quoted one with steady transactions, nearly as badly as if the investment were in a private company. If £100 m. is invested, it would be a monumental task to spread this around even a thousand companies and even then the average purchase would be £100,000 – over 10% of any company with a market capitalisation of under £1m. The result is that large investments have to be made in the giant companies, most of which have performed rather badly in recent years – in both the U.K. and the U.S.A. – or in gilt-edged which can be bought (and sold) in very large quantities.

This holds down the "total-return" performance of the insurance companies, in spite of receiving special "large-customer" service[15] from brokers and others. It is not surprising that they are gradually going into the property business, not just as lenders at fixed interest but as profit (and loss) sharers.[16]

It may be that insured schemes will gradually offer better terms. Even now, they perform as well or better than indifferently run self-administered schemes, but the insurance arrangement provides many excuses for top management who can easily avoid any responsibility for performance. Slowly, in self-administered schemes, targets are being raised and increased "know-how" sought and gained. In some cases, the main objects of having a fund are being realised, and the employees as well as the company are proud as well as glad to belong to a particular scheme, where benefits are raised and raised again without increases in the scale of contributions.

In other words, attainment of a total return of 10% p.a. compound over the last ten years is currently providing more than the state Reserve Scheme will dream of twenty-five years hence, with contributions only just over twice those which seem likely to be required by that scheme which seems to be based on much lower yields than 10% – indeed the concept of "total return" does not seem to be appreciated by more than a tiny handful of M.P.s on either side of the House. There are also those who would be far from pleased if the investment performance of the scheme proved as good as or better than that of the insurance companies.

The latter is unlikely to occur. Sheer size will almost certainly exact its price. What is seldom mentioned is the fact that both prospective pensioners and the stock market would benefit much more from five thousand actively and expertly invested self-administered schemes than from large insurance and Governmental schemes owning blocks of shares so large that the portfolio is restricted and any realisations can seriously depress the share prices even of multi-national giants.[17]

One more comparison between gilt-edged and equity yields. If an equity is bought with an average *dividend* yield of 3·5% (the FT-Actuaries All-Share index yields about that at the time of writing) whilst a gilt-edged stock will yield 9·5%, there is a differential of 6%. In other words, two interpretations are open:

1 If inflation is not more than $5\frac{1}{2}$% p.a. the real yield on gilt-edged will be a "reasonable" figure of 4% p.a.

2 The equity dividend and (especially) the share price must, on average, grow at least 6% p.a. for it to have been worth while to buy the equity rather than gilt-edged. If the equity dividend yield of a particular share is only 1% or less, then the average growth of the share price must certainly exceed 8·5% and, because of the risk of growth slowing down or stopping, the short-run growth should be much more, say 18·5% p.a.

Great care is necessary, therefore, before buying current glamour stocks with very low dividend yields. If many are held for long, the income of the fund will suffer, and for any but the best managed companies in favourable circumstances, constant growth at 20% p.a. or thereabouts is almost impossible to achieve in the long term. There have been, and still are, companies like I.B.M. which achieve this, but they are far easier to see in retrospect and the chances of these successful companies continuing at the same rate in the future is fairly small. Otherwise we should only have a handful of companies now. The giant companies in particular find anything but modest growth rates difficult. If corrections are made for inflation, few giant companies have grown very much in terms of earnings per share over the last five years.

To sum up. In an age of inflation:

1 The performance targets of most pension funds are very modest.

2 Too few pension funds measure their performance in a modern way.[18]

3 Fixed-interest stocks should only be bought for two reasons:
  (a) Liquidity, i.e. as part of the contingency plan.
  (b) During bear markets in the equity sector, after some capital gains have been realised.

4 Strategies suitable for the fixed-interest market are inappropriate to the equity market. An active, expertly conducted, strategy is needed – selling "dear" and buying "cheap" – every year or two in many cases.

5 Trustees must seek out and be willing to pay for expert equity investment know-how. A considerable increase in expert but independent investment-consultant services is needed, especially for the private investor and for the smaller pension funds which the investment-consultant sections of the large institutions are unlikely to find worth their while to look after. There will shortly be a seller's market for investment consultants in this country, as pension-fund trustees are beginning to realise that most insured schemes do not perform as well as the expertly invested self-administered schemes do – with resultant better benefits or lower contributions – or both.

NOTES TO CHAPTER 22

[1] "The Measurement of Investment Performance – Internal Assessment", a private seminar paper reprinted in *Investment Analysis and Portfolio Measurement*, Ed. Basil Taylor, Elek Books, 1970, pp. 117–128. See also T. G. Arthur, "The Measurement of Past Investment Performance as an Aid to Future Investment Policy", unpublished paper presented to the Birmingham Actuarial Society, 5th October 1972.

[2] Table 79, "Financial Statistics", October 1972, p. 92 *et seq.*, Central Statistical Office. Further detail is now given in Supplementary Table B of "Financial Statistics", e.g. February 1973, pp. 136–8, including the very large purchases and sales figures compared to the net changes.

[3] See "Financial Statistics" Supplementary Table B. Very rapid growth of self-administered funds is taking place in the U.S.A. too and the percentage of Common Stocks doubled to 62·6% between 1955 and 1968 and is still rising. See *U.S. Securities and Exchange Commission Statistical Bulletin*, May 1969.

4 E.g. comments by Richard A. Brealey, "Security Prices in a Competitive Market", M.I.T. Press, 1971, pp. 20–21; and T. G. Arthur, *op. cit.*, Section 4.

5 A brief but very clear exposition by George Ross Goobey, Investment Advisor to and Director of Imperial Tobacco Ltd. and President of the National Association of Pension Funds, can be seen in *Professional Administrator*, December, 1972, pp. 59–60.

6 See for example W. Nursaw, *Principles of Investment for Pension Funds*, Hutchinson, 1966, especially pp. 69–73; Hosking, *Pension Schemes and Retirement Benefits*, Sweet & Maxwell, 1968, pp. 248–60; P. J. Naish, *The Complete Guide to Personal Investment*, Evans, 1962, pp. 241–2.

7 A similar position occurred in the U.S.A. in the 1960s and some funds adjusted their strategies: see D. and A. West, "Risk Analysis in the Sixties", *Financial Analysts' Journal*, Vol. 23, No. 6, November–December 1967, pp. 124–6.

8 Cases where earnings per share have risen regularly for at least five years and there is considerable confidence that E.P.S. will continue to rise for a further period of two or more years.

9 One recent American author recommends the use of shares with very large swings in share price: see M. G. Zahorchak, *The Art of Low-Risk Investing*, Van Nostrand Reinhold, 1972.

10 Except for the now illegal "bond washing" and the more recent switching arrangements – in some cases agreed to be carried out by the broker automatically. For examples of switching, see Nursaw, *op. cit.*, pp. 76–78.

11 This is despite the tax-exempt nature of pension funds, e.g. Richard A. Brealey, *op. cit.*, p. 20.

12 E.g., Manchester Corporation.

13 See comments regarding the Manhattan· Fund in The Value Line contest, John P. Shelton, reprinted in *Security Evaluation and Portfolio Analysis*, edited by Edwin J. Elton and Martin J. Gruber, Prentice Hall, 1972, p. 387.

14 Courtauld's pension fund recently sold half of a large holding in Triumph Investment Trust. This, coupled with a rights issue, seems to have had a considerable effect on the market price in the second half of 1972.

15 There is a danger, often overlooked, that they receive dubious as well as genuine information quicker than smaller investors: see *Fortune*, December, 1969, pp. 163–68.

16 Some very large pension funds, including Imperial Tobacco Co. Ltd. and the National Coal Board, are also by-passing the stock market (and Corporation Tax) by going directly into property and property development.

[17] For a discussion of "block transactions" in the U.S.A., see Friend, Blume and Crockett, *Mutual Funds and Other Institutional Investors: A New Perspective*, McGraw Hill, 1970, p. 100.

[18] Interesting methods have been published in 1972 by: 1. The Society of Investment Analysts at 35p, and 2. Phillips & Drew – part of the March and October reviews (a simpler one). For other evaluations, see Jack N. Treynor, "How to Rate the Management of Pension Funds", *H.B.R.*, Vol. 43, No. 1 (January–February 1965), pp. 63–76. A further article by the same author and Kay K. Mazuy, "Can Mutual Funds Outguess the Market?" *H.B.R.*, Vol. 44, No. 4 (July–August 1966), is not recommended as there is a flaw in the logic: curvature of the characteristic line is not necessary.

Chapter 23

LONG-RANGE PLANNING FOR PERSONNEL

Ralph L. Hopps
General Manager, Personnel Division,
National Westminster Bank

My purpose in this chapter is to share some thoughts on the human resources in financial institutions and the influences that may cause changes to be made in the years that lie ahead. This will help to indicate what action can be taken to prepare for the future.

Some readers, I know, will be familiar with the trend towards "human asset accounting" which seeks to quantify the value of a company's human resources and show it as an asset in the balance sheet rather than, as occurs at present, purely as a cost in the Profit and Loss Account. The theory is that one might try to estimate how long it would take to get back into business at the present level of activity in the event of losing one's entire staff. If this was an average of, say, three years over the whole staff then it would be fair to enter three times the annual staff costs as the value of the human asset. Having obtained that figure it is not difficult to incorporate such refinements as determination of the percentage that might be allocated to the maintenance of the human asset.

Now I appreciate that no two companies are alike and it is necessary to develop one's own solution to what must be a unique problem. Moreover, the boundaries of some of the financial institutions are changing and the edges are becoming blurred. Also, the sizes of the organisations represented here vary so much. Nevertheless, I hope the principles which will be covered will apply with equal force to large and small companies alike.

Earlier contributions have emphasised the need for an effective Business Strategy, particularly in view of the accelerating

pace of change. The questions being asked today are:
"What are the big issues that affect us now?"
"What are the alternative opportunities?"
"What are the constraints?"
"What is really important?"
Looking to the future, we ask:
"What business shall we be in in 5/10/15/20 years' time?"
"How can we prepare for this?"
"Can we go it alone and, if not, with whom should we work?"

My first plea is that in all areas of Strategic Planning the human resources should be given proper and timely consideration. In Personnel Management this is the responsibility of the manpower planner and he must be brought in and consulted at an early stage in the consideration of any new project, whether it be to consider new services, modification to existing services, new computer systems, or other technological change. Gone are the days when it was possible to decide on a particular line of action and then merely ask the Staff Manager to provide the required staff of the right quality and experience. What, then, are the forces generating change?

TECHNOLOGICAL CHANGE

What is possible in terms of Research and Development and Manufacture and makes good business sense in terms of efficiency could have a big effect on staffing requirements and these may not be acceptable to the Staff Representatives. In seeking to plan forward, therefore, one must try and predict not only those things that are feasible but also what is acceptable. This is not to say that efforts should not be made to take staff with management in new developments, but time is of the essence to ensure the position can be properly discussed. People generally like time to adjust to change.

SOCIAL CHANGE

There is a growing demand for leisure in terms of hours per day and days per week. How and when are further developments likely to take place? Will this lead to an extension of shift working? Companies are now experimenting with flexible working hours, pioneered successfully in West Germany. Then there are the growing pressures for more holidays. How much? When? All these social developments must, in the end, lead to increased costs of human resources.

Youth. Then there is also the so-called "cult of youth" in which more and more young people look for and expect responsibility and promotion early in life. The need to reconcile the forty-year career with the expressed desire of at least some young people for responsibility early in life is certainly one of the more difficult problems of our time. Indeed, in the United States a backlash is being experienced arising from the practice of appointing too many young executives.

Women. Large numbers of women are employed in financial institutions – in the big banks over half the staff are women. However progressive has been the outlook of the organisation in seeking to give equal opportunity, most women have not started to compete with men for responsible positions until they have reached their middle or late twenties. However, here again it is clear that social attitudes and the rôle of women are changing and in the years ahead more of them will look for long-term careers as opposed to jobs, leading to shared domestic responsibilities. The practice of women leaving to start a family and then returning some years later may well become more prevalent in the future. For the manpower planner this provides uncertainty, for the present position with its built-in female wastage may be said to suit many employers.

Environment. In terms of environment there appears to be a growing reluctance on the part of some people to travel long distances to work. This may in time extend to a resistance to moving home. One may be tempted to question the degree of commitment to the job in such cases, but it is perhaps only a natural developing desire of a growing number of people to live satisfying lives both at work and in the home environment. One must recognise it – not just ignore it.

Other social questions include the desire of some people to retire early so that they can have second careers. This could be offset by others – perhaps late entrants – who desire to retire later. Encouragement is given to this last line of thought in view of the delay in the ageing process which the medical profession is promising to provide.

The basic problem in a career-dominated organisation is to reconcile the number of people needed to fill today's vacancies with rewarding career opportunities for all those on long-term engagements. Each company can solve its own problem by redundancy/early retirements, etc., but we have all seen the adverse social consequences caused by the cumulative effect of these measures not only in terms of the unemployment situation but also the self-respect of individuals concerned. Whilst lifetime career employment has been rather out of fashion recently, the social needs of the community may make it increasingly valuable in the next generation.

These social factors give an indication of some of the developments that a manpower planner must consider as he prepares his forecasts. They have a real bearing on future business plans.

POLITICAL CHANGE

First comes education. This year (1972) we see the school-leaving age raised and this will have a direct effect on the number of workers available. Some people are advocating a greater involvement of industry and commerce in the content of school education, no doubt seeking to influence developments so that the education given is suitable for modern employment. This does not remove from the employer the responsibility for providing jobs suitable for modern school-leavers, and it is interesting to note that Mr. B. M. Rooney of the Inter-Bank Research Organisation is at present planning research on these lines in conjunction with the Social Science Research Council.

The graduate represents for many a smallish but important proportion of manpower intake but, in view of the likely continuing increase in output from the Universities, Business Schools and Polytechnics, it is essential that clearly-defined policies be evolved regarding their employment, taking full account of career opportunity, company needs and the level of expectation of the remainder of the staff.

Other political factors influencing human resources include Government directives concerning race, the disabled, and legislation on such topics as the guaranteed minimum wage, minimum/maximum hours, and holidays. Pensions policies have received considerable publicity recently, particularly in regard to the effect the State Scheme will have on occupational schemes and inter-company mobility. This latter factor, of course, has a direct bearing on such things as resignation rates and promotion from within.

Other political factors which have affected staff and staff costs are regional policies, social benefits, S.E.T., National Health Insurance, to some extent transport and housing, and, of course, the Industrial Relations Act.

All this shows that a business of any size seeking to do strategic planning must bear factors such as these in mind and, therefore, involve the manpower planner at a very early stage in any new development in the concern.

Bearing in mind, therefore, technological, social and political changes that are taking place now and are likely to take place in the future, the manpower planner seeks to provide – at acceptable cost – adequate staff of the necessary aptitudes and skills to implement the action programmes required to fulfil corporate objectives.

MANPOWER PLANNING

Manpower Planning starts as a "numbers game" directly affecting recruitment, promotion, and retirement, but really covers everything that has a bearing on the attraction and retention of the right people. It extends to training and development policies, and to personnel relations. All these will be dealt with in detail a little later on, but it cannot be over-emphasised that a company should keep its terms and conditions of service under constant review. These include a salary strategy, arrangements for pensioners and widows, sickness benefits, arrangements for early retirement, sports facilities, and fringe benefits generally. There is a tendency to remove the paternal aspects from management, but it will be a sad day when staff do not receive the kindly interest and human concern often associated with the phrase.

In my preamble on human asset accounting I referred to staff as a capital asset and not merely a charge in the Profit and Loss Account. Indeed, the manpower planner views each member of staff as a unit of manpower which appreciates in value with training and experience. In some situations units may be reduced in value because of changes in systems, in management style, and in philosophy. This shows how careful one must be before introducing new systems in view of the effect on the "human asset" side of the Balance Sheet. In banking most units used to be – so to speak – "written off" after forty-three years – a lifetime's service. Now more than half the staff – mostly female – write themselves off by leaving the company after forty-five years.

The computer is fast becoming the principal tool in helping to formulate manpower plans. By constructing a manpower model which takes the form of a computer programme it is possible to obtain rapid answers to the vital question "What might happen if . . .?" It does not remove the need to study long-range forecasts, technological, social and political, and it must be left to the manpower planner to ask appropriate questions. Some people look on manpower planning as a science; in view of the many subjective judgements that are involved I see it as more of an art. Forecasting really is prediction based on observed regularities of the past, allowance being made for foreseeable changes which may break established trends and relationships.

The manpower model that has been constructed in my own organisation is based on a detailed study of the bank's personnel and career structures. The basic purpose is to help formulate and test the effect of major personnel policies. This is achieved by projecting year by year into the future the possible manpower position in the bank, starting with the present position given certain assumptions about retirement, wastage, promotion, recruitment, and the number of jobs to be filled at each level of responsibility.

The power of the model is that it enables the decision-maker, without being lost in a mass of calculations, to experiment very rapidly with different sets of assumptions, seeing what happens in each case. This power of experimentation is an extremely valuable aid in revealing potential problems and identifying better policies for the future. The model provides a useful mental discipline by requiring precise data to be fed in and also shows how sensitive the various policies selected are. It acts as an impartial arbiter in the event of disagreement and, finally, encourages decision-takers to look at problems in the round and not to give too much weight to one factor.

However, the success of the model depends on the accuracy of the records, and this is encouraging us to consider the integration of payroll with staff records on the computer.

As I mentioned earlier, manpower planning starts with effective recruitment and selection of individuals; this is vital if unnecessary wastage and frustration, which are costly, are to be avoided. This is the starting-point for all career development.

CAREER DEVELOPMENT

The control of career development is a central task for all large companies, for availability of competent staff at all levels is essential for sustained company progress. Staff may be classified in varying levels of potential so that plans for their development can be made. People are different, but more often than not a person can be extended that little bit further with benefit to the company and, above all, greater satisfaction and fulfilment to the individual.

Of course, much of the development must be self-development, and the company should seek to provide an atmosphere in which individuals can themselves grow in stature. In these competitive days I believe the companies which will succeed will be those which encourage their staff to use that priceless gift of intelligence – to be creative – to provide new ideas. The company must be effective in translating the best ideas into practice. It must ensure as far as possible that the work it provides is interesting, satisfying, and worthy of human beings. This needs careful scrutiny, for though automated procedures are introduced to remove the need for human beings to perform routine tasks, there is always the danger that even more monotonous tasks may nevertheless remain, though for fewer people.

There are some people who express themselves as being content to perform routine tasks. Nevertheless, with enlightened education, I think we shall find more and more that young people will reject job opportunities which do not offer an adequate level of job satisfaction.

For people with high potential special arrangements can be made. Their careers can be monitored and they can be given tasks of increasing interest and responsibility. As we are likely to see greater diversification in financial activities it is important that they should be given opportunities in various branches of finance. They, like everyone in the business, must be encouraged to exploit their main strengths and develop their lesser strengths. In doing so they may well change the nature of the job. This must be accepted. Human beings are a dynamic force. It is interesting to see, in banking, how some human qualities which have perhaps been undervalued in the past now begin to receive appropriate recognition. This is particularly true of organising ability and marketing skills.

SUCCESSION PLANNING

Given ideal conditions, correct career development would lead naturally to careful and effective succession planning. Who will follow this executive at the appropriate time? Who will follow that executive in the event of an emergency? The unpredictability of life will never permit of ideal conditions, of course, but our efforts must always seek the ideal goal. Succession planning must look as far ahead as possible so that adequate preparation and experience, both inside and outside the company, can be given to those destined for high places. The whole-hearted support of top management is absolutely essential to success when the time comes for drafted plans to be put into effect. Ineffective succession planning may remain hidden for a long time – the theory of the time-span of discretion certainly applies here, particularly at high levels, and the future of the company can be greatly affected.

TRAINING

Closely linked with career development and succession planning is training, and this includes induction, technical training, and managerial development. It covers training in branches and departments both on and off the job, and it also covers attendance at day and residential colleges. The first task must be to make new employees welcome, aware of the organisation they have joined, and quickly capable of doing a full day's satisfying work. Some companies do most of their training away from the place of work, whereas others give training partly at college and partly in the job environment. In the latter instance teaching machines can be of great assistance; an hour a day on a teaching machine before doing a new task can be beneficial both in giving confidence to the individual and enabling the organisation to maintain a high level of service.

Care must be taken in all courses, but particularly in some of the advanced development courses, to see that individuals move to positions of greater responsibility as soon as possible after their return. Better that some people do not go on courses than that they should have their hopes dashed for increased responsibilities and new opportunities.

In these days, when there is greater awareness generally, assistance can be gained by sending staff to courses run by outside organisations, Business Schools, the Universities, Ashridge, Cranfield, Harvard, Henley and so on. Mixing with people from other organisations and seeing problems through their eyes is a stretching experience. Whilst there is greater movement between companies these days attendance at these outside courses provides a similar form of experience.

In terms of cost the expenditure on company training may be viewed as part of the maintenance cost of the human asset in an organisation. Such expenditure may also be seen as an investment, the return on which is the more effective performance of work.

PERSONNEL RELATIONS

Speaking of awareness brings us naturally to a discussion of Industrial Relations, or Personnel Relations as I prefer to call it. One of the more important issues of today, if not the most important, is the desire of people at all levels to be involved in and contribute to many of the decisions that affect their work. The word is "participation". It is not enough merely to consult – there must be provision for participation. Over past years there has been an almost complete absence of industrial strife within the City, and by avoiding the mistakes of other industries we can, I am sure, continue a developing relationship with our staff and their representatives. There are no blue-prints for different industries or different companies – indeed, it is wise to avoid other people's prescriptions and to resist the appeal of current fashion.

Personnel Relations is not only about salaries and wages –

it is also about productivity, progress, need of change; above all, it is about attitudes and relationships. Some say that the autocratic style of management is going – so, too, is the over-paternalistic form reminiscent of Victorian times. Individuals seek more and more to participate in decisions. Of course, good employers consult their employees before decisions are taken. On some matters they then decide, and that is that. On others they negotiate. But in all things the trend is towards consultation.

Over recent years there has been a growth in white-collar unions; in banking there are Staff Associations and the National Union of Bank Employees. Other developments are taking place in Insurance, Finance Houses and in Building Societies. It is not for an employer to choose the form of representation but to speak to whatever organisation has the confidence of his staff.

The Industrial Relations Act has served to focus attention on relationships between employer, employees and their representatives. Generally speaking, we welcome the Act, but we must remember that human relations are too complex to be contained in a legal formula and we would be foolish to rely on a legislative framework to the exclusion of balanced judgement. Nevertheless, we support the spirit and purpose of both the Act and the Code.

The Act has made employers look at their procedures and, in particular, their methods of communication. The Clearing Banks especially, with their many small units, have special problems but also special opportunities of holding explanatory groups and encouraging "feedback". Some have central Joint Staff Offices, each consisting of one Staff Association representative and one N.U.B.E. representative, whereby grievances which have not been settled by normal line management may be aired and resolved. Some say that too much reliance is placed on the views of the Staff Representatives – they have a tendency to paint a picture rather blacker than it really is. However, their views provide a cross-check against the information coming through normal management channels. Need I say that management continually needs to improve its lines of communication? How much information should we provide? Some people press for more and more, but still feel dissatisfied when they have it. Some like what they hear and others do not – human nature being what it is, one usually only hears from the latter category. Certainly the request for more information will continue and some form of balance must be struck.

I believe that what matters most in the field of Personnel Relations is the quality of the relationships. If employer/employee relationships are positive and constructive, if there is mutual respect between the individuals concerned, then that company should prosper. But some negotiations are on a national level – what happens there? The same principles apply but I have sympathy with the views of the Donovan Report that the most satisfactory solutions are likely to be found nearest to the problem areas. Of course there will be differences, that is natural. But they will mostly be long-term versus the short-term, the Staff Representatives wanting the benefits now – not perhaps very dissimilar to shareholders – whereas management will wish to look a little bit further ahead. Hence the need for Strategic Planning and the associated need for good communications. In the future, with the spread of multi-national companies, we shall no doubt see Trade Unions spanning national frontiers in order to protect the interests of their members.

EUROPE

This brings us to a consideration of the impact on personnel matters of this country joining the European Economic Community. The yearning for greater participation is as strong in other parts of Europe as it is here. The objects there are said to include:

(i) A better distribution of power.

(ii) A greater co-operation of the staff.

(iii) An increased personal involvement and fulfilment.

Mention should also be made of European Supervisory Boards, one third of which is elected by the staff and whose principal function is the appointment and control of the Board of Management. Whether this pattern of management will be adopted in this country is not known, but we may expect to see more training and a greater professionalism in everything, particularly personnel matters.

PERSONNEL FUNCTION

Personnel Managers must earn respect by their expertise – they must be able to have their views and recommendations accepted by line management because of their greater knowledge and professionalism. There cannot, of course, be career paths for everybody in such a specialist function and, indeed, a company is the better for having men with high potential pass through such a function on their way up the ladder. Nevertheless, there must be specialist personnel career paths if the organisation is to retain good people and maintain at a high level its standards of personnel management.

We have tended to think of there being three parties to any commercial enterprise. They are:

the customers,

the shareholders – who put their money into the business,

the staff – who invest their lives in the business.

There is a fourth dimension which will be receiving more and more attention as time goes on, and that is the social dimension. In general banking we are very close to our customers and the public. One behavioural scientist I know referred to our organisation as being all skin, all pores – so close are we and so sensitive are we to outside influences and pressures. That is probably a good thing. It augurs well for the future; it should help us to react promptly to such influences.

We need to take advice from outside specialists. In this chapter I have referred, either directly or indirectly, to long-range planners, operational researchers, computer specialists, behavioural scientists, statisticians, economists and psychologists. All have their part to play in helping us to see as far forward as possible and to do our job better. We must not buy packages from the specialists but work out with our staff what the appropriate solutions to our problems are.

We live in a changing world. Some tell us to stop doing yesterday's things in yesterday's ways. Well, the more we equip ourselves to manage change for the well-being of the company, and particularly the staff, the better. The management of change might be the greatest lesson yet to be learned. In this I believe our greatest asset is our staff; their integrity, their ability, their experience. If goals can be carefully defined; if we, our staff, and their representatives spend time time and effort in looking well ahead, then we can encourage greater commitment by our staff, for they have their individual goals to aim at for their own benefit and that of the company. Above all, it will help them to put their energies, their strengths, their creative intelligence, where worthwhile results can be seen to be achieved.

Chapter 24

STRATEGIC PLANNING
IN A COMPOSITE INSURANCE GROUP

K. G. Addison
*General Manager and Director, Sun Alliance and
London Insurance Group*

The following comments on long-term planning refer particularly to a large composite insurance group. There is, therefore, limited reference to matters which are common to long-term planning in all industrial and commercial undertakings such as the formation of the planning team and the mechanics of its operation. However, a few preliminary points are worthy of special mention.

1 If the plan is to be meaningful and a sound basis for future action, the planning team must include adequate representation at senior management level and its terms of reference and underlying purpose must be known and understood throughout those parts of the organisation whose activities will be affected.

2 The scope of the plan must be clearly defined and any basic assumptions on which the plan is prepared must be clearly stated. For example, does the plan assume no major changes in legislative control, does it assume that inflation will continue at a certain rate, does it make any assumptions on merger activity among its intermediaries or policyholders? On some of these questions the planning team may feel sufficiently confident to make a firm assumption and they can then base their recommendations firmly on that assumption. In others, the team may find it necessary to consider in detail two or more possibilities and make a number of alternative recommendations which can be reassessed as events unfold.

3 However well researched and however skilful the forecasts,

the plan will be of limited value unless it is regularly brought up to date. The frequency with which this is done depends largely upon the organisation concerned, but it can be confidently said that any period over twelve months is too long. Whatever the interval between general reviews, the planning team, or at least a representative section of the team, should be constantly comparing actual events with the forecasts in the plan and assessing the extent to which those events make necessary changes in their recommendations. If the plan is allowed to lose its dynamic quality it can become a straitjacket which will hinder rather than promote the company's development.

ENVIRONMENTAL FACTORS

In preparing a long-term plan an examination must be made of environmental factors both outside and within the insurance industry. Factors outside the industry include:

1 Future developments in the markets served by the industry; commercial and industrial changes in both technology and organisation; the development in the various classes of insurance intermediaries; changes in the buying habits of the insuring public.

2 Demographic and economic trends; changes in the distribution of wealth; improvements in the standard of living and its effect on property ownership and attitudes to financial security.

3 Future legislative changes, for example, statutory control of the industry; changes in taxation; legislation affecting particular classes of insurance such as pension schemes, public and employers' liability indemnities and motor insurance.

4 Major international developments such as the entry of the United Kingdom into the Common Market; growing nationalism in overseas territories; the emergence of an increasing number of large international industrial undertakings with major trading and manufacturing units spread throughout the world.

The insurance industry is unusual in that it has a market in practically every branch of business and personal activity. A market in this sense may be a class of insurance business, a geographical area, a particular industry or profession, some identifiable section of the population, such as a social or income group, or a class of intermediary. The insurance requirements of each of these markets varies widely both in relation to cover and service, requirements which are constantly changing. In the personal insurance field, for example, the number of "two-car", "two-earner" households is growing rapidly and the population is increasing at the rate of some 7% every ten years. In the business area small trading units, both in the commodity and service fields, are diminishing in favour of supermarkets and larger business units. Industrial undertakings are becoming larger by business expansion and by merger and a vast accumulation of risk in comparatively small compass is seen in the latest oil tankers, in jumbo-jets and in computerised production lines.

A long-term plan must not stop at the consideration of existing markets and their likely development over the period of the plan. The planning team must examine the possibility of new activities, some perhaps differing widely from the traditional activities of insurance groups.

In considering environmental factors within the insurance industry an assessment must be made of the strengths and weaknesses of competitors and their likely courses of action. In a highly competitive market comparatively small improvements in marketing methods, in selective underwriting and in administration can mean significant improvements in profits. Manpower and salary planning, major procedural changes, such as computerisation and decentralisation from city centres, a carefully planned training programme for staff at all levels are essential elements in the long-term plan. Without proper attention to these elements the objective of the plan will, at best, be achieved only with serious waste of resources or, at worst, will become impossible of achievement.

Reference has already been made to the growing size and complexity of industrial units. As mergers and takeovers continue, these giant undertakings naturally consider from time to time whether they should themselves bear certain risks previously covered in the insurance market. To this extent they are themselves competitors of existing insurance groups. In undertakings of this size practically all the major insurance groups work in concert to provide the market capacity required and the competition in this situation is not between one group and another, but between the insurance industry and the large industrial groups. If the insurance industry seeks to limit this trend it must plan to provide service and cover at a cost which shows a clear advantage over self-insurance.

THE MARKETS IN WHICH A GROUP SHOULD OPERATE

Reference has already been made to the numerous sections of the insurance market and an individual group is faced with a choice of operating at any particular time in all or in a selection of these markets. At present, practically all composite insurers operate on a selective basis. Although entry into new markets by an insurance group does not present the same problems which face an industry making, say, heavy capital goods, any serious attack on a section of the existing market previously outside the scope of a Group's activity demands a clear long-term appraisal of present and future trading conditions. If a Group plans to go further and decides to operate in a market previously outside the traditional area of activity of the insurance industry as a whole the need for careful planning becomes even more obvious. Such an incursion into new fields could demand new staff skills, major changes in the marketing organisation and possibly an entirely new Group philosophy.

In whatever section of the market a Group operates, it is unlikely that within the period covered by the current long-term plan, it will have a sufficiently large share of any section of the market to enable it to trade significantly above or below the market rate. In making the plan, therefore, it must aim in each market to expand to the level and only to the level at which marginal revenue and marginal costs are equal. This demands sophisticated management information and sufficient flexibility to react quickly to changes in trading conditions. History suggests that conditions in at least some sections of the market will make it impossible for a Group to trade at a satisfactory level of profit for at least some of the years covered by the long-term plan. Which markets and at what times these potentially unprofitable conditions exist will depend upon a variety of factors, some within the influence of the Group and some over which it has little or no control. The plan must contain adequate research and statistical arrangements for recognising well in advance these unprofitable areas.

The application of marginal costing techniques present particular difficulties in a long-term business such as insurance where a large proportion of costs are represented by claims which are predictable only within comparatively wide margins over short periods. However, in principle the same considerations apply to insurance as to other industries.

THE FIELD ORGANISATION

All large composite insurance groups have a network of Branch offices which, in general, give the kind of service which has been a feature of the industry for the past forty years. Certainly over these years and particularly during the last decade there have been changes, but these changes have reflected mainly administration and documentation improvements following computerisation and organisational improvements following better manpower planning and training. They have reflected to a lesser extent changes in the marketing side. The next ten years will almost certainly see significant changes in the insurance needs in practically every market; the rôle of various classes of intermediaries will change; the buying habits of at least some sections of the insuring public will change; policyholders may seek new financial services and perhaps welcome a closer partnership with insurers in connection with risk improvement and control. The long-term plan, backed by market research, must attempt to match these needs of a developing market with the country-wide organisation of the Group. If forecasts in the plan are inaccurate the Group may embark on wrong courses of action which will be expensive to correct. Correction could demand, *inter alia*, the acquisition or disposal of premises, retraining of staff and major changes in selling and servicing arrangements. In the case of overseas operations, inaccurate planning would be even more expensive and errors more difficult to correct.

CONCLUSION

Planning enthusiasts suggest that in the absence of a long-term plan a company staggers from one crisis to another. This overstates the case; many of the decisions taken following recommendations in the plan would have been taken anyway, although in a less formal manner. Others less enthusiastic suggest that the only value of a long-term plan comes from the mental discipline it imposes on the planners. This is too narrow a view; even a simple plan, properly documented, should enable a company to avoid repeating the same errors of judgement. The truth lies somewhere between these two extreme views. Companies who shape events are usually more successful than those who allow events to overtake them. Planning is no panacea but it makes success more likely.

Chapter 25

STRATEGIC PLANNING
FOR A UNIT-TRUST MANAGEMENT COMPANY

David H. Maitland
Managing Director, The Save and Prosper Group

No two companies are exactly alike even if they operate in the same industry. Thus strategic planning for Save and Prosper Group in the context of unit-trust management companies is a problem on its own, though some principles must be common to the industry as a whole. Thus the first stage in strategic planning is to analyse the nature and positioning, not only of the industry in which Save and Prosper operates, but also of the company itself.

The nature of its business is at the long-term end of the financial services industries. A unit trust is established usually for a period of twenty years and it is normal to extend the trust deed at the end of its period. It offers long-term investment to its customers for capital growth or income growth and the objective is for the customers to stay with the unit trust for a long period. In this the industry is largely successful and the average length of holdings is not far short of ten years.

Unit-trust management companies earn their fees principally in two ways – a one-time initial charge when the customer buys units, and an annual charge based on the value of funds under management. These fees are fixed by the trust deeds and all management expenses are set against them and are not chargeable additionally against the unit-holder. For a new management company there is pressure to garner enough new money in order that annual charges cover the basic costs of running the business. In theory, once an economic size has been reached, the pressure to sell should diminish. In practice, the annual fees receivable move sharply since they depend directly on general stock-market levels. Management expenses are almost all constant (and rising annually on inflationary pressures). Thus the margins fluctuate sharply and in the light of conditions which cannot easily be planned forward. Inevitably, therefore, the pressure to sell units and collect initial charges to add to management profits continues. There is also a natural dislike of easing up and watching the competition garner money which might have come to oneself.

Thus there is a natural tendency to want to grow all the time. Moreover, fashions change and the public is always more attracted to something new. Unit-trust management companies are always under temptation to start new unit trusts to take advantage of new trends or to cover competitive activities. But each of these new trusts is a long-term venture to be kept in existence for twenty years or more. The discipline of testing new products against long-term responsibility needs to be watched very carefully. There is no point in starting a new product which is not going to give long-term satisfaction to its customers, just because there is short-term advantage to do so.

Within the financial-services industries, unit trusts are closely analogous to the life-assurance companies which are even more at the long-term end of the market. Life assurance stopped being mainly concerned with death protection many years ago and is now far more involved with long-term investment. Life assurance has a number of legal and structural advantages against the unit trust and so inevitably the companies running unit trusts have moved much closer to the life-assurance sector – a movement which is likely to accelerate over the next decade.

Analysis of the actual and potential market for unit trusts has still been carried out very imperfectly and superficially. There is still too much of the "since only 15% of dentists own unit trusts, there are 85% still to be sold" thinking. The truth is closer that "only 30% of dentists are likely to be interested in equity-type investment, so that the industry has already captured 50% of them". The market is, however, of two kinds. A growing number of people – not yet very far down the market – want to protect their investments and savings against inflation. Life assurance and unit trusts are the media through which this can be done. Secondly, a number of Stock-Exchange investors are finding stockbrokers increasingly disinclined to service them on cost grounds and are seeking the unit-trust mechanism. It has to be accepted that this second category may be used to a more active switching policy and may result in increasing volatility and a reduction in the average holding period.

Save and Prosper is unique in its own industry because of its size. Managing some £750m. on behalf of around one million customers, it represents over 30% of the unit-trust industry and is certainly twice as large as its nearest competitor. It cannot, therefore, be compared with other companies in its own industry. But once one includes the life-assurance industry in the standards for comparison, there are a number of institutions of the same or larger size against which to compare the company. At least one interesting fact that emerges is that, given that long-term investment is the basic business of both, a life company is much more profitable than a unit-trust company. It emerges this is not because the latter has higher expenses – very much the reverse. Effectively the revenues of a life company are much higher than those of a unit-trust management company, i.e. the former takes more from the customer for doing a similar job.

Examining the profile of Save and Prosper's million customers, they clearly cover the whole spectrum of the existing market. Broadly they understand the long-term nature of their involvement in the company's products. They appear to have further resources and a requirement for other long-term services. They appear very willing to support further services which are offered to them by the company. At the same time they have a fair involvement in competitor products too, and are equally prepared to buy from them.

It is critical to any strategic appraisal of financial services to assess how distribution patterns are likely to develop. Traditionally the main channels for unit-trust distribution have been the bank branches, stockbrokers and newspaper advertisements. These channels are now changing and need serious re-evaluation together with alternative possibilities which are emerging. The current trends towards the financial conglomerate or supermarket are two most important situations. A company such as Save and Prosper which is not a part of either situation must consider whether strategically this is tenable and what action it must take.

Finally, it is important to consider the organisation structure and personnel of the business. Companies' structures and people are living parts of the whole and are hard to change quickly. They show strengths and weaknesses. It is no use planning without understanding the areas on which it is possible to build constructively.

This chapter has so far discussed the basic conditions of the unit-trust industry and Save and Prosper's position in it. This is the most critical issue in all strategic planning. Without a real understanding of the basic factors of the business, there can be no platform from which it is possible to plan.

Analysis of the basic factors will certainly establish lines along which further study seems interesting. The possibilities will need in-depth research – mainly into the marketing and distribution areas. This must now be carried out but with considerable discipline as to the profiles to be examined and the feedback required. It is far too easy for research results to be unnecessarily diffuse through lack of clarity at original briefing. But, in due course, the research should further narrow the promising areas on which full profitability studies can be carried out. And as these are completed the parameters of a strategy become definable.

Mechanisms for the control of the planning business have to depend on the structure of the company concerned. Save and Prosper set up some two years ago a Secretarial and Co-ordination Department as a central communications vehicle. Headed by the Company Secretary, the main objective of the department is to service all inter-departmental committees (starting from the main Board), to co-ordinate all development projects and to be responsible for the whole flow of inter-departmental communications. Thus its main function is not to do a lot itself, but to make sure both that things get done and that everybody knows what is going on. The relevant work is carried out by line or staff departments as necessary. Against this background the company has not set up a separate planning structure, since it has seemed preferable to operate within the overall organisation. However, the planning process in Save and Prosper is not yet complete and it would be premature to say that this will work right through satisfactorily.

For financial-services companies operating in the long-term sector, servicing very large numbers of customers, strategic planning is essential to secure the future. But it is no less important to retain flexibility. Opportunities can develop with great rapidity and it has always been the strength of the City that such opportunities are grasped. We do not have big problems of tooling up and developing complex manufacturing processes before embarking on a new project. Therefore, no strategy must deny the possibility of rapid change to meet any challenge that may occur.

Chapter 26

STRATEGIC PLANNING IN STOCKBROKING

Anthony Rudd
Rowe Rudd & Company

As in Einstein's theory of relativity, how you look at strategic planning depends on where you stand. In my firm we look at the problem from the point of view of a relatively small, recently founded business; to us having a strategic plan and following it as best we can is not a luxury but a way of life, to which we must adhere if we are to survive.

It is not difficult to see why this is the case when you consider the environment in which we operate. We employ (with the partners) about a hundred people and compete with about 170 other firms, of which I would guess about thirty-five to forty are larger and of which all but a handful have been longer-established. Like most of them we operate as a partnership with unlimited liability; we are not allowed, under the present club rules, to advertise (except abroad); we may only compete in the services we offer – and not by price.

We are in an area where costs are rising steeply (both labour and rent) and where the actual number of clients is diminishing fast, as the rôle of the private investor diminishes and that of the institution increases. Yet the demands made upon us are increasing fast: the professional clients are demanding better and more wide-ranging research, speedier methods of communication, improved methods of dealing and an international service. As a result the economies of large-scale operations are becoming ever more attractive and mergers are frequent (in 1950 there were 364 firms, now there are 168).

I take the view that in such circumstances the strategy of the small firm needs to be based on specialisation. It has to avoid trying to compete "across the board" with the larger well-established firms and it must not try to offer an overall inclusive service covering every aspect of all markets (the cost of trying to do so is prohibitive without the huge volume of business on which the large firms depend). Instead the strategy has been to select a few defined parts of the market and concentrate on them. Where the firm must offer an all-round service – say to private clients – the policy is to avoid doing all the research within the organisation and to rely instead on published sources.

The great advantage of specialisation is that it is always open to the small firm to excel on a defined front and, in its chosen field, to provide a better and more attractive service than the big general firm offers in that particular area. For example, during the past decade one new firm has made an excellent name for itself in the Eurobond market, another has specialised most successfully in computer-based rating systems, a third in the new issue market, and so on. Of course, the process is re-generative: the small specialist of ten years ago grows success-fully (or even merges) into a larger concern offering a broadly-based service and so, under its lee, smaller firms take over its former specialist rôle and so the process continues. In my firm we chose to start by specialising in the electronic and electrical industries; next we added property shares, then oil, and we are starting up in two other areas. We also developed expertise in the new-issue field and to keep a balance we foster our private-client business.

We found that successful specialisation demanded a particular type of structure. With the first area we started (electronics and electricals) there was no problem; the people running the area were, so to speak, part of the team running the firm. But when the next area (property) began, the first team could only hand on their experience and their contacts; the new team had to build up their own product and make it successful themselves. And this is the pattern we have adopted since.

It means that the team must be largely self-contained. Each needs an "anchor man": the person whose expertise and ex-perience leads the institutional clients to trust the product. His success is assured when the institutional clients become reluctant to make an investment in his area without at least consulting him. Such a trust is not born overnight and the key to it lies in finding a first class "anchor man". He can be "home grown", in which case the process can take several years, or he may come into the firm with ready-made expertise from industry, elsewhere in the City or from journalism. To be successful he must take responsibility for the business and sell his product and himself to the customer. The team will probably number between three and five: the "anchor man", two or three analysts capable of talking to the clients, as well as doing research, and a dealer in the market to transact the business and to give a minute-to-minute service in terms of prices and stocks on offer.

Basing our strategy on research represented a conscious choice. Institutions aim their business at particular brokers for a variety of reasons, of which analytical ability is only one and not necessarily always the most important. Indeed many institutions claim that dealing ability and placing power are more important. So why did we base our effort on analytical work? Starting from scratch we would not have cut any ice by pretending that we were better dealers than our established competitors – it would have been too unlikely a claim. At least with our analytical work the clients could see whether it was valuable by monitoring it. Another angle to this was that when we started, not many of the established broking houses were run by research-orientated people. Yet we could see that more and more of the power to give business was coming into the hands of younger men who were, or had been, trained as investment analysts themselves. Making our approach research-based meant making contact with this group who in the years to come would be at the top in the institutions.

On private clients there is less to say: our strategy is based on the proposition that there are plenty of people with modest wealth who want a stockbroking service and can generate sufficient commission to be entitled to it. We have organised a team of young "account executives" who each run a group of clients on a personal basis and yet operate as a team, drawing on all the resources of the firm as well as a central policy manufactured for and by themselves at weekly meetings.

In the new-issue field we again depend on specialisation: our strategy has been to issue companies whose size precludes them from going to an issuing house or where their problems are simple enough to be dealt with by a broker alone. Our aim has been to build up a group of expanding companies for which we provide a continuing service, keeping them in touch with the market in their shares and being ready to advise on all matters appertaining to the Stock Exchange.

Now that the business is established, the strategy has had to be redefined. A broker must be conscious that, acting alone in the issuing and corporate finance field, he may be regarded as competing with his institutional clients, many of whom, in the case of merchant banks, are members of the Issuing Houses Association. If this competition is too direct he will never stand a chance of partnering such an Issuing House as a broker. It may even hurt the rest of his stockbroking business, particularly when he suffers the inevitable unsuccessful issue (it must be remembered that when a merchant bank offers a broker under-writing he is doing the latter a favour; when a broker offers a merchant bank underwriting he is asking one). So the right strategy must be to go on concentrating on the area, largely ignored by the established issuing houses, namely the smaller companies with profits of between, say, £150,000 and £400,000, but where nonetheless the demand for financial services is intense. Large issues should in most cases be handled jointly with merchant banks and companies which we originally brought to the market but which have grown large and need advice on acquisitions and mergers, should (prudently) be introduced to a merchant bank.

Implementing these strategies successfully depends, as with any other service organisation, on the quality of the people whom we can attract. In our experience the two most important attractions to good staff are opportunity and financial rewards geared to personal success.

Opportunity we provide by having the firm organised in a cell-like structure; more room at the top is created every time a new area is added or expanded. On rewards, each team (including those in the private-client part) has a percentage of the gross commission which they earn allocated to them as a participation for their members. This is then split according to the relative contributions made by the individuals in the team, the "anchor man" being the most important, followed by the others. When a new area is started the partnership underwrites the cost until it becomes viable, when a degree of participation is introduced, although in the first year or two the partner-ship may still guarantee a minimum take-home level. After this the "net" is withdrawn and the team are on their own.

Everybody gets a fixed salary, but each year, as the operation succeeds, this becomes a significantly smaller proportion of their take-home pay. Ultimately, when the fixed salary disappears, the team joins the partnership and exchanges its participation for a share in the firm's equity.

Almost every member of the firm engaged in getting business participates in this manner; I know that other firms have considered this approach and rejected it as being potentially unfair, particularly when, through no fault of their own, a team may suffer a poor year because the level of business in their field drops away. The answer to this, we think, is to allow teams to expand into defined related areas so that they build in some protection from these market swings. The great advantage of the system, which in our opinion is paramount, is that the business-getters are not involved in the overall profitability of the firm which is the responsibility of the partnership (and depends on many aspects out of their control). The only people to be rewarded by reference to the overall profitability of the firm are those operating on the "service" side of the business, either in the front office or in the general office.

Turning to the vital management tool of budgets, they are made up of three elements:

1 General overheads (which cannot be individually ascribed to any of the selling teams) such as the general office, the printing services and secretarial services, the dealing system and such items as rent, rates, heating and lighting.

2 The overheads of the individual selling departments, and in particular their salaries (but not including any of the profit participation earned by the individual teams).

3 The commission budgets produced by the individual areas.

The partners are responsible for the general overhead budget; the individual groups, for producing their budget of expenses and their expected levels of commissions. The whole lot are put together at the end of March, one month before the beginning of the New Year, when the overall budget is produced; the exercise is probably the most important element in implementing the firm's strategy. During the course of the year the budgets are used by the partners as a measure of progress and to some extent as a tool of management.

Planning further ahead than a year means taking a view about some of the many changes which could occur in the structure of the market and which are likely to affect stockbrokers and their business. I can only touch on a few here. Firstly, we see the institutional customers wanting even more in the way of services in return for the commissions they pay out and, as a result, more of the work behind investment decisions will get pushed on to the brokers and out of the customers' offices. Some institutions may want to go in the opposite direction and bypass the market, thus avoiding its costs, entirely. We can't really see this developing too far; buying and selling stock needs more than just a computer to match bids and offers; it requires a market where the Byzantine business of real dealing can take place; nobody can haggle with a computer. On the other hand, we do see pressure developing for brokers to lower commissions, not (as in New York) to abolish the minimum scale altogether but to lower them on some kinds of business, say on very large bargains. The only valid strategy in these circumstances is for brokers to earn their commissions by the quality of the service they offer. During the past decade the private client has been the Cinderella of the broking business, mainly because few brokers took adequate steps to make this business pay. Now more and more brokers are fixing higher minimum commissions, say, of £5 to £10 per bargain (and in due course we see this being applied to Clearing Bank business too) which will make the business viable and sought after again. This in turn could well result in a swing back by the individual investor (particularly when he is too small for the merchant bank and too large just to rely on managed funds) to direct involvement in the stock market. Our strategy is based on this assumption.

Lastly, I expect to see an expansion in stockbrokers' activities, particularly in the field of corporate finance and money raising (though in the context of what I said earlier they must take care not to appear to be trespassing overtly on ground which the merchant banks regard as theirs). This expansion will be made easier when brokers themselves are allowed access to the capital market – as they are now on Wall Street. When this comes it is possible to foresee brokers linking with other complementary (rather than competitive) financial services like insurance, property and perhaps fund management. Of course the essential nature of a broker's unlimited liability will have to be preserved. But in looking at the possibilities it must be remembered that in the U.K. there is no tradition (as there is in the U.S.) of anti-trust legislation working to prevent natural partners from getting together. In the U.K. traditional forces can impede such development, of course, but market forces and the opportunities thrown up by them will be much more important.

Planning a strategy for the Seventies in stockbroking is going to demand plenty of imagination but the opportunities, in the changing world of the City, are likely to be immense.

Chapter 27

STRATEGIC PLANNING
FOR A CLEARING BANK

Richard E. B. Lloyd
Chief Executive, Williams & Glyn's Bank

The best laid plans, wrote Burns, "gang aft agley". He might have said, too, that the best laid plans are not worth a scrap if the process of putting them into action is not itself of the highest order. In our view, successfully organising and implementing strategic planning is more important than any other part of the planning process. I would like to explain the reasons for our belief, and then describe the way we carry out our own planning process at Williams & Glyn's Bank.

First, and most important, putting the plan into action is the only part of planning that contributes to growth in profits. One often hears criticism these days of large planning departments whose annual cost, because of expensive business graduates or professional planners, is pretty high, and whose contribution to the company's profits is very indirect and hard to quantify. Probably the criticism arises because the planners spend too much time on conceptual work and general analysis, and too little time on implementing action via the line divisions. In our view, professional planners are important and have a place, but it is not every company which needs them. Once line executives learn to raise their sights from short-term problems and solutions, they are capable of doing their own planning. Consequently, because they are undertaking most of the process themselves, one achieves greater commitment to the plan, and a more practical action programme.

Secondly, organising and implementing the plan is probably the most difficult part of the planning process, because it demands a wider variety of skills. For instance, setting the company's objective as, say, 10% per annum growth in earnings per share is not in itself a difficult process: the difficulty is in implementing courses of action, motivating managers and controlling results so as to achieve this objective.

Finally, in our view, business success depends, like stock-market investment, on getting your timing right. You can choose the right objectives, know the right stocks to buy, and excel at investment analysis, but all this will be worthless unless your timing is right, and your investment decisions are put into action in the market. In the same way, correct timing, which we consider to be an integral part of organising and implementing strategic planning, is vital to business success. For example, the leading Assurance-Linked Property Bond probably owes much of its success to the timing of its launch.

To enable the reader to appreciate the nature of our own planning process, I will now outline some of the background to the formation of our Bank in 1970 – the character of which evolved through a heavy process of planning over two or more years. (Readers interested in a more detailed case-study of the merger, written when the merger had just taken place, are referred to the next chapter.)

Formed from three old-established banks of differing character, Williams & Glyn's Bank came about mainly as a result of the merger of two Scottish parents in 1967/68. One of these, the Royal Bank of Scotland, owned both Williams Deacon's and Glyn Mills & Co., while the other, National Commercial Bank of Scotland, owned The National Bank, which after the sale of its Irish business in 1966 to the Bank of Ireland Group, was left with thirty-seven branches in England.

All three English banks were small enough to share an entre-preneurial approach to business but had very different manage-ment styles. Glyn Mills, for instance, worked in some ways like a partnership with merchant banking overtones; most of its Executive Directors sat in one room – The Parlour – and there were only four branches, all in London, each with a large degree of autonomy. The National Bank had an intimate style of management which revolved closely round the General Manager himself; it being a small bank, he could influence, in a highly personal way, all his branch managers. Williams Deacon's, by contrast, had 283 branches, was based in Manchester and had a strongly centralised and authoritative management, with a mainly non-executive Board. All three banks were profit-orientated, seldom missed business opportunities, and each had its own strong connections with particular groups or market sectors.

The new bank, however, did not spring fully formed like Athene from the head of Zeus. First of all, study groups were set up in 1968, drawn from the three English banks and both Scottish parents, to consider three possible alternatives, only one of which involved a full merger of the three English banks. There was no rush into a single merged bank: the alternatives were dealt with thoroughly and empirically for nearly twelve months, until during the winter of 1968/69 the thinking of the Directors of the three banks and the holding company developed into gradual acceptance of the idea of a single new bank.

During this period (December 1968 – February 1969) considerable priority was given to objectives and organisation structure in discussions about the alternative strategies open to the three banks.

The organisation structure was given the earliest priority during this formative stage of thinking, and it was considered vital to balance the desirability of logical tidiness and accountability on the one hand with, on the other, the available executives and their particular abilities. With this in mind, various organisations for the new bank were discussed from December 1968 to February 1969 – that is, for some four months before it was finally decided by the Group to go for a single English entity. The structures proposed avoided committee responsibility and "one over one" relationships. In discussing and getting agreement on the organisation, a pragmatic approach was adopted in order that all executives responsible for Divisions had a fair allocation of responsibility. Consultants were not called in at any stage to advise on structure.

As part of the organisation structure, a chief personnel executive was from the outset to be recruited at Board level from outside with vocational experience of carrying out personnel work as an advisory function. He was to provide a personnel skill at the highest level and to persuade the line Divisional Heads to become the "employers" of their own staff, rather than to rely on the staff departments to do it for them.

A further problem on structure was how best to preserve the

goodwill of the existing banks' staffs and customers. To achieve this, it was initially proposed that The National Bank branches, Williams Deacon's branches and Glyn's branches should each be organised in separate Divisions, despite overlapping situations between all three banks in the South and between The National and Williams Deacon's in the North. Logic demanded a regionalised structure, but it was initially intended that this should follow as a second stage to be implemented after one or two years of the new bank's life, so that customers and staff could continue to deal at first with those they knew.

In March, 1970, however, one year after the announcement of the intention to undertake a full merger, and six months before the implementation was to begin in September, the future banking divisional heads agreed to a much more radical structure; they agreed to a regional split between banking divisions, involving the breaking up and reallocating of the branch organisations of the constituent banks. By thus hastening slowing during the planning stage, general agreement was gradually achieved for a far more radical structure than would have been possible at the outset.

Reflecting on lessons which we learned about implementing our plans for this merger, I would like to highlight certain points:

(i) The style of planning had been participatory throughout the whole process. Line Divisions had been involved in designing strategy for the bank and in discussing the output of the Planning Division, whose rôle was advisory rather than directive.

(ii) The majority of those involved in the strategic planning process were of an age where they were able to take a long view of what was required. In other words, having some fifteen to twenty-five years still to go before bowing out from the executive scene, our top management had and have greater commitment and greater willingness to accept risk than they would if they were nearer retirement.

(iii) There was no pressure to produce plans or profit-forecasts to fend off unwelcome bidders – as is sometimes the case in mergers and acquisitions where public shareholders are involved.

(iv) The absence of public shareholders also meant that there was time for second thoughts, since a deal on share prices was not relevant.

All the above factors have, I think, contributed to a successfully implemented merger.

Let me turn now to consider our current planning process, and to draw out certain observations about organising and implementing strategy.

First of all, one hears so much these days about the importance of good communications that it may seem trite to reiterate this point. Nevertheless, I feel that it is worth saying how much care should be taken to ensure that the right people receive the right messages, and that enough of the decision makers in ordinary middle management become involved in the discussions that lead to formulation of plans. In our case, in 1970 and 1971 our Corporate Plan was used not just as a summary of action to be taken, but also as a means whereby each Division would learn what other Divisions intended to do. We call this the "open" approach to planning. In 1970 and again in 1971 we held a major Top Management Conference at which each Divisional Contribution to the Plan was extensively discussed by other Divisions. About fifty people were present each time, including some senior "in-line" branch managers. Subsequently, the Corporate Plan itself, a ninety-page document, was printed and issued to all Branch Managers, together with the strong suggestion that they communicate the key features to their own staff. We did this as part of a conscious effort to build a new single bank out of the constituent parts by encouraging all levels of management to participate in the planning process.

Another part of our effort was directed towards the introduction of Management by Objectives. This is serving us well in two ways: first, by ensuring that each manager in the bank is clear about the extent of his job and his targets in the new scheme of things, and secondly by providing a vehicle for each level of management to communicate bank plans and policy through a regular programme of Review meetings between the manager and his Deputy Director, or Director. In fact, when it comes to detailed implementation of strategy, we find the system of MbyO to be of great value through its discipline of setting objectives, working out action plans, and regular reviews of progress.

We have this year revised part of our planning process in the light of changing priorities. Incidentally, we have slightly modified our organisation structure as well. For instance, our full-time planners – there are less than three of them – now report to the Director of Finance and Administration, a new position which we have recently filled with an experienced non-banker. This year's planning process began with a review of Divisional activity carried out by the planners in the Autumn.

Later in the year we went through a kind of self-appraisal as a bank, looking at our strengths and weaknesses, especially in the light of the new competitive banking scene. We have also extended our planning outlook to five years, superseding our original concentration on short-term matters such as naturally concerned us in the merger and post-merger situation.

And now for the procedure. In previous years, Divisions used to write their own contribution to the Corporate Plan which was then discussed and edited centrally, agreement being reached with the Division about any major changes. Once the merger was completely behind us and its immediate objectives achieved it was appropriate to continue to speed the process of change in a more radical way.

This year, therefore, we formed small working parties each under the Chairmanship of an Executive Director or Deputy Director, with one of our planning team as Secretary. The other members were usually drawn from more than one division and were of senior managerial rank or above. Each working party tackled one of our major business areas – for instance, City Banking – with a brief to come up with three things: first, a summary of likely developments in the market and competitors' action over the period 1972–77, next an analysis of where our bank stands now in relation to these markets, and finally recommendations on strategy and courses of action open to us.

These findings were then discussed at a two-day Conference of Executive Directors, with each working party presenting its points to the Conference. Some fifty or more decisions were reached on those two days – although in some cases, it was only a decision to make further study of the problem! The major strategic issues then went in the form of recommendations before the full Board of our bank, during April. The next stage involves each Division preparing by the end of June a five-year operational plan, based on the outcome of the two-day Conference, and the recommendations to the Board. The final stage is the production of Divisional budgets before the end of our financial year in September.

In this way the reader will see that while we have full-time planners, they work with and through Divisional management. We believe that those responsible for implementation gain a greater commitment to their plans by shepherding them through the various stages and by defending them against sundry and sometimes unexpected critics. The planners' task is to enable Divisional executives to broaden their horizons. He also has to gain a consensus of opinion about what will happen in the market, and he must be able to keep people informed about competitors' actions.

Our present planning has now become much more of a two-stage approach – on the one hand, strategy-formulation in working parties and the two-day Conference, and on the other the implementation through Divisional operating plans and budgets. In the first part there is a lot of discussion within the groups, but in the second part one gets down to detail and this has to be left to Divisional management without undue interference. All the same, these detailed plans and budgets have to be agreed by me with the Divisional head concerned.

To sum up our experience in organising and implementing strategic planning, I would say that certain things stand out:

(i) In terms of gaining acceptance at Director-level for a specific strategy, we try to get a complete consensus of opinion, even if this takes a long time, because we believe that if one were to force change without acceptance the strategic moves would be made with less impact and less conviction.

(ii) Full-time planners have an important part to play, as advisers and catalysts, but should not attempt to undertake someone else's planning for them.

(iii) The difficult thing is to prevent people from discussing points of detail in the early stage of strategy formulation, when they ought to be comparing alternative strategies. But then it is so tempting to talk about what is familiar – and so much easier.

(iv) One should not expect everyone to take to this "open"

approach very easily, but, once established, it helps build up mutual understanding and assistance.

(v) Plans only have a value if action results from them. If no action results, they are merely pipe dreams.

Chapter 28

CASE STUDY OF A BANK MERGER

Richard E. B. Lloyd
Chief Executive, Williams & Glyn's Bank

In October 1970, Williams & Glyn's Bank started trading in the place of the three banks, Glyn, Mills & Co., The National Bank Limited and Williams Deacon's Bank Limited. To get to this point took nearly two years of negotiation and planning.

It would not be true to say that the three constituent banks merged because of the rash of other and earlier bank mergers, but they probably would not have merged unless the Scottish parents of the three banks had not themselves decided to merge in the winter of 1967/68. These Scottish parents were The Royal Bank of Scotland, a quoted chartered bank owning Glyn's and Williams Deacon's, and National Commercial Bank of Scotland Limited, also a quoted company which owned The National Bank. The vehicle which was formed for their amalgamation was a holding company, National and Commercial Banking Group Limited, which became the owner of the two Scottish banks and, through them, of the three English banks. Subsequently in March 1969 the businesses of the two Scottish banks were merged into The Royal Bank of Scotland Limited.

At that stage, the new holding company found itself the owner of four banks. The three English banks were used to being treated as large trade investments with a trading life of their own. It was by no means clear what rôle they would play nor what structure they would adopt. Only the Scottish scene was certain. The new Royal Bank of Scotland Limited enjoyed 43% of total Scottish bank deposits, and was dominant in terms of branch representation in Scotland. Its importance compared with the English banks within the new Group is shown in the middle of Appendix II.

324

INDUSTRY BACKGROUND

One of the contributory factors to the various mergers in the banking industry was the publication of the Prices and Incomes Board's Report on bank charges in 1967, with its veiled intimation that mergers of banks would no longer be disapproved of by the Authorities. Late in 1967, Martins Bank, the share price of which had for some time been speculatively high, let it be known to the industry's leaders that it was prepared to enter into merger negotiations. The Midland decided not to put in a bid. The National Provincial and Westminster banks announced on the day after initial bids were due that they themselves were already engaged in merger talks; their proposed National Westminster Bank was also to incorporate The District Bank, previously a subsidiary of National Provincial, although Coutts & Co., a fellow N.P. subsidiary, would continue to trade separately. Barclays and Lloyds banks thus merged as the only bidders for Martins. The attempt of Barclays, Lloyds and Martins to merge into a single vast bank, controlling some 47% of English Clearing-Bank deposits, was referred to the Monopolies Commission, which, by a narrow majority and with subsequent Board of Trade confirmation, turned the merger down, leaving Barclays as the only bidder for Martins.

The main reason given for these mergers was the need for size to provide funds on a sufficient scale to satisfy the demands of British industry and of multi-national corporations, which were, themselves, going through a period of merger and rationalisation. In this way, the banks were responding to national trends. As further benefits, it was hoped that cost savings could be achieved in such fields as computers and that overlapping branch representation should be cut out. These last two points were uppermost in the minds of the Directors of The Royal Bank of Scotland and National Commercial Bank of Scotland, who had studied in depth before their merger was announced the steps which would be taken to rationalise their branch network in Scotland, which was at the time a notably overbanked country.

There were a number of other factors in the back of the minds of the Clearing Banks:

(a) The probability that their true profits and inner reserves would eventually be disclosed, since the Board of Trade had requested in the late Autumn 1968 to be given, in confidence, the true figures following the new 1967 Companies Act.

(b) Severe competition from the American banks rushing to open in London and lobbying by U.K. consumer organisations, which substantially influenced the Monopolies Commission's recommendation, which meant that the banks were under a certain amount of external pressure to change.

(c) The new management style which was gradually evolving in the major banks which resulted in a more profit-conscious approach to traditional services and an examination of areas for expansion and diversification. The word "marketing" was being heard in the corridors of Lombard Street and Poultry.

However, the Clearing Banks, or most of them, had traditionally adopted a centralised type of management and this, with their large size even by international standards, meant that developments and changes came slowly.

A side effect of the bank mergers which had some, but not crucial, influence on the Williams & Glyn's Bank merger was the future contraction of the banks' trade association, The Committee of London Clearing Bankers. This was to be reduced from eleven to eight members, three of which would be the English subsidiaries of the National and Commercial Banking Group.

THE CHARACTER OF THE THREE
CONSTITUENT BANKS

Glyn's had only four branches, all in London, including two long-established ex-banking partnerships which were purchased in the 1920s – Childs in Fleet Street and Holts in Whitehall, both of which were given a large degree of autonomy. Glyn's worked in some ways like a partnership, with merchant-banking overtones; most of its ten Executive Directors sat in one room – The Parlour – with policy and execution effectively lying in their joint hands as a Committee of General Management. The nature of Glyn's Lombard Street business was essentially corporate, and it drew a disproportionately large amount of its business from overseas banks. The bank's staff of some 1,000 were represented domestically by an active Staff Association, and Glyn's relationship with its staff was close and paternal. Glyn Mills Finance Company was a thriving bidding subsidiary and contributed significantly to consolidated profits.

Williams Deacon's was, like Glyn's, a long-established bank (two of the founder partners of Williams Deacon's and Glyn's were cousins!). As the figures in Appendix III show, Williams Deacon's was substantially the largest of the three constituent banks with 283 branches. Originally a London partnership, it became particularly strong in the North-West of England following its merger in 1890 with the joint-stock Manchester and Salford Banking Company, and its branches, although spread over the whole country, were concentrated in Lancashire and Cheshire. Because of the bank's dual geographical origins, its predominantly non-Executive Board was headquartered in Manchester but met also in London. A Committee of the Board in each city supervised, respectively, the business in the North and South. The management style of Williams was strongly centralised and authoritative, the bank being very effectively controlled by the General Manager, who was, at the time of the merger, the only Executive on the Board. The staff of some 2,500 were represented domestically by the National Union of Bank Employees (NUBE).

The National Bank, an English-owned joint-stock bank founded in 1835, derived two thirds of its deposits, up to 1966, from its branches in Ireland. Then a rationalisation of Irish clearing banking resulted in the sale of its Irish branches to the Bank of Ireland Group and of the English part, still called The National Bank, to the National Commercial Bank of Scotland. The National Bank had a strongly Irish flavour in its U.K. business, and was particularly strong in banking for the Roman Catholic community in England. Following a steady policy of opening branches in large centres in England, it had, by 1969, thirty-seven branches, half of which were outside London. Its style of management was intimate and revolved closely around the General Manager himself; it being a small bank, he could influence in a highly personal way the conduct and new business-getting of his branch managers. The National Bank's deposits had shown excellent growth in the late 1960s and had (unlike Williams Deacon's and Glyn's) exceeded the average rate of increase for the English Clearing Banks as a whole. The bank's staff of some seven hundred were represented domestically by NUBE.

The original Royal Bank of Scotland Group ("the Three Banks Group") operated on a federal basis, exemplified by the fact that Williams Deacon's was a larger contributor to that Group's profits than The Royal Bank itself. With the foreshadowed merger of the businesses of the two Scottish banks into The Royal Bank of Scotland Limited, this federal structure naturally came under review. The three English banks found themselves fellow subsidiaries by historical accident.

DEVELOPMENT OF POLICY IN FORMING WILLIAMS AND GLYN'S BANK LIMITED

After the formation of National and Commrcial Banking Group, the question of possible structures for its English banking side was considered. Study Groups were set up, drawn from the staff of all five banks, and, after six months' work, reported on various alternatives:

(a) "Co-operative management" of certain of the functions of the future four banks, such as management of their gilt-edged portfolios and foreign exchange.

(b) "Integration" – i.e. full merger of the three English banks into a single new bank, following the Scottish example.

(c) "Federation", which could roughly be described as the "status quo".

The Chairmen, Deputy Chairmen and Directors of the three banks and of the holding company considered these Study Groups' reports during the Autumn of 1968 and their thinking developed, during the winter of 1968/69, into gradual acceptance of the idea of a single new bank.

With the benefit of hindsight, there were some interesting features of this method of considering alternatives:

(a) There was no rush into a single merged bank; the alternatives were dealt with thoroughly and empirically.

(b) The discussion was based mainly on considerations of the similar nature of the underlying businesses, and of the potentialities of harnessing their management efforts, presently carried on in very diverse ways, into a single new-style entity.

(c) Within the context of examining the existing businesses, the executives likely to run a single English unit occasionally resorted to conceptual plans for their ideal bank in the existing market circumstances.

(d) The main requirements, which emerged gradually in discussion, were for a clear distinction (which did not previously exist) between line and staff responsibility, and for the individual accountability of the executives from Board level downwards, as well as for the development of techniques such as marketing, budgetary control, corporate planning and personnel development.

(e) In all these discussions, the absence of public shareholders meant that there was time for second thoughts, since "a deal" on share prices was not relevant and there was, therefore, no need for the accompanying quickly-prepared polemics about management quality and company forecasts.

The organisation structure was given the earliest priority during this formative stage of thinking, and it was considered vital to balance the desirability of logical tidiness and accountability on the one hand with, on the other, the available executives and their particular abilities. With this in mind, various organisations for the new bank were discussed from December 1968 to February 1969 – that is, for some four months before it was finally decided by the Group to go for a single English entity. The structures proposed avoided committee responsibility and "one over one" relationships. In discussing and getting agreement on the organisation, a pragmatic approach was adopted in order that all executives responsible for Divisions had a fair allocation of responsibility. Consultants were not called in at any stage to advise on structure.

As part of the organisation structure, a chief personnel executive was from the outset to be recruited at Board level from outside with vocational experience of carrying out personnel work as an advisory function. He was to provide a personnel skill at the highest level and to persuade the line Divisional heads to become the "employers" of their own staff, rather than to rely on the staff departments to do it for them.

A further problem on structure was how best to preserve the goodwill of the existing banks' staffs and customers. To achieve this, it was initially proposed that The National Bank branches, Williams Deacon's branches and Glyn's branches should each be organised in separate Divisions, despite overlapping situations between all three banks in the South and between The National and Williams Deacon's in the North. Logic demanded a regionalised structure, but it was initially intended that this should follow as a second stage to be implemented after one or two years of the new Bank's life, so that customers and staff could continue to deal at first with those they knew.

ANNOUNCEMENT OF THE MERGER

The merger of the three English banks was announced in March 1969, to be implemented in September 1970. The time interval of eighteen months fitted in with the minimum calendar time required to put through Parliament a Private Bill which, by then, had become the best method for achieving mergers of English bank businesses.

One month after the announcement of the merger, the make-up of the Board and senior appointments were announced, so that those responsible for the new bank could personally plan the structures of their own Divisions, and select the staff for them in liaison with their colleagues. The Board was twenty-four strong and to arrive at even this large number, seven non-executive directors of the constituent banks and two of their executive directors were not appointed. The announcement of the new bank and of the appointments caused interested Press comment, and the embryonic new bank (formed as a £100 company for the purpose of planning the merger) sought to draw attention to the following facts about itself:

(a) Nearly half the Board were Executive Directors (a departure from normal Clearing-Bank practice), and the next layer of management were called "Deputy Directors", this different terminology being deliberately chosen to differentiate from the usual General Manager/Assistant General Manager rankings: Of the Executive Directors, eight had been career bankers, five with Glyn's, one with The National Bank and two with Williams Deacon's; and two had been recruited to Glyn's from merchant banks. The Personnel Director was not finally recruited until a year before the merger.

(b) The headquarters were to be in London, rather than in Manchester, but to be located at the City office of Williams Deacon's, the largest of the three banks. The name, Williams & Glyn's Bank Limited, omitted mention of The National Bank only after much debate, and partly because so many banks already had "national" in their names.

(c) Because of the new Bank's lack of nationwide branch coverage, it would concentrate on assembling, into a single organisation, a range of services which would not only meet customers' expressed needs, but also anticipate their unexpressed needs. From formation, it was envisaged that this would involve merchant-banking work and some new services, such as insurance broking and/or travel (managers would be compensated for the loss of their own personal insurance agencies).

(d) Marketing would be introduced as a staff function so that it could be taught to the line Divisions and the idea of an outward-going approach and of the introduction of new products would be disseminated from the centre.

(e) The management style would consciously encourage an entrepreneurial approach at all levels and, to back this up, a more performance-based salary structure would be initiated to complement the introduction of Management by Objectives.

(f) Profit targets would be set by the Divisions, and a system of budgetary control introduced to monitor their performance.

(g) The scope for creating a banking unit which would make a contribution to management methods in the financial sector and, to some extent, set a standard by which potential staff recruits and others could judge progressiveness among the Clearing Banks, was present as an idealistic motive. It gave the whole enterprise a *raison d'être* over and above the mere mechanics of merger.

MERGER IMPLEMENTATION

No staff, other than the Chief Executive and his secretary, and ultimately some members of the Planning Division, were withdrawn from their existing responsibilities. This ensured that each Divisional Head could oversee the design of his Division's structure and manning, whatever duties he had to carry on at the same time in his existing bank. Mostly under the chairmanship of the Divisional Heads, sixteen working parties were set up, covering all merging areas of the new bank.

The absence of a full-time merger secretariat was partly deliberate and partly of necessity. Because of the small size of the bank, staff could not have been seconded. But the system had the de-merit of causing a certain amount of untidiness in administration on, and before, merger day. For example, a new comprehensive book of rules on banking procedure still has not been written. The concept of accountability by each Divisional Head, however occupied in his own bank, for the design of his Division in the new bank was considered to be of overriding importance and on balance this has been justified; their mistakes are their own and so are their achievements.

The question which took longest to resolve was how the merchant-banking work should be carried out. The solution of incorporating Williams, Glyn & Co. as a wholly-owned merchant banking and bidding subsidiary with a capital of £5m. was not finally reached until February 1969, nearly a year after the announcement of the new bank. The evolution of the policy on this matter was most important in evolving the character of the new bank as part clearing and part merchant. It was at this point that it was decided to strengthen the merchant-banking talent by recruiting from outside a second Director to the Williams & Glyn's Bank Board, himself already distinguished in the new issue, merger and acquisition fields.

As thinking developed on the organisation structure, it gradually became clear to all concerned that a non-regionalised bank structure would not seem sufficiently radical or efficient to the staff as a whole, and one year after the merger was announced the future banking divisional heads agreed to adopt a regional structure, involving the splitting up and re-allocation of the branch organisation of the three constituent banks. By thus hastening slowly during the planning stage, general agreement was gradually achieved for a more progressive structure than would have been possible at the outset. It was, of course, always proposed to pool the three central organisations, and, *en route* to the merger date, the computer departments of

Williams Deacon's/Glyn's (which had had a joint computer department for a number of years) and of The National Bank were merged in October 1969, and the Inspection and Premises Departments of all three banks in March 1970.

As foreshadowed in the first organisation chart, the Planning Division's brief was to cover the following areas:

Long-range Corporate Planning.

Marketing.

Branch Development Policy.

Communications (both internal with the staff and external with the Press and through the advertising agents).

No professional corporate planners were recruited into this Division, but Urwick, Orr proposed, and the Bank accepted, that they should act as consultants on planning as a prelude to their advising on Management by Objectives.

The style of planning has been participatory throughout. Line Divisions have been involved in designing the strategy for the bank and in discussing the output of the Planning Division, whose status is that of an advisory service division. In reverse, the presence of bank-trained executives in the Planning Division has meant that considerable attention has been paid to the problems of implementing its recommendations. The programme adopted for planning was as follows:

(a) An embryonic Planning Division was established, July 1969.

(b) Line Divisions outlined areas for development within their respective spheres of influence, Aug–Nov 1969.

(c) A strategic assessment was prepared by the Planning Division summarising these reports and indicating fields for initial development, Dec 1969.

(d) A draft corporate plan was prepared setting out line Divisional plans and suggesting bank objectives and strategies, Jan–Mar 1970.

(e) A top management conference for the bank was held to discuss the draft corporate plan and to enable senior executives from each of the three banks to see their future colleagues in action, April 1970.

(f) The Corporate Plan 1970 was discussed at Executive

Director level, section by section, and then submitted to the Board, April–July 1970.

(g) The Corporate Plan was distributed down to branch-manager level to involve all executives of the bank in its future development, July 1970.

The Corporate Plan endeavoured to set objectives and five-year targets for the bank in the context of a competitive and economic survey. Line Divisional plans, and tentative marketing and branch development strategies were outlined. Personnel policies to implement the style of management envisaged in the new bank were also described.

Despite this programme and its good intentions, there is not total acceptance of planning and only partial use of it by line Divisions.

MORALE AND INVOLVEMENT OF STAFF AT ALL LEVELS

Inevitably, the merger of three long-established English banking institutions, each with its deep traditions and special loyalties from staffs expecting a lifetime's career in the bank of their choice (there is very little staff movement within the banking world), involved staff in a certain amount of anxiety about change. It was particularly necessary to establish terms of service which were felt fair by all three staffs. To ensure objective assessment of this problem, a programme of job analysis and evaluation was instituted with the help of the Hay–M.S.L. organisation, but this is a long-term project. As an interim measure a rough salary batting order was worked out by *ad hoc* evaluation to remove anomalies. A new pension fund was set up with some benefits significantly better than existed in the present three banks' funds, and it was announced that rights of transfer into the new fund would later be offered. On the whole, the highest common denominator of terms of service, with limited exceptions, was applied across the board. These factors, and above all else the early announcement of senior appointments in the new bank, gained the confidence of the banks' staffs and helped to minimise their anxieties. At the same time, the staff representatives, split between the Staff Association and NUBE, found common interests in dealing in their own familiar terms with the Personnel Director, who insisted on negotiating on a tripartite basis, rather than with only one of them.

It may have helped, too, that as a general principle, the consultants employed by the bank (which, besides Urwick, Orr and Hay–M.S.L., included Colin McIver Associates for marketing and McLeish Associates for public relations) were confined to their own specialist areas and the limits of their work carefully explained to the staff, so that management stayed in control of the changes being introduced. A prime example of such explanation to the staff was in the field of Management by Objectives which was started in the Northern Division; great efforts were successfully made to get branch managers to set their own objectives and think about their business prospects.

The new bank was careful to use outside recruits at senior levels of management only in those areas where expertise was quite clearly absent in the bank. An ex-Manchester University don – expert in management education – was recruited in this way, as was a Marketing Manager and a Staff Training Officer, besides the Personnel Director and the joint head of the Financial Services Division at Board level.

The new bank also found various gaps in the three banks' previous practices. One of these was in the area of management information. A committee on management information has been formed with representatives from Line, Planning and Management Services Divisions, and this is considering what management information is required on such projects as customers, staff, capital resources, income and costs. Lack of adequate information has so far proved a major handicap to effective planning and control.

MERGER PUBLICITY

Advertising agents were appointed in May 1970 and visited all Divisions of the bank before recommending an approach by way of advertising (newspaper advertisements – post advertising on super sites and direct mail) based on the concept of "we are small and take more trouble". The advertising was intended to be striking and aimed at the corporate sector, the ABC sector, existing customers and staff. The advertisements used the device of a thinking man, reflecting "What you want a bank to be".

The total advertising appropriation was £150,000, treble the three banks' combined spending in the past, and disproportionately high in relation to other banks' spending compared with the new bank's share of Clearing Bank deposits.

Two days before the bank started to trade, the newly appointed public-relations consultants arranged for the Press to be invited to a lunch conference when the bank's aims and objects were outlined to them by the Executive Directors and the Press were shown the details of the advertising campaign. As a result the Press coverage of the merger was significant and favourable.

REFLECTIONS ON A NEW BANK

It is far too early (at the time of writing) to evaluate whether this merger has worked. But there are so far some aspects which may distinguish it from other mergers. In the first place, this was a genuine merger between partner-banks, each with its own traditions, and similarly high profitability. In practice, there has been no element of management take-over by one bank of the whole; none would have been a suitable base for the other two. Secondly, the principle on which the co-operation of top management was obtained was that all policies and developments were thoroughly debated at Board level and by the Executive Directors in conference before they were adopted. In this way, it gradually became apparent to all concerned that the contributions of individual executives at all levels mattered and would be noticed, that the bank would be small enough to combine efficiency with humanity and personal touch, but big enough to be able to make a significant impact on the banking scene.

APPENDIX IV

DIARY OF SIGNIFICANT DATES

March 7th, 1966   Split of The National Bank effective.

May 15th, 1967   PIB report on Bank Charges.

December 9th, 1967   Martins preparedness to merge indicated.

January 26th, 1968   Plans announced to merge National Provincial, District and Westminster.

February 8th, 1968   Plans announced to merge Barclays, Lloyds and Martins.

February 12th, 1968   Merger of Barclays, Lloyds and Martins referred to Monopolies Commission.

February 17th, 1968   Plans announced to merge The Royal Bank of Scotland and National Commercial Bank of Scotland

October 7th, 1968   Internal working party reported on potential Williams & Glyn's structures.

October 1968–March 1969   Discussion within three banks.

December 1968   First organisation chart.

March 20th, 1969   Merger announced.

March 31st, 1969   Merger of two Scottish banks effective.

April 17th, 1969   Initial Board announced, and post of Executive Director (Personnel) advertised.

June 30th, 1969   Planning Division working party reported.

December 19th, 1969   Strategic Assessment approved by Board.

April 2nd–4th, 1970   Draft Corporate Plan 1970 considered at Top Management Conference.

July 7th, 1970   Corporate Plan 1970 approved by Board.

September 25th, 1970   Merger of three English Banks effective.

September 29th, 1970   Merger of English Bidding Companies and Trust Companies effective.

September 30th, 1970   End of Accounting Year.

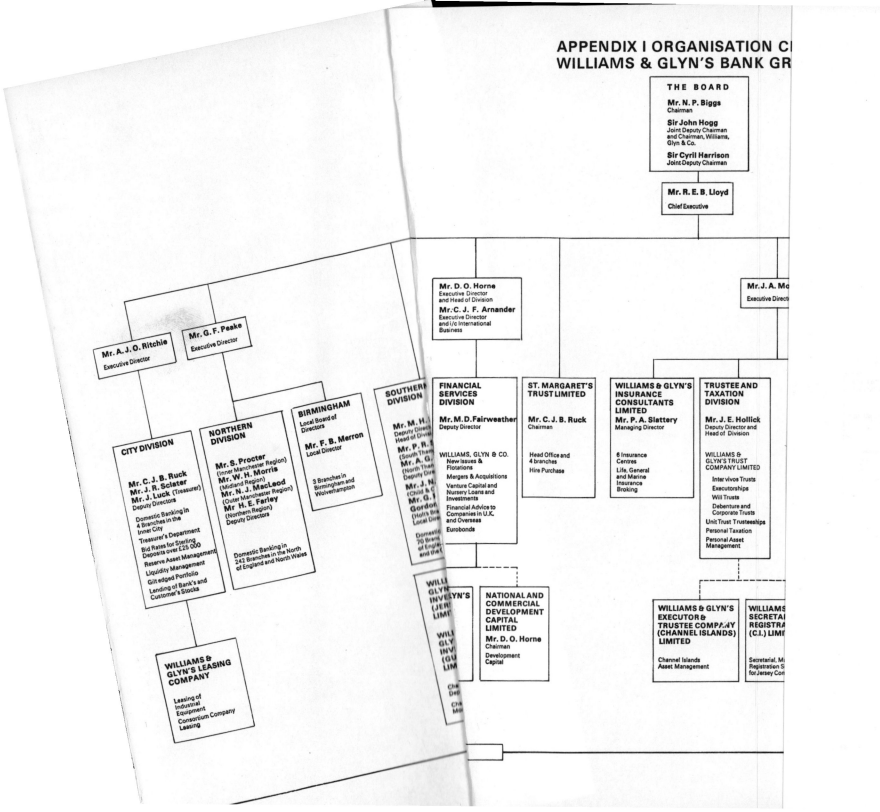

THE BOARD

Mr. N. P. Biggs
Chairman

Sir John Hogg
Joint Deputy Chairman
and Chairman, Williams,
Glyn & Co.

Sir Cyril Harrison
Joint Deputy Chairman

Mr. R. E. B. Lloyd
Chief Executive

Mr. D. O. Horne
Executive Director
and Head of Division

Mr. C. J. F. Arnander
Executive Director
and i/c International
Business

Mr. J. A. M[...]
Executive Direct[...]

Mr. A. J. O. Ritchie
Executive Director

Mr. G. F. Peake
Executive Director

CITY DIVISION

Mr. C. J. B. Ruck
Mr. J. R. Sclater
Mr. J. Luck (Treasurer)
Deputy Directors

Domestic Banking in
4 Branches in the
Inner City

Treasurer's Department

Bid Rates for Sterling
Deposits over £25 000

Reserve Asset Management

Liquidity Management

Gilt edged Portfolio

Lending of Bank's and
Customer's Stocks

**NORTHERN
DIVISION**

Mr. S. Procter
(Inner Manchester Region)
Mr. W. H. Morris
(Midland Region)
Mr. N. J. MacLeod
(Outer Manchester Region)
Mr H. E. Farley
(Northern Region)
Deputy Directors

Domestic Banking in
242 Branches in the North
of England and North Wales

BIRMINGHAM
Local Board of
Directors

Mr. F. B. Merron
Local Director

3 Branches in
Birmingham and
Wolverhampton

**SOUTHERN
DIVISION**

Mr. M. H. [...]
Deputy Direct[...]
Head of Divis[...]

Mr. P. R. [...]
(South Tham[...]
Mr. A. G. [...]
(North Tham[...]
Deputy Dire[...]

Mr. J. N. [...]
(Child & C[...]
Mr. G. [...]
Gordon [...]
(Holt's Bra[...]
Local Dire[...]

Domestic [...]
70 Bran[...]
of Engla[...]
and the [...]

**FINANCIAL
SERVICES
DIVISION**

Mr. M. D. Fairweather
Deputy Director

WILLIAMS, GLYN & CO.
New Issues &
Flotations

Mergers & Acquisitions

Venture Capital and
Nursery Loans and
Investments

Financial Advice to
Companies in U.K.
and Overseas

Eurobonds

**ST. MARGARET'S
TRUST LIMITED**

Mr. C. J. B. Ruck
Chairman

Head Office and
4 branches

Hire Purchase

**WILLIAMS & GLYN'S
INSURANCE
CONSULTANTS
LIMITED**

Mr. P. A. Slattery
Managing Director

6 Insurance
Centres

Life, General
and Marine
Insurance
Broking

**TRUSTEE AND
TAXATION
DIVISION**

Mr. J. E. Hollick
Deputy Director and
Head of Division

WILLIAMS &
GLYN'S TRUST
COMPANY LIMITED

Inter vivos Trusts

Executorships

Will Trusts

Debenture and
Corporate Trusts

Unit Trust Trusteeships

Personal Taxation

Personal Asset
Management

**WILL[...]
GLYN'S
IN VELYN'S
(JER[...]
LIMI[...]**

**WILL[...]
GLY[...]
INV[...]
(GU[...]
LIM[...]**

Ch[...]
Dep[...]

Ch[...]
M[...]

**NATIONAL AND
COMMERCIAL
DEVELOPMENT
CAPITAL
LIMITED**

Mr. D. O. Horne
Chairman

Development
Capital

**WILLIAMS & GLYN'S
EXECUTOR &
TRUSTEE COMPANY
(CHANNEL ISLANDS)
LIMITED**

Channel Islands
Asset Management

**WILLIAMS[...]
SECRETA[...]
REGISTRA[...]
(C.I.) LIMI[...]**

Secretarial, M[...]
Registration S[...]
for Jersey Co[...]

**WILLIAMS &
GLYN'S LEASING
COMPANY**

Leasing of
Industrial
Equipment

Consortium Company
Leasing

Appendix II

RELATIVE SIZES OF THE RESPECTIVE BANKS BEFORE, DURING AND AFTER FORMATION OF WILLIAMS & GLYN'S BANK LIMITED

The shaded areas indicate clearing deposits and the non-shaded areas bid deposits.

All figures are taken from annual balance sheets, on an undisclosed basis for consistency.

The height of each box is in proportion to the level of deposits.

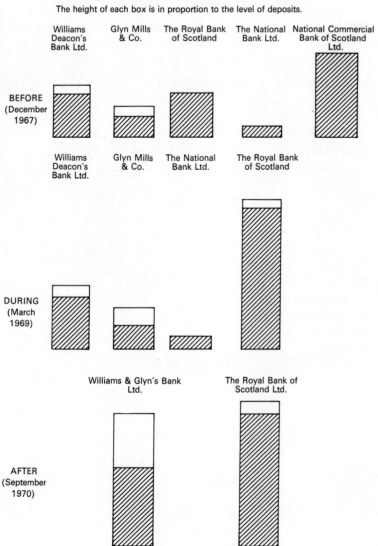

APPENDIX III

BASIC STATISTICS OF THE CONSTITUENT BANKS OF WILLIAMS & GLYN'S BANK LIMITED

AS AT SEPTEMBER 30TH 1969

£m.	Glyn, Mills & Co.	The National Bank Limited	Williams Deacon's Bank Limited
Clearing Deposits	75·3	44·6	159·5
Bid Deposits	126·0	none	26·1 (Manchester)
			32·0 (Channel Islands)
Shareholders' Funds	15·6	9·3	28·6
Pre-tax Profits	2·10	1·18	4·62
Branches	4	37	283
Staff	1,000	700	2,500
% Deposits derived from Banks and Discount Houses (average 69/70)	39·6%	13·7%	5·6%
% Advances made to agriculture, professions and charities (average 69/70)	14·2%	29·4%	19·2%